AF664324

Globalization and Humanity

Globalization and Humanity

Samir Dasgupta

RAWAT PUBLICATIONS
Jaipur • New Delhi • Bangalore • Hyderabad • Guwahati

ISBN 81-316-0349-0
© Author, 2010

No part of this book may be reproduced or transmitted in any form or by any means, electronic or mechanical, including photocopying, recording or by any information storage and retrieval system, without permission in writing from the publishers.

Published by
Prem Rawat for **Rawat Publications**
Satyam Apts, Sector 3, Jawahar Nagar, Jaipur 302 004 (India)
Phone: 0141 265 1748 / 7006 Fax: 0141 265 1748
E-mail: info@rawatbooks.com
Website: www.rawatbooks.com

New Delhi Office
4858/24, Ansari Road, Daryaganj, New Delhi 110 002
Phone: 011 2326 3290

Also at Bangalore, Hyderabad and Guwahati

Typeset by Rawat Computers, Jaipur
Printed at Chaman Enterprises, New Delhi

Dedicated to
my beloved and sweet mother,
Renuka Dasgupta,
whose loving spirit
still continues to guide me.

Contents

Foreword

Surely globalization is human, profoundly so. It is their species adaptability that enables humans, as 'unfinished animals', to dwell in every climate zone all over the planet. This gave rise to the ancient population movements of the 'time walkers'. Here then is humans' oldest worldliness and world making, deeply embedded in the recesses of evolutionary time. The ancient migrations shaped the backbone of globalization to come. The rest is history—pastoralism, cultivation, trade, urbanization, city states, conquests, empires, civilizations.

Nietzsche might say globalization is human, all too human, which opens another register. Perhaps weariness with humanity is part of being human; a sensibility of heightened sensitiveness to human traits.

Humans are animals so human traits include animal traits. Humane, then, is that which distinguishes humans from animals. Is globalization humane? It would hardly make sense to say so unless one goes out of one's way to be sarcastic. Of course, aspects of globalization are humane, but does it make sense to say globalization is humane? Humane aspects of globalization include movements and organizations that seek to empower and emancipate people and institutions that monitor and alleviate human suffering, music and art, communications and advertising that profile and celebrate beauty, humour and joy. The humane aspects of globalization are probably overlooked, underrated. Cynicism comes easy, as a protective reflex, yet also a tunnel vision. Humane aspects include not just what is done but how it is done—human work with a human touch, humane in gestures great or small, humane in minuscule details that do not or seem not to matter. Humane because we have no choice but to express our humanness; humane, then, with small h; humane as in the human touch.

Is there a calculus that would enable us to assess which traits, overall, prevail in the human touch—indifference, rudeness, cruelty, warmth, finesse, joy? Is there humanity in our limitations, in our being embedded in time and in space? Surely that is deeply human, but to say it is humane would be too benevolent a gaze. I am sure, it is, too, in ways that are not superficial, yet find it difficult to pinpoint them. Humane was the romantic movement and the concurrent movement for the abolition of slavery, which connects with the great 19th century emancipation movements—of minorities, nations, the working class and women.

Humanist globalization carries several meanings. First, globalization by humanists—free thinkers of the late middle ages and Renaissance such as Giordano Bruno, Ariosto and Montaigne who established nodes and networks of knowledge that paved the way for the 17th century 'scientific revolution' and 18th century *philosophes*. This includes globalization in the footsteps of the great scholars and travellers, poets and architects, Sufis and marabouts of the Muslim world such as Ibn Khaldun, Ibn Battuta, Ibn Rushd and Rumi. This precedes and accompanies humanist globalization à la Erasmus—a familiar figure in several European cities and a bridge builder of European culture, with an old yet wearable patina. Arguably, the slow ripple effects and rivulets of humanist globalization include the Jacobins, the French revolution, Feuerbach's work, perhaps the effervescence of 1848 and the sway of national movements. Surely they include the humanist movements of the late 19th and early 20th centuries. These inspired feminism too and are part of the internationalism of that epoch, as Akira Iriye discussed, and are thus part of the decolonization movements, which are all predecessors to the cosmopolitanism of our times.

'Humanitarian' has acquired an ominous ring in contemporary globalization—besides humanitarian aid and relief, 'humanitarian intervention' has been used so selectively and implemented so bluntly as an instrument of hegemony and coercion that Noam Chomsky's term 'humanitarian militarism' is appropriate.

The project or the idea of 'humanizing' globalization is chancy. In the first place, globalization is human already, thoroughly so. Hence humanizing it in effect means adopting a special, moralizing gaze on humanity, which, no matter its virtuous intentions, is a partial gaze that elevates some dimensions and skips others. Doing so might be 'civilizing', but this calls to mind Freud understands of civilization and its discontents. Another reservation is the postmodern reluctance towards humanism. As Lyotard said, Auschwitz took the ground from under the belief in humanity—as one of modernity's metanarratives. Foucault, too, distanced himself from humanism. Poststructuralism, then, is also post-humanism, a position that most modernists would not agree with. Ecology and deep ecology are also reluctant toward perspectives that are anthropocentric and fetishize humanity, for indulgent anthropocentrism has wrecked the planet.

Humanizing globalization, then, would imply the claim that humans can fix the planet, eradicate global inequality and implement global justice, which are pretty good ideas. Pending this, what we all—pre-modern, modern, postmodern—can share with Maimonides is perplexity as part of the human condition. It is surely part of globalization, too. These are themes that are inspired by Samir Dasgupta's engaging project of viewing globalization side by side with humanity.

Jan Nederveen Pieterse

Preface

Globalization is a word understood by many, in the Third World countries, as a kind of political strategy invented by some industrial nations to exploit the poor developing countries. This is because they observe that its consequences have been that the rich is becoming richer and poor is turning poorer. Therefore, the real concept of globalization and the problems associated with this phenomenon must be better understood.

Humanity, through the process of evolution, has grown from the condition of single families into tribes, then emerged into city-states and nations and now the world has reached the state of what is known as "global village" where all the nations and the peoples of the world have become highly interdependent. The problem that many feel about globalization is the abuse of some powerful groups or nations, taking advantage of this new reality for their own immediate egoistic benefits determinant to others.

Globalization and Humanity leads the reader well beyond a reiteration of current and past observations on this complex and often controversial subject.

Of special interest of this book is to relate the research of sociologists, economists and other contemporary academic social scientists to classical theology and philosophy—especially that rooted in the Vedic tradition of ancient Indian culture.

Thus, it is able to discern the commonalities, as well as the points of contention, in a vast range of viewpoints on humanity's evolution toward a single population, culture, and society.

Also noteworthy is my insistence that globalization in itself, is neither a positive nor a negative trend. Rather, its ultimate effects on the well-being of people depend critically on several, still unresolved factors. These include who is involved in the decisions that drive the process, which values are to dominate it, and whether the often vast inequalities that now exist between regions, ethnic groups, socio-economic classes, and the like will endue, increase, or diminish.

I have tried to point out throughout my study that to humanize globalization means to participate in the struggle for social justice. This is an ethical obligation that applies to both individuals and collectivities. First and foremost, however, it applies to the millions in the global North that have benefited for so long from existing global inequalities offering a diagnosis of global injustice as well as a vision of how to combat it,

Firstly, I want to thank my friends and excellent academicians Prof Manfred Steger, Prof Jay Weinstein, Prof Jan Nederveen Pieterse, Prof George Ritzer and Prof Pujan Kumar Sen and Prof Swapan Kumar Bhattacharyaya. I am really impressed of their humane nature and academic brilliance. I feel much and much pleasure to acknowledge them. Heartfelt gratitude is due to Chaitali for her deep sense of support and inspiration.

The appreciation and encouragement of my friends and colleagues, Prof Robyn Bateman Driskell, Prof Sing Chew, Prof Yvonne Braun, Prof Nicola Yeates, Prof Sheila L Steinberg and Joy A. Alemazung have inspired me to write such a book for a brighter tomorrow.

I am very much indebted to Prof Nico Stehr, Prof Abbas Mehdi, Prof Ismail Siriner, Prof Peter Kivisto, Prof Rosalind Sydie, Prof Ray Kiely, Dr Rajesh Pillai, Prof Julia Silvia Guivant, Prof Steven J. Steinberg, Prof Damayanti Banerjee, Prof Rajat Subhra Mukherjee, Prof Mahbuba Nasreen, Prof M. Mizan Uddin, Prof William K. Tabb, Prof Leslie Sklair, Dr Partha

Sarathi De, Dr Ananda Dasgupta and my dearest Diba, Mani, Manu, Tanu and Bristi for their love, good wishes and academic support.

Thanks are also due to distinguished Prof Immanuel Wallerstein, Prof Amitai Etzioni, Late Prof Andre Gunder Frank, Dr Paul Frank and Prof Samuel P. Oliner for their unflagging inspiration and academic support.

I am especially grateful to my wife Sumitra who always tempted me to work with this volume.

It has been my pleasure to work with Rawat Publications. I thank them for their unfailing enthusiasm.

Samir Dasgupta

1 Global Humanism

Humanity and trust underlie the common values. Without them, liberty/justice, rationality/sympathy, legality/civility and rights/responsibility will not have the wholesome ethical environment in which to become fully realized. To combat the grave dangers that threaten our viability, the need for wisdom and compassion is compelling. Wisdom always connotes holistic understanding, profound self-knowledge, common sense and good judgement. There are some ways such as art of listening, face-to-face communication and timeless ways of learning which make and teach us to be humane. Humanity enables us to establish a shared interaction with the other. Justice helps us to put our humane feelings for the other into action. The emergence of a global civil society suggested that global players, transcending ethnic, linguistic, cultural and religious boundaries, require new rules of the game to contribute humanity in the process of globalization. Depoliticized civility always speaks the truth of humanity. There are four mainstays of global humanity: a craving and determining for peace, for justice, for partnership and for truth. Sin against sin, vengeance against vengeance and brutality against brutality kills humanity. Some say that the number of clashes at present in action is still sizeable and the number of people affected directly or indirectly from war is very soaring.

Human Security Report, University of British Columbia states, "Although wars and war-deaths are down, there are some 60 armed conflicts raging around the globe. There are still gross abuses of human rights, widespread war crimes, and ever deadlier acts of terrorism."

Why are we creating this humanitarian tragedy for the Afghan people? It was the dehumanizing desire of the global player to bomb Afghanistan that put millions of people on the shift without food, clothes, shelter, water or medical facilities, and that has engendered this humanitarian cataclysm for every-where from 5 to 7 million Afghans. After the United States declared its strike against Iraq, the Holy Father in an address said, "When war, as in these days in Iraq, threatens the fate of humanity, it is ever more urgent to proclaim, with a strong and decisive voice, that only peace is the road to follow to construct a more just and united society." It is irrefutable that brutality and guns can never decide the problems of man and humane living. Recently, more than 280 are dead so far in the Gaza Strip and hundreds and more are severely injured—rocket bombs are striking *Ashdod* deep inside Israel for the very first time, and the sides are mobilizing for invasion. A global outcry has begun, but it'll take more than words—the immediate violence won't end, nor will wider peace be secured, without firm action from the international community. The humanists should immediately launch an emergency movement which will be conveyed to the key world powers, influencing them to act to make sure an instant truce and speak to the budding humanitarian predic-ament—only with strong global oversight and action can civilians on all sides be protected and real steps be taken toward a wider peace (http://www.avaaz.org).

Love for the impoverished, passion for the weak and feeling for the 'others' boost the attribute of humanity and global justice. If you say man a man, not a terrorist and if you open dialogue with him, he will not violate social peace. If you open dialogue with him regarding the cause of his discontent and try to solve his problems and plight, he will not be a terrorist.

Without kindness and understanding, solemnity deteriorates into obsessiveness, promise into passion, moral resentment into hostile rage, wisdom into a tool of annihilation, sacrifice into colossal distress, morality into conceit and audaciousness into cruelty. Humanity as sensitivity and sensibility nurtures other values so that the traits mentioned above can enrich our inner resources and strengthen our resolve to cultivate a mindset of peace. The definition of 'enemy' should be changed now. Confucius says, "The ruler rule with virtue, not force". The global players are very arrogant of their hegemonic power which leads to difference, dissension and inequality that lacks real respect for humanity. Mahatma Gandhi says about seven sins of human being which destroy our humanity and bind with globalization now, "Politics without principles, wealth without work, enjoyment without conscience, knowledge without character, business without morality, and science without humanity". Gandhi says, "All life is one.... Non-violence is not a mechanical thing. You do not become non-violent by merely saying 'I shall not use force'. It must be felt in the heart... When there is that feeling it will express itself through some action". That action, for Gandhi, was endless overhaul of mankind. His positive approach to life cropped up out of passionate love, his profound sagacity of uniqueness with all life and with the whole of humanity. He states, "My constructive programme is rooted in non-violence". So, not hatred but love, not hostility but kindliness, not revenge but heart-feeling, not exploitation but reconstruction and not exclusion but inclusion are the prime traits of ideal humanity in the present era of globalization. All men and women must be equal and be given equal openings. The people of our planet would be identical and all would sustain the poise of each and help accomplish devout progress and humanity.

The way I see it today, globalization does not have any advantages at all but to use, enslave others in other parts of the world. Once upon a time peace and humanity were the two aspects of human living. Men were the worshipper of beauty and aesthetics. They loved flowers. They loved nature's divine green. Son obeyed his parents as the prime agents of socialization and humane learning. The kids were enchanted and thrilled by the fairy tales. Help thy neighbours was the mission of human beings. "Attainment of highest ideal of humanity is the attainment of divinity" was the only ideal of human living. Men liked to live in the joint family under a common roof. They had a cordial interaction with their friends and relatives and frequently visited their kin's houses. They had a nice fellow feeling and they were emotionally perturbed at any sad incident. They used to love traditional value system and tried to obey moral and ethical values. But with the emergence of globalization all such systems have changed. We witnessed a new society with the new economy, new culture and new politics. The traditional kitchen utensils dumped in the museum. We began to take fast food coming and processing from alien countries. We began to take quantity food at a very fast pace which served by the waiters with efficiency and speed. The joint families began to break down with the emergence of consumerism. The family tie began to be distorted because of occupational and spatial mobility. The singleness of the world, which we call global village, becomes one and one is the only number which breeds into selfishness, egocentrism and isolation from the next kin. Then something is happening. Are we approaching towards a world of postmodernism which is very much alien to us? Kellner (1998) states, "Acting in the present age involves understanding the matrix of global and local forces, of forces of domination and resistance, and of a condition of rapid change and a 'great transformation' brought about by the global restructuring of capital and multidimensional effects of new technologies. The future is up for grabs, as are characterization of where we now are, where we are going, and what concepts and perspectives best characterize our present dilemma. I have suggested that we are living in a period between the modern and something new for which the term 'postmodern' stands as a marker. One could, of course, describe the tensions between global and the local, the modern and the postmodern, and the old and the new, as a process of postmodernization, of increasing complexity, fragmentation, indeterminacy, and uncertainty. Yet it is my position that although a postmodern turn is visible, continuities with the modern are so striking that it is a mistake to posit a postmodern rupture and exaggerate discontinuities". Might be. We are perhaps entering into such a world where space takes over humanity, where technology controls the humanity and where capital dominates over humanity. Kellner (1998) argues, "New technologies are changing the nature of work and creating new forms of leisure, including the hyper-reality of cyberspace, new virtual realities, and new modes of information and entertainment. Capital is producing a new techno-culture, a new form of the entertainment and information society, and everything from education to work to politics and everyday life is dramatically changing".

If we change the jingle from "Think globally, act locally" to "Think locally, act globally" the problems pertaining to global ecology, the development of a global information superhighway, and the need for new global forums for discussing and resolving the seemingly intransigent problems of war and peace, poverty and inequality, and overcoming divisions between the haves and the have nots may produce new conceptions of global citizenship and new challenges for global intellectuals and activists (Kellner, 1998).

While enquiring into the threefold *Sraddha* (endued) in the sacred Vedas in Indian society the utterance of '*Om*', '*Tat*' and '*Sat*' denote the philosophy of pure humanity. '*Om*' means the acts of sacrifice, gift and austerity as enjoined in the ordinances of Vedas; '*Tat*' denotes the various acts of '*Yajna*' without aiming at fruits; and the word '*Sat*' is used in the sense of reality and goodness. Vedic hymns really denote the humane or altruistic type of globalization. Ours globalization is mostly '*Rajshika*' and '*Tamashika*' type which lacks sacrifice, serenity of rationale, kindliness and honesty of motive.

Most of the development policies to eradicate social problems mostly depend on sociological insights. Its theories and knowledge are based on the construction of the real society. Bruce (1999: 99) observes, "Sociology recognizes the socially constructed nature of reality; it identifies the hidden cause of action; it describes the unanticipated consequences of action". If the sociologists assume such issues, the endeavour would be totally non-professional. The amateurism's view of sociological explanation is rhetoric and concerned with the world but professional sociology serves the real purpose of the real world. If it is the discourse of the real world, then it has a humanistic perspective.

We are now living in the age of globalization. We have taken shelter in a global village under a common borderless roof but, under the hegemonic and military domination of capitalist societies. We are using cell phones breaking down the face to face interaction with our relatives and neighbours. We are becoming more and more affluent in our style of living, showing our interest in cultural consumerism but disregarding our traditional culture and social living. We are now visiting fast food centres but suffering from severe diseases. We are getting cheap and easily available Viagra for sex pleasure but dying due to lack of high-priced life-saving drugs. This is our globalization. The theorists sometimes define globalization as a process of reorganization of the production, labour, capital and the world's reserves between people and countries. Globalization has also incorporated the scattered and distributed activities. In this process, there are recipients as well as sufferers. Some countries as a whole would benefit and the others lose. In the eventual analysis some may be included and others may be excluded. They include countries, communities, groups and individuals. Globalization can thus be defined as worldwide social relations which link distant localities in such a way that local happenings are shaped by events occurring in some other distant parts of the globe and vice versa. This is a dialectical process because such local events may move in an obverse direction from the very distanciated relations that shape them. Local conversion is as much a part of globalization as the lateral extension of social links across time and space (Giddens, 1990: 64).

If you think of humanity and worried of dehumanizing activities of human beings, you are suffering from the phobia of humanity erosion. Then, you are a radicalist. But I do not know what the actual sense of the term is. I only understand from literatures that if you claim yourself as a humanist, then, you are a radicalist. If you desire to see any problem from its root, then, you are a radicalist. If you view this world and its human beings in terms of humanity, then, you are a radicalist. The globalization of humanity is an organic and evolutionary process. Yet we face a massive crisis because the most central and important aspect of globalization—its economy—is currently being well-thought-out in a manner that so austerely infringes the basic principles by which healthy living systems are planned that it threatens the annihilation of our entire civilization. The organic view of humanism reflects that all living systems self-organize and maintain themselves by the same biological principles, which we can identify and abstract. Among the principles essential to the health of living systems are empowered participation of all parts and continual negotiation of self-interest at all levels of organization.

Humanity constitutes a living system within the larger living system of our earth. Essential to the health of humanity is the empowered participation of all humans and negotiated self-interest among individual, local and global economies as well as the world itself (Sahtouris, 1998). Thich Nat Han, in his *The Heart of Understanding* notes that survival means the continued existence of humankind as a whole, not just a part of it. If the South cannot survive, the North is going to crumble. If countries of the Third World cannot pay their debts, you are going to suffer here in the North. If you do not take care of the Third World, your well-being is not going to last, and you will not be able to continue living the way you have been for much longer. The global humanism is peace not war, light not darkness, happiness not anxiety and accomplishment not uncertainty. You may have cell phones, I-pod, internet access, you may travel across the world following time over space reality, you may be thrilled to have MacDonald pizza, you may be a regular visitor to shopping malls, you may have exported cars and foreign essentials, you may be the right man who follows globalization or neo-liberal philosophy. But, are you that man who disobeys your parents and sends them to the old age home? Are you that man who is the follower of unkindness, hatred, short temperament, selfishness and moral values destruction? Are you that man who likes to live in conjugal family, who always shows disrespect and disregard to his superiors, who hates tradition and local cultural values, and who is a fundamentalist and likes war? If it is the case, then, I can claim that humanity in the era of globalization is at stake. The planet is not dying; it is being killed, not by multinational corporations or institutions, although they certainly play their roles, but by the supreme power holders whose actions and choices mean war, death, hunger, illness, deforestation, flooding, drought, the global warming, eco-disaster, global terrorism, religious fundamentalism and "the end of the Cenozoic Era" (Brouillet, 2008). Humanists view human values as making sense only in the context of human life. Humanism is a philosophy of care. Humanist ethics are solely concerned with meeting human needs and solving human problems. It is a realistic philosophy. And, the humanists recognize the existence of moral predicament and the need for careful consideration of immediate and future consequences in moral decision-making. Humanists are devoted to civil emancipation, human rights, the extension of participatory democracy not only in government but in the workplace and education, an expansion of global consciousness and exchange of products and ideas internationally, and an open-ended approach to solving social problems, an approach that allows for the testing of new alternatives (Edwards, 1989).

Alvin Toffler (1970) forecasts, "Today, the whole world is a fast-breaking story. ... In the three short decades between now and the twenty-first century, millions of ordinary, psychologically normal people will face an abrupt collision with the future. Citizens of the world's richest and most technologically advanced nations, many of them will find it increasingly painful to keep up with the incessant demand for change that characterizes our time. ... This new disease can be called 'future shock'. ... Future shock is the dizzying disorientation brought on by the premature arrival of the future. It may well be the most important disease of tomorrow". *Future Shock* accurately foretold globalization and defined exactly how we would suffer from its effects. On the basis of such future paradigms we can say that globalization has really silhouetted our lives, styles of living, mindset and our tradition-bound identity. And, for billions of the world's people, capitalist globalization means uprooting old ways of life and threatening traditional styles of living, livelihoods and cultures. We have perhaps talked too much, and for much too long, about globalization. Globalization is a key organizing thought of our time. Social transformations, whether they be conceptualized as from local to global, or from modernity to postmodernity, are having diverse impacts on the production of social scientific knowledge not only in the discipline of sociology but also in diverse related fields. Conceptualizations of globalization and its social impacts are becoming ever more stylish. Understandings of who gains from globalization and who bears the burden of it are also evolving. As Immanuel Wallerstein (1974) argued, the global system is a hierarchy of power based on social inequalities between rich and poor nations. And, as conceptualizations are also moving beyond the crude dichotomies of global and local to hug 'glocalization' (Appadurai, 1996) so too imaginaries of integration, interaction, and harmony associated with the idea of the 'global village' are also giving way to accounts to capture the extent of discord, discrimination, and oppression arising from these global transformations (Purkayastha and Schwartzman, 2008).

You may not be interested in globalization but globalization is interested in you (Dasgupta, 2004). From the late 1980s or the early 1980s some prime incidents began to happen in the world's socio-political and economic spheres. Fall of the Soviet Union, the subsequent termination of the 'Cold War', demolition of Berlin Wall and the 'Asian Crisis' are some major events which accelerated the rejuvenation of globalization at the beginning of the new millennium. This may be called as the 'burst of globalization'. But, the theorists who have a deep sense of concern with the social reality are suffering from the crisis of intellectual and humanitarian stimulation.

The idea of a global village was based on the pledge of an extensive privileged circumstance, of economic globalization, and the additional belief that this wealth went hand in hand with distributing social justice and liberal democracy. The deceit of these undertakings, however, is apparent in growing discrimination and vicious circle of poverty. Kellner (1998) argues that 'globalization from below' refers to the ways in which marginalized individuals and social movements resist globalization and/or use its institutions and instruments to further democratization and social justice. While on one level, globalization significantly increases the supremacy of big corporations and big government, it can also give power to groups and individuals that were previously left out of the democratic dialogue and terrain of political struggle. 'The west and the rest' dichotomy makes our world not compressed but divided. The dismay of contrast between winners and losers, between lions and foxes at all levels of human existence feeds an insidious mood of ambiguity that creates a situation of 'either-or' mentality and exclusion-inclusion fear psychosis. The result is the expression of fundamentalism, religious bigotry, ethnic cleansing, separatism, genocide, cross-border terrorism and struggle for food and shelter. It has become the central point of attention in the social sciences since the late 1980s and has appeared as a paradigmatic concept in analyzing economic, social, political, environmental, ecological and cultural metamorphoses occurring in major parts of the modern world. The currency that the concept reflects the agenda that the world is now interconnected and interdependent mainly as a result of changes in the global economy and the quick changes in communication and information technology which have a great impact on the cultural, social and political shift. Globalization is used to describe the process by which the world is transformed into a single arena. At the heart of this is the incongruity that the concept of globalization as such should be applied to the tangible structuration of the world as a whole. It is not simply an economic phenomenon; rather it covers all the aspects of modern life: economic, cultural, political, humanitarian, social and ecological. In relation to these aspects, the social scientists increasingly turn their attention to global phenomena. Simply globalization can be defined as a process, which designates a transformation in the spatial organization of social relations and transactions. The prime features of this process are associated with historical trajectories, i.e., the universal adoption of state system, globally interdependent economic, political, cultural, technological and communication system. Globalization is now both an exciting opportunity and a formidable threat. For the most affluent it entails a shrinking world but it is very illusory and misleading for the destinies of the disadvantaged majorities. It is for an American child whose glittering eyes have been fixed on the enchanting Disneyland. Side by side, the dark face of globalization depicts a rather tragic picture when we see the face of a dejected child beggar who leaves the door empty handed. So, it seems very impractical to go beyond the world of us and them. Capitalism, which underwent different stages and the present phenomenon of globalization, ushers in the ongoing process of escalating social and economic inequality. For example, at the beginning of the 20th century, about 40–45 per cent of the world's population remained below the poverty line. Globalization can thrive and flourish either by perpetuating or escalating poverty. Globalization cannot reverse this ongoing process, it could only intensify it. As M.S. Swaminathan (2000) concisely says that there is no level playing field in this area since we have to pitch in this battle the economics of scale and money against the economics of livelihood, security and basic human needs. Industrial efficiency is being measured by increased production and decreased human employment, leading to what is being referred to as 'jobless growth'. Capitalism under the guise of globalization has excluded a vast bulk of populace. It survives and nurtures through exclusion and poverty boom. Globalization is like the amoeba. Nevertheless, its signs are poverty and hunger, exodus, illiteracy, unemployment and underemployment, health hazard and a multitude of other discriminations and injustices. Sorokin (1954) states, "By the mysterious forces of destiny mankind is confronted with a stern dilemma: either to continue its predatory policies of individual and tribal selfishness that lead to its inevitable doom, or to embark upon the policies of universal solidarity that brings humanity to the aspired for heaven on earth. It is up to every one of us which of the two roads we prefer to choose".

Sorokin's view presents the global people with a stern challenge: which path do we choose for our future? Should we choose to act individually for our own benefit, or collectively for the benefit of the whole? While this may often be interpreted on a micro level of individuals and small groups, it also applies to larger structures such as nation-states and international non-governmental organizations (NGOs). Indeed, Sorokin's debate is alive today, and is one of the most persuasive issues as we tackle with escalating globalization (Elvira del Pozo, 2006). One may easily raise the question: can globalization be oriented with the policies of universal solidarity?

It appears that the notion of globalization sounds with the lines of Dante's 'Inferno': "the motto on the gate of hell was: abandon all hopes yea, who enter herein". It means the present-day globalization is becoming a misnomer mostly because of the threat of exclusion and the crisis of new global ethic. Is it true that the danger of nuclear catastrophe has already been removed? Can we say that the risk of proliferation of weapons of mass murder is out of our imagination? The makers of globalization have failed to move to world vision of inclusion, participation, humanizing the differences, discrimination and dissonance. The gap between rich and poor countries has widened considerably. Amartya Sen (2002) comments, "To see globalization as merely Western imperialism of ideas and beliefs (as the rhetoric often suggests) would be a serious and costly error". He sees issues related to globalization that link imperialism. But it would be a great mistake "to see globalization primarily as a feature of imperialism. It is much bigger—much greater—than that". Only, making policies of universal solidarity, with the mission of distributive social justice and love, feeling and passion for human being, applying sense of all possible humanness, compassion and altruistic instinct, can built into the objectives. Globalization should be 'for the people, of the people' and must be by the do-gooders.

2 Dialectics of Globalization: An Antithesis of Humanity

The term 'global' is an indicator of the change. In the year 1960 this came to be used to mean "belonging to the world" or "worldwide". Marshall McLuhan (1962) uses the term 'the global village' capturing a property of modern culture like the possibility of global communication and suggests that the instant reception of far-off lights and voices changed the concept and content of culture. His idea focuses on the worldwide network of communication as a key organ of transforming local life of equal significance to the impact of capitalist markets. The advent of the global village as an imagined community is a sign of not only integration and coexistence but it indicates differences and dissonance. Wallerstein (1974) analyzes his 'world system theory' in terms of the power play which the centre or core extends and links to periphery, i.e., extension of power from metropolis to satellite. The image of influence in the idea of global culture gives extra impetus to those who recognize culture as an independent factor in the creation of one world.

Robertson (1992) develops a paradigm to mean the historical-temporal aspects of globalization which he might be intellectually inherited from Rostow. Considering political inputs, Robertson analyzes directly the canvas of development in terms of globalization process, which binds the question of reality. This links with the growth of communications, on which globalization depends. Robertson asserts that globalization refers both to the compression of the world and the intensification of consciousness of the world as a whole. The European Commission defines globalization as the process by which markets and productions in different countries are becoming increasingly interdependent due to the dynamics of trade in goods and services and flows of capital and technology. This indicates a new type of capitalism known as 'flexible accumulation' (Harvey, 1989). "The need of a constantly expanding market for its product chases the bourgeoisie over the whole surface of the globe. It must nest everywhere, settle everywhere, establish connections everywhere" (Marx and Engels, 1848). Wallerstein's (1990) world system theory has widened the Marxist version of understanding global capitalism. 'Global capitalist class' generally operates from a nation-state of hegemonic type who dominates the transnational practices in economic, political and cultural spheres. Castell's (1996) interpretation rejects the concept of 'global capitalist class' and accepts the view of integrated global capital network. Albrow (1990), on the basis of the warming debates of globalization, raises the issue of using sociology to global network and thus pleads for a global sociology. The term 'globalization' has come to be emotionally stimulating in public converse and has become a buzzword now. In fact, the brand of globalization is the surfacing of a single social system—the process, which is hastened by a worldwide network of economic, political and social relationships—able to produce a unique social order. The present-day globalization, as we see it or as we feel it, is a collection of processes in which economic, political, cultural and other ties are made between different countries. This interdependence has been contributory in forming a new pattern for our daily lives. Nowadays, internet and fax machines are connecting people who were once secluded, job availability for a person is widening, cross-border monetary transactions are increasing manifold, and trade patterns are altering quickly and the aftermaths of an event are not being merely confined within the national boundary but considerably affecting other countries too. The economic action patterns of local actors and institutions are moulded by external agencies, which epitomize the global changes in this regard, taking place around us. But, the concept does not just point out the concern of interconnectedness. Globalization is best perceived in terms of time-space distanciation. Giddens (1991) states that globalization concerns the intersection of presence and absence, the interlacing of social events and social relations at a distance with local contextualities. Contemporary globalization indicates to a phenomenon identified interchangeably as a process, an historical event or the end result of shifting "ethno-, techno-, media-finance, and ideo-scapes" (Appadurai, 1996). The present-day social scientists discuss globalization as a process by which the world is becoming increasingly interconnected and unified, subject to homogeneous and uniform process of cultural, technological and economic unification. This process replaces the concept of modernization, which mainly depends on the dualistic interpretations like 'centre-periphery', 'north block-south block' 'developed-third world' distinctions. But, as Martin Albrow (2001) emphasizes that globality is not the latest form of modernity. It is non-teleological and, in fact, consists of multiple globalizations without the totalizing character of the modern project, which neglected everything that resisted the advance of modernity. Theoretically, the concept of globalization may be viewed as the expansion of the world system, accompaniment of modernity, creation of a single world market and resultant of modernity. Of course, Beck (1992) refers it to as a 'second modernity'. Social scientists have to accept the intensified impact of globalization not simply as an imaginative terminology but as a contemporary social reality. Globalization dwells in the contemporary thought world and public discourse because it encourages change and the distant has come near.

But, side by side, it also tends to be associated with the feeling of subjection and economic depression in that the speed and scale of current global socio-economic change appears to overwhelm political leaders, planners, policy makers and academics. The unevenness of globalization compounds such dejection and strong are becoming stronger and the weak weaker. So, we may claim that globalization is an uneven process, which divides winners and losers. As stated earlier, the most affluent it entails a shrinking world but it is very deceptive for the destinies of the deprived majorities. It is for an American child whose glittering eyes have been fixed on the enchanting Disneyland. Side by side, the dark face of globalization depicts a rather tragic picture when we see the face of a dejected child beggar who leaves the door empty handed. The interconnection between globalization and inequalization sheds a head-spinning glimpse of alien future because we are confronted with two contradictory forces: globalization and localization on the one hand and progress and misery on the other. So, it seems very unreasonable to go beyond the world of us and them. As the 20th century has already come to a close, we all felt the incredible and positive changes of mindset among people and nations on the one hand and anecdotes of tragedies, fear of identity and uncertainty, on the other. As we move beyond the dichotomies of globalization and localization, developed and deprived, we become an increasingly interconnected global village. And, there is a global village, which we have not yet visited. There is also no scope to visit the global village either spatially or empirically. It is only our intention to imagine what would be the physical and socio-economic realities of global village and how the structural and functional components would interact. We are afraid of thinking the future of such a global village. We are also afraid of thinking its identity, nature of interaction, its economy, culture, politics and ecology. It is true that our planet is one but it is also the bleak reality that in our earth "22 children die of starvation in every minute ... one million dollars are spent on arms in every minute ... in the meantime three children died and the arsenal of the instruments of murder in the hands of adults grew by $1,50,000" (Dadayan, 1988). Would global village be able to remove all such contradictions and provide us the single economy, single culture, single society and single polity? Unification is not an averaging out. If some values become universal, for instance, all people the world over equally value peace and hate violence, then we would welcome such unification and we do not see in what way it can contradict such concepts as individuality or personal freedom. The bequests of globalization to the Third World are many. It generates macro social problems. More than half of the people of the world are living in conditions approaching misery. Their food is inadequate; they are victims of disease, ill-health, starvation, illiteracy, environmental and technological risks and cultural marginality, glocalism, terrorism and ethnic violence. So humanity in the global era, one may claim, is at stake. It is very much elitist by nature. Accordingly, the social policies will be constructed. It is very difficult for the applied sociologists to cross such a hell and high water. It is an important social agenda. Looking at the issues of poverty, inequality, economic growth and its relationship to trade liberalization, Kiely (2005) observes that there has been a substantial increase in inequality when comparing the poorest and richest countries. Growth can alleviate poverty. This is an important issue for social policy framing mechanism, but at least as important is the extent to which neo-liberal globalization can promote growth. But Kiely argues that the matter is not the simple matter of policy making, but it depends on the national and international power relations. And I hereby include the issue of humanity for the purpose of social generation and social reconstruction. Martin Luther King (Jr) states, "We must develop and maintain the capacity to forgive. He who is devoid of the power to forgive is devoid of the power to love. There is some good in the worst of us and some evil in the best of us. When we discover this, we are less prone to hate our enemies". Humanity is not just a catchphrase. It is associated with instinctive reality and perception of biological and mental state of human being. Here, we may think of forgiveness, love and apology of the human beings. Stephen Post (2003) says, "In essence, unlimited love is an abiding other-regarding perspective and emotional attunement that affirms and serves all of humanity unselfishly and unconditionally, without any exception whatsoever." Boundless love is a form of love that rises above every plausible limit to embrace all of humanity in joy, creativity, compassion, care, and generosity; it lies at the heart of all valid and sensible spiritual, religious, and plagiaristic philosophical traditions. It is often associated with a divine presence that underlies the cosmos and makes life a meaningful gift. Indeed, the life of unlimited love probably begins with the sense that every life is a gift. The concept of *forgiveness* is an important part of this paper. Forgiveness is the willingness to abandon the right to resentment, negative judgment, and indifferent behaviour towards one who has unjustly injured us, while fostering the undeserved qualities of compassion, generosity, and even love towards the offender (Enright, 1998). Apology does not make superficial excuses, but rather is a sincere attempt to ask the offended person for forgiveness in an attempt to restore harmony and reconciliation (Oliner, 2007).

While globalization is progressing at an extraordinary speed and power, the occurrence and profundity of local identities have resurged as key agenda. The ideal-type 'global village', which was created with the imagination of opening discourse of integration, interaction and harmony, can triumph over discord, differences, demarcation, discrimination and dissonance of local villages. But, the people in the Third World have been misled into believing that the world has changed and globalization means homogenization. The hegemonies and domination of the globalists indicate the black hole of exclusion and threats. It is a very debatable concept, explained in all sorts of different ways. But, the rhetoric of debate often hides more than it expresses. So, the debate over the merits and demerits of globalization continues. Behind the architecture of New World Order (benign globalization?) the malignant globalization creates a three-tier structure across national boundaries. The globalists reside in the core of the circle, in the second circle we find the people who "labour in insecure forms of employment and thrown into cut-throat competition in the global market" and the outer ring represents the exclude. If the world were a global village of 100 people, 70 of them would be unable to read, and only one would have a college education. Over 50 would be suffering from malnutrition; over 80 would live in what we call substandard housing. If the world were a global village of 100 residents, six of them would be American. These would have half the village's income; and the other 94 would exist on the other half. How would the wealthy six live "in peace" with their "neighbours" (Huizer, 2003)? To some observers, the process of globalization is linear, unidirectional. But this is a superficial perspective. For, upon reflection, it is clear that inconsistencies and disharmony characterize the process. At root, there are profound contradictions between globalization in progress and globalization in conflict. What seems to be globalization for some appears to be localization for others. Under these circumstances, a key question is whether globalization is bringing people new freedom to act or if it portends an uninvited, unwanted and cruel fate for the majority of the world's population. For the clash continues between fear, anxiety and uncertainty for the dejected majority and freedom, comfort and happiness for the few elites. Being local in a globalized world, is a sign of social deprivation and degradation (Bauman, 1998). Those local areas where global inputs exert the most pressure are losing their meaning-generating and meaning-negotiating capacities. The people in those areas are increasingly dependent on the economic and cultural hegemony of global powers. The gap between the global and the local, although often unobtrusive and dynamic, is potentially explosive. In brief, globalization is now oscillating between global winners and losers. Thus, globalization has to be perceived as a process which both includes and excludes peoples and nations. The process is embedded in a hierarchical system of power, exchanges and benefits (Petras, 1999). Can globalization lead us to a brighter world or will it generate more conflicts, poverty and contradictions in our already anxiety-ridden world? Dialogue is the only instrument to understand the present status of globalization. Thus, the need for discourse among the people of different nations has never been more acute. The focus of this book is on globalization as a worldwide phenomenon and an attempt has been made to draw theoretical and applied illustrations from different parts of the world. Until recently, the leading philosophical perspective on globalization emphasized crossing the economic and cultural divide. Ethically and morally, the purpose of globalization was to bring different races, cultures, ethnic groups and socio-economic classes into closer contact with each other. The rationale for the movement was altruistic: to replace hatred with love, violence with peace, destruction with construction, their culture with our culture, and an 'either' with an 'or' mindset. The elements of this globalization paradigm were the elimination of hostility, the construction of an ideal-type civil society, the restructuring of a sick economy, and the integration of all cultures.

Now, however, we fear the injuries that globalization can inflict in each and every facet of our economic, cultural, political and social lives. The concept demands revision, reassessment, re-evaluation and re-projection. It demands reflections on diversity, an open vision of humanity and free discourse. It is a grim fact that many nations and peoples are now confronting reality with what appear to be two mutually contradictory faces: the global and the local. Along with the increasing pace of globalization in science, technology, economy, culture, education, communication, global and local conflicts are also increasing at an unprecedented pace. This situation weakens the positive potentials of globalization.

According to Martin Albrow (2001), nothing better illustrates the difference between globalization, on one hand, and modernization, on the other than the debates about the relationship between global and local interests. From Albrow's perspective, the local is always defined in contrast to a specific frame of reference. That is, the local is the neighbourhood in relation to the community; it is the community in relation to the nation-state; and it is the nation-state in relation to the international system. Conflicts emerge with the metamorphosis of localism into globalism. This is the locus of economic, cultural and political marginality, which can easily generate a situation of crisis, adoption-rejection conflict, disintegration, pandemonium and disarray. It was once believed that the primary mission of globalization was to integrate the parts into whole. But, in fact, the parts have lost their socio-cultural, economic and political identity. The result is severe economic disparity, painful cultural identity crisis, loss of the sense of belonging, ethnic violence, secessionism and, ultimately, civilization shock. The tragedy of globalization is that it began with the aim of restructuring and rebuilding civilizations; yet the mission has produced discord, more separatism and identity crisis. The global village, once a symbol of integration, unification and harmony, now stands for difference, differentiation, isolation, discrimination and dissonance. The world, compressed into a single economic, ecological, cultural, electronic and political system, has never been so highly stratified (Picco, 2001).

The estimated global population is around 6 billion, of which 3 billion live in Asia. The total worldwide assets of all countries were estimated at $150 trillion at end of 2005.

The richest 2 per cent of the adults, approximately, 120 million people, control 50 per cent of the global wealth. Out of this, 1 per cent or 60 million control 40 per cent of it. The balance 1 per cent or 60 million people control the rest 10 per cent of it. Fifty per cent of the world population has an asset or net worth of less than US $2,200 or around INR 88,000. The rest 48 per cent do not have any assets at all.

The richest country in the world—USA—has the highest per capita income of $1,80,837. Japan follows it with $1,43,427. Canada has a per capita income of $89,252 and has 0.2 per cent of the wealthiest 1 per cent in the world. The bottom 125 countries have per capita income of less than 500 dollars. In some of the poorest countries, people earn just a dollar a day or even less (Ward, 2006). The catalog of horrors attests not only to the failures of the ideals of globalization, but even more vividly to the harsh unintended consequences the process has produced. Consider, for example, the severe famine in Somalia, extreme economic genocide in Rwanda, the rise of fundamentalism and fanaticism in India and Pakistan, and moral and ethical corruption and political and economic turmoil in Bangladesh. Recall, too, the debt burden in Brazil, Argentina, and Bolivia, and economic disintegration in Peru. In these and related instances, globalization has brought hopelessness, disparity and ethnic explosion.

Charlie Chaplin, in his excellent film *The Great Dictator,* expresses the true spirit of democracy and altruism, "We want to live by each other's happiness, not by each other's misery. We don't want to hate and despair one another ... in the name of democracy.... Let us all unite. Let us fight for a new world—a decent world that will give men a chance to work—that will give youth a future and old age people a security. Let's fight to free this world to do away with national boundaries to do away with greed, with hate and intolerance...".

Chaplin resonates a satiric *raga* about an ideal type of globalization. But forty years have passed (since the coinage of the term 'global village' by Marshall McLuhan in 1962), and our society remains as it was. In terms of disparity, we remain parts rather than wholes. In terms of a single humanity, we are divided. In terms of wealth, we are either rich or destitute. From the porthole of a space vehicle high above the earth, it is obvious that the divided and rival peoples comprise only one human race; for the borders that separate nations are not visible from the outer space. But, in the inner space of the earth, we see the heartbreaking division of humanity into hostile groups. Terrorism, sectarianism, bigotry, fundamentalism, and its horrible descendant, fanaticism, have all possessed this beautiful planet. They have filled the earth with violence, drenched it often with human blood (Vivekananda, 1893). Does this represent altruism and humanism? Does it indicate the philosophical, idealistic spirit of the globalization mission?

3 Globalization Phobia

The upsurge of excessive media culture and consumerism, which appear to the people as hallucination, not only damage mental health but also destroy the emotional mindset and social, moral and ethical values which may cause severe humane crisis in future society and certainly will divert people from social ideals and ideas that may ultimately enervating civil society. I feel tired—I feel badly tired of the rat race. I feel bored of the cell and mail culture. I feel disgusted of the invited technological hazards. I spent breathless nights at the loud and enchanting spell of rock-and-roll music associated with global instruments mix like *Tabla* (an Indian instrument), Spanish guitar, African drum, Egyptian flute and heavy metal anthem. All the global cultures, rituals, races, databanks, the toys of technological Disneyland, cyberspace and its hydra-headed piercing antenna, mysterious and simulacra-fashioned language game are intermixing like a smorgasbord in an earthquake that severely damaged our tradition and our identity. I do not know how far it is possible to integrate the differences in cultures, styles of living, rituals, socialization, mindset, temperament, customs, folkways, norms and politico-economic behaviour of the local people into global. I was saying about tradition—that soothing and symphonic tradition, which always invites me to be with its orbit. I want to enjoy our traditional folk songs and dances like *Baul,*

Bhatiwali, Tusu, Saree and *Chou of* West Bengal, *Bihu* of Assam, classical dances like *Bharat Natyam, Mohini Attyam* and *Kucipudi* of South India, *Kathhak* of Manipur, *Oddisi* of Orissa etc. I do not want to enjoy a global dance with the image of "East Indian head, a male Navaho left leg, the right leg of an Afro-American modern dancer, a torso half-covered by a suit and tie...and two more female arms in a lyrical dance pose from India" (Powel, 1998).

I want to get back to our traditional roots where there was love, emotions, kindness, devotion, forgiveness, tolerance, truthfulness, loyalty to parents and other kith and kin, obedience, humane feelings and so on. Here, there was no room for technological despotism and value trafficking. One very crucial question comes into my mind: Does globalization disintegrate *'Togetherness'* and individual style of thinking and living? Might be. It has mostly swallowed our traditional interaction pattern and 'we-feeling' within the local orbit. The social and political evolutions during this era of globalization are giving rise to a moral dismay and sarcasm, as can be heard in phrases and laments like 'the end of modernity', 'against ethics', 'the closing down of humanism', 'simulacra fashioned human existence', 'moral aestheticism and relativism', and so on. Another factor fuelling this moral bafflement of our age is the radicalization of the stress between a much needed long-term dream for human aspirations on the one hand and the always bullying importance and short-term applicability of policies on the other. The moral perplexity of the era of globalization has rendered us a temporal lack of forethought.

The Disparity

I am not a global naysayer. Global pessimists are those who claim that the gains of global capitalism are unequally distributed. They suggest that large disparities of wealth feed international terrorism and are worried about the benefits of a technological and consumerist society. Masters of alarm and anxiety, they prey on fear of the future and have authored one of the great narratives of our time: globalization is bad. I am not going to call globalization bad; rather, my intention is to describe and explore some uncertainties and errors of globalization.

The Reality

It is evident from the United Nations Development Programme's Human Development Report, 2003 that the income of the richest 25 million Americans was equivalent to that of nearly 2 billion of the world's poorest. In 1920, per capita income in Western Europe was three times that in Africa; by the 1990, it was more than 13 times as high. Adding human meaning to these numbers, the report said, "the statistics today are shaming; more than 13 million children have died through diarrhoea disease in the past. Every year over a half million women, one for every minute of the day, die in pregnancy and childbirth. More than 800 million suffer from malnutrition" (cited in Sen, 2004). Fiedel Castro imagines a new type of social and economic order as an alternative to present globalization: "The world needs an order. There is a need for universal, global, just and democratic order. There is an order coming, one that can be seen coming at a full speed, unstoppable—it's the neo-liberal globalization, going global. We have to start thinking about an order of a different kind and, in the meantime, denounce and struggle."

The Divided World

The west and the rest dichotomy makes our world not compacted but alienated. The horror of contrast between winners and losers, between lions and foxes at all levels of human existence feeds a pervasive mood of uncertainty that creates a situation of either-or mentality and exclusion-inclusion fear psychosis. The result is the expression of fundamentalism, religious bigotry, ethnic cleansing, separatism, genocide, cross-border terrorism and struggle for food and shelter. It appears that the notion of globalization sounds with the lines of Dante's 'Inferno': "the motto on the gate of hell was: abandon all hopes yea, who enter herein". It means the present-day globalization is becoming a misnomer mostly because of the menace of barring and the crisis of new global ethic. Is it true that the danger of nuclear catastrophe has already been removed? Can we say that the risk of proliferation of weapons of mass murder is out of our imagination? So, we have to say, "We appeal as human beings to remember your humanity and forget the rest. If you can do so, the way lies upon to a new paradise" (Russell and Einstein, 1995).

Globalization as Humanity: Threatening Phenomenon

The unbridled commercialization and commodification of social life threaten the humanitarian fabric of societies of the rest world. Here, the global ethics like craving and striving for peace, justice, partnership and truth appear as a misnomer code of global conduct. What is clear is that the global-local dichotomy is giving birth to an uncertain globalization where there is no room for humanity. In inner space of the earth we see the tragic events of the division of humanity. Globalization, as a humanity-bullying phenomenon, has possessed this beautiful earth. The commonalities that unite the people of the rest might have been possible if they were not dejected. The globalizers have created a 'global gloom' where we can see a dichotomy of 'revolutions of rising expectations' and 'revolutions of rising frustrations'. For example, in our country, the media has entered into the remotest rural areas and the cultivators are now ready to accept the gift of globalization knowingly or unknowingly which creates the temptations of 'rising expectations', to have better yields and less profit-risk. A good number of cultivators purchased seeds from foreign agencies at minimum cost and got the full benefit of selling and profit return. In the next year some conditions were imposed upon the local cultivators. They had to give tariff and satisfied the conditions of the foreign agencies. In course of time it was seen that the cultivators began to suffer from the fear of rising frustrations because their local seeds had already being damaged and they were being totally dependent on the global companies. The ultimate result of such trapping is mass suicide. This type of authoritarian globalization creates uncertainty among the rest. Does this incident show the expansion of opportunities for unparalleled human advance? In the unending debates that are raging about globalization, it is often found that people are taking extreme views, like the end points of a pendulum. One side is totally in its close and ready to swallow its hook, line and sinker. The other side is equally ardent to reject it viewing it like an ogre, ready to swallow the poor countries. It is quite a tough task for a sociologist to find out the exact point along the swinging track of the pendulum. Contemporary segmented realities, nevertheless, suggest that the spirit of we-ness and the process of globalization as such represent a myth; it is perhaps, a tragedy that the spirit so much endowed with the promise of reconstructing the world had to express symptoms of uncertainty, dissonance, fundamentalism, threat, exclusion and identity crisis. It demands re-thinking of the globalization discourse. Social scientists and altruists are divided over how globalization promotes homogeneity, integration and co-existence on the one hand and disparity, dejection, differences, dissension and unevenness, on the other.

Open Heart Surgery

As we move beyond the dichotomies of globalization and localization, developed and rejected, we become an increasingly interconnected global village. We are afraid of thinking the future of such a global village. What would be its identity? What would be its nature of interaction? What would its economy, culture and environment? Our planet is one but it is also the bleak reality that in our planet "22 children die of starvation in every minute ... one million dollars are spent on arms in every minute ... in the meantime three children died and the arsenal of the instruments of murder in the hands of adults grew by $1,50,000" (Dadayan, 1988). Would global village be able to remove all such contradictions and provide the village with single mindset? Unification is not an averaging out. If some values become universal, for instance, if all people the world over equally value peace and hate violence, then we would welcome such unification and we do not see in what way it can contradict such concepts as individuality or personal freedom. The scars of misery and deprivation mar the face and heart of the world. It presents a "picture of horror and dejection for majority of people who were born to face a slow and agonizing death" (Dadayan, 1988). In *New Times* it is reported that "in the Third World there are now starving over 500 million; life expectancy under 60–1.7 billion; lacking medical care—1.5 billion; living in extreme poverty—over 1 billion; unemployed and underemployed—more than 500 million; annual per capita income under $150–800 million; illiterate adults—814 million; children having no access to school education and unable to attend school—over 200 billion" (cited in Dadayan, 1988). Tinbergen (1976) notes, "we have a situation where, in the Third World, millions of people toil under a broiling sun from morning till dusk for miserable rewards and premature death without even discovering the reasons why". The ratio of per capita product in the underdeveloped countries and developed countries was only 1 and 1.2 in 1770. The per capita income at the turn of the 19th century in the developed and underdeveloped countries was $190 and $150 respectively, and the ratio at the beginning of the 20th century was 1 in case of developing countries and 14+ for developed countries. This ratio denotes a horrible picture of dejection and inequality.

The reason was certainly the appearance of managerial capitalism, which made the disparity and the divided selves. The process of exploitation of the people by the capitalists has changed its image from time to time. Marx, on the exploitation by the colonists, wrote: "The discovery of gold and silver in America, the extirpation, enslavement and entombment in mines of the aboriginal population, the beginning of the conquest and looting of the East Indies, the turning of Africa into a warren for the commercial hunting of black skins, signalized the rosy dawn of the era of capitalist production". A Soviet social scientist, N.P. Shmelyov (1970) writes that the treasure gained from beyond Europe by means of robbery, enslavement of the people of America, Asia and Africa, murder, treachery and subordination flowed into the metropolises where it was turned into capital. And, "the capital comes dripping from head to foot, from every pore, with blood and dirt" (Marx). The Third World countries have their own problems like one-sided dependence on, and economic and technological illness. The contracts between wealth and poverty in the developing countries are sharper than in their developed counterparts. Whilst in 1983 (the concept of shadow globalization opened its petals in 1960) Switzerland had per capita GDP 4.3 times that of Greece ($13,338 and $3,558 respectively), the per capita GDP of the UAE was no less than 187 times that of Bangladesh ($23,546 and $126 respectively). The 15 richest countries in the capitalist world included seven developing states ... there are 55 countries in the group where the per capita GDP exceeds $1,500, 55 between $150 and $1,500 and 50 with less than $500 of which the group of 38 least developed countries have a GDP equivalent to $20.1 per capita, which is 50 times less than the developed capitalist countries and 52 times less than the United States. The statistics reveals that since 1960 (the mission of globalization started) income disparity among countries had increased worldwide. It is evident from the World Development Report that the wealthy countries have experienced a steady growth in their share of the world GNP, while the poorest countries have experienced with a tragic decline in their share of world GNP. "Between 1960 and 1991, the richest fifth of all nations had its share of world income rise from 70 per cent to 85 per cent, while the poorest fifth of all nations had its share fall from 2.3 per cent to 1.4 per cent" (UNDP, 1994). This trend towards greater disparity gives a very chronic indication of continuing into the next millennium (Sandler, 1997). This sort of chronic disparity sounds the opus of dilemma whether the globalization policy would be able to reduce the tension of conflict arising from such an inequality or inequality itself would be a prime mover in economic equality, social integration and crisis reduction. This is perhaps the globalization impasse.

With the emergence of the jingle of globalization the rate of global disparity is increasing with a very a steady and rapid pace. The top poorest 40 per cent nations are suffering from chronic development sore. They are not even curable even by the application of any development steroid. The income disparity between top 20 per cent richest countries and down 20 per cent poorest countries shows a distinct mark of horror and dejection. The ratio of GNP between these two types of nations, i.e., 61:1 is not even alarming but fatal too. The motto on the gate of global village for down 40 per cent poorest country sounds: "Abandon all hopes, yea, who enter herein". But, the heads of the global village are sermonizing the message to the depressed people through economic, cultural and political satellites that they would minimize such an increased inequality and would arrest the greatest threats to mankind. But, their golden voices contradict with the grim reality. They are conferring that they would establish an ideal type of global village with a single roof for all but the reality stands for confusion, which might be the future shock for the people in Third World countries. The trend toward greater inequality gives every indication of continuing into the new millennium, as the underlying factors show no signs of abating. "Will increasing world inequality worsen or alleviate global conflicts? Furthermore, will increased inequality make these conflicts easier or more difficult to address in the future?" (Sandler, 1977). The people in the Third World countries are now in confusion whether they would be the beneficiaries of the global change or they would be the worsen victims of increased global inequality. The 'free-ride aid', a new type of foreign aid, a section of the development experts assume, may reinstate "traditionally tied and untied foreign aid of the post-World War II period" and the according behaviour pattern on the part of the poor may limit even greater worldwide inequality. But this possibility is merely the utopian possibility because the worldwide income inequality pattern and the trend of global income disparity limit the impact of free-ride aid and free-riding behaviour as the accelerating inputs of globalization process. It is evident from the report of the United Nations Development Programme (1996) that the wealthiest 1 per cent of people owned 36 per cent of the world's financial assets in 1990. Is the one per cent people are the head of the global village? If it is so, then, the concept of forming and creating global village is a misnomer. The other name of such a utopian globalization is global identity crisis. For instance, millions of poor, unemployed, underfed and illiterate Indians are not even familiar with the term 'globalization'. The former President of India, K.R. Narayanan in a speech comments: "the three-way fast lanes of liberalization, privatization and globalization cannot be placed above everything else and cannot be an end in itself". The President's caution is intended for the negative directions of liberalization, privatization and globalization and a vast majority of the people has been left untouched by this transformation. The President observed, "We find that justice—social, economic and political—remains an unrealized dream for millions of our fellow citizens". It is undeniable that we have the largest number of people below the poverty line and the largest number of children suffering from malnutrition. The Asian Development Bank estimates that every third Asian is poor, judged by the World Bank interim of a per capita daily income of one US dollar. South Asia, one of the poorest regions in the world, now has more than 900 million poor people of whom 450 million are in India. The UN Commission for the nutrition challenges in the Twenty-First Century, in its report (2000), has pointed out that "about one in four new-born children in developing countries—around 30 million each year—suffer retarded growth in the womb. About 35 million, or a third of our children between the ages of 6 and 10, have no opportunities for school education. Large numbers of poor children are "pushed out" of the school system within 2 to 3 years of their entering it. We are thus beginning this century, frequently referred to as the knowledge and innovations century, with every third child being handicapped at birth in brain development due to poverty-induced maternal and foetal under and malnutrition and every third child left out of the educational system (Swaminathan, 2000).

Besides, when people suffer from economic insecurity, fear of shelterlessness, health hazard, fear of war catastrophe, ecological threatening, cross-border terrorism, ethnic violence, loss of family-interaction identity and moral and ethical value erosion, humanitarian globalization appears as a jargoned spell of discourse. Specifically, the term has its own social science discourse and mostly textual. In the textbooks of social sciences the term 'globalization', along with the concept of postmodernity, has crossed its cognitive and metaphysical boundary. This has become more popular among the academicians, intellectual elite, media personalities and activists. But, to the common people, the term becomes visible as a hydra without tentacles. The explanatory and meaningful as well as realistic variables of the concept are not clear and lucid; rather, it is mostly a buzzword. Humanizing globalization means inclusion of marginalized countries and people.

In intellectual discourse, globalization raises a debate about the relevant economic issues. Among the processes of globalization, economy is a vital part, which has accelerated the very process of globalization to a great extent, and in essence, which means the rise of the giant companies operating on national economies all over the globe. By the early 1990s, there were around 37,000 Trans-National Corporations (TNCs) controlling over 2,00,000 foreign affiliates worldwide, generating sales of more than $4.8 trillion (UNCTAD, 1994: 86). Today, the TNCs are enjoying an enviable 50 per cent share of the world's largest selling economic units. Their influence on world economy is unrestrained now and is increasing day by day. For example, the combined sales of the world's largest 350 TNCs totalled nearly one-third of the combined GNPs of the 'advanced' capitalist countries (New Internationalist, 1993: 18). Moreover, the leading 600 TNCs are responsible for one-fifth of the world's total industrial and agricultural production. Thus, for these institutions, the globalization of the world economy means the ability of capital to move freely "across national boundaries" (Ohmae, 1991). So, in the prevailing condition, we cannot think of a single, independent indigenous economy because the financial capital in the global network is highly

Table 1

Total External Debt

(in $ million)

Country	Total external debt		Long-term debt		Public and publicly guaranteed debt		Private misguaranteed debt		Use of IMF credit	
	1990	2002	1990	2002	1990	2002	1990	2002	1990	2002
Afghanistan	—	—	—	—	—	—	—	—	—	—
Argentina	62,233	1,32,314	48,676	1,03,140	46,876	74,661	1,800	28,479	3,083	14,340
Australia	—	—	—	—	—	—	—	—	—	—
Brazil	1,19,964	2,27,932	94,427	1,83,710	87,756	96,565	6,671	87,145	1,821	20,827
Bangladesh	12,439	17,037	11,657	16,445	11,657	16,445	0	0	629	71
China	55,301	1,68,255	45,515	1,20,370	45,515	88,531	0	31,839	469	0
India	83,628	1,04,429	72,462	99,860	70,974	88,271	1,488	11,589	2,623	0
Iraq	—	—	—	—	—	—	—	—	—	—
Mexico	1,04,442	1,41,264	81,809	1,31,364	75,974	76,327	5,835	55,038	6,551	0
Pakistan	20,663	33,672	16,643	30,100	16,506	28,102	138	1,998	836	2,032
Peru	20,064	28,167	13,959	25,596	13,629	20,477	330	5,118	755	237
Poland	49,364	69,521	39,261	60,637	39,261	29,374	0	31,263	509	0
Russian Federation	—	1,47,541	—	1,24,738	—	96,223	—	28,514	—	6,481
Rwanda	712	1,435	664	1,305	664	1,305	0	0	0	85
Sri Lanka	5,863	9,611	5,049	8,805	4,947	8,455	102	351	410	310
Turkey	49,424	1,31,556	39,924	94,278	38,870	61,823	1,054	32,455	0	22,086
Vietnam	23,270	13,349	21,378	12,181	21,378	12,181	0	0	112	381

(in $ million)

World	Total external debt		Long-term debt		Public and publicly guaranteed debt		Private mis-guaranteed debt		Use of IMF credit	
	1990	2002	1990	2002	1990	2002	1990	2002	1990	2002
Low Income	4,11,419	5,23,464	3,51,318	4,48,932	3,32,366	3,99,076	17,953	49,857	11,317	20,258
Middle Income	9,40,479	18,17,163	7,49,931	14,69,476	7,07,793	9,83,880	42,138	4,85,596	23,334	75,550
Lower Middle Income	5,83,682	11,49,118	4,77,625	9,25,294	4,53,753	6,51,767	23,872	2,73527	7,811	59,160
Upper Middle Income	3,56,797	6,68,045	2,73,306	5,44,182	2,54,040	3,32,112	18,266	2,12,069	15,523	16,390
Low and Middle Income	13,51,898	23,40,627	11,01,250	19,18,408	10,41,159	13,82,955	60,091	5,35,453	34,651	95,809
East Asia and Pacific	2,34,092	4,99,133	1,94,633	3,88,064	1,72,998	2,72,783	21,635	1,15,281	2,085	11,618
Europe and Central Asia	2,17,224	5,45,842	1,76,378	4,34,625	1,71,457	276350	4,921	1,58,275	1,305	34,245
Latin America and Caribbean	4,44,227	7,27,944	3,52,476	6,13,916	3,27,447	384961	25,029	2,28,956	18,297	38,302
Middle East and North Africa	1,55,134	1,89,010	1,20,603	1,48,851	1,19,101	142396	1,502	6,455	1,815	2,219
South Asia	1,24,395	1,68,349	1,07,527	1,58,723	1,05,799	144785	1,727	13,938	4,537	2,416
Sub-Saharan Africa	1,76,826	2,10,350	1,49,632	1,74,229	1,44,355	161681	5,276	12,548	6,612	7,009

Source: World Bank World Development Report, 2004. pp. 242–244.

mobile and is playing a key role in determining the fate of the Third World economies.

The term 'globalization' is now a demanding subject of analysis. Many countries initially susceptive to it are accepting the inputs of globalization either as a forced inception due to political and economic constraints or as a matter of continuing process of development. The triad, i.e., the United States, Europe and Japan being the initiators and backed by IMF and World Bank, is now partially successful to spread its arms to developing as well as developed countries. It has bipolar realities: (a) creating a global situation of open market it has created high hope and aspiration in developing countries to be at par with the global nucleus; and (b) creating an unbound disparity between the periphery and the core. The two opposite contending forces of globalization process, i.e., growth decade and global malady have created a dilemma in the scenario of the Third World country. And, the crisis is very acute in case of India.

It is estimated that the amount of debt in the year 1980–81 was Rs 819 crore which increased to Rs 5,480 crore. The second major criterion of disparity is evident from the estimate of the ratio of income inequality. In the year 1970 the ratio of income inequality between the highest rich and the lowest poor country was reported to be 30:4, which increased to 74:1 in 1997. The net result of such a disparity is hunger, high mortality due to malnutrition and disease, unemployment, illiteracy, industrial stagnation and trade crisis.

In India, the globalization with its economic liberalism and reformation has failed to produce a very glowing impact. The annual rate of industrial development in India was 13 per cent in 1995–96, which decreased to 2.3 per cent only in the year 2001–02. The annual rate of growth of GDP in the year 1993–94 was 7.1 per cent, which reduced to 5.1 per cent by the year 1997– 2001. The gloomier picture of our economic growth indicates a frustrating representation of the impact of globalization in India.

In India, with the acceptance of globalization, the quantitative restrictions on 715 foreign commodities were omitted from 1st April, 2001. And masses are attracted to these low-priced foreign goods which causes stagnation of national industrial development. This stagnation leads to the dependency and the Third World countries are becoming periphery of the triad—United States, Europe and Japan. And, the triad is accumulating capital from the peripheries. Ultimately, the time will come when the destiny and fate of the Third World countries will be totally controlled, regulated and managed by the initiators of the globalization process.

World Development Report (2000–01) accepts the view of poverty as encompassing not only low income and consumption but also low achievement in education, health, nutrition and other areas of human development. By definition, poverty now includes powerlessness and voicelessness and vulnerability and fear. These dimensions of human deprivation emerged forcefully from "Voice of the Poor" study, conducted as background for World Development Report, 2000–2001, which systematically sought the views of more than 60,000 poor men and women living in 60 poor countries. The basic outcome of the study reveals that (i) increasing education leads to better health outcomes; (ii) improving health increases income earning potential; (iii) providing safety nets allows poor people to engage in higher risk, higher return activities; (iv) estimating discrimination against women, ethnic minorities and other disadvantaged groups; (v) gross under-optimization of the precious and wonderful human potential endowment as its immediate determinant; and (vi) lack of equal opportunities for all stemming from such evils.

The bipolar concept of globalization, i.e., dualism and marginalization, are the key windows to open or close. Dualism is very much a new form of dependence on capitalist development while marginalization refers to the expression of exclusion and discarding by the triadic centre. The rationale of the globalization process marks some negative aspects of development such as property ownership and income consumers in corruption, social hierarchy etc. as its intermediate determinants and outmoded non-egalitarian social structure, unjust international economic order, vicious human psyche and mindset erosion of ethical values and spiritual and moral degradation and value crisis as its ultimate determinants. And, the sole cause of such a disparity is the transnational triadic capitalism. Historically speaking, the features of the current stage of capitalism have taken its shape on and from post-war period. The dualism of the national monopoly capitalism leads to the marginalization of the current transnational triadic capitalism (Bruno, 1998). The present practice of globalization is ostensible by the poor countries as a means to accumulate capital by the initiator countries. But, the followers and the initiators both speak of globalization as a means to control market and available resources so as to increase worldwide profits and to reduce poverty of the Third World countries and to make a cohesion between rich and weaker parts of the globe without the constraints of bureaucratic red tapes. But reality says another version. A strong voice of protest against globalization rises from more or less all parts of the globe. This 'anti-globalization' saying has a strong base of reality. A senior administrator for Porter Novelli writes: "A friend of mine told me a story very soon after the genocide in Rwanda. He was there as a military representative accompanying an NGO tour of the area. The situation was awful. There was also no infrastructure to get to the people in need. And so there were United Nations conveys that just could not get through. This delegation literally sat there on the road for hours going nowhere. By the time they finally reached their destination, they discovered that Coke had already been there for two weeks distributing what they needed. What a fascinating thing—Coke got there before the UN. It shows you just how powerful the global market is and this brand in particular .... I suppose if Microsoft needs to be there, they'll be there too" (Hunter and Yates, 2002).

So, one may argue that globalization is, in both source and character, American. McDonaldization or Americanization as the synonym of globalization is now being viewed by the social scientists. For example, McDonald serves fast food to 20 million people worldwide each day, Coca-Cola serves billions of people worldwide everyday, MTV reaches half a billion people per year, etc.

Role of Alternative Development Forum

A section of the development specialists holds the view that the motive of spreading global net is partially being performed and activised by the non-governmental agencies. The increased interest and funding of NGOs are generally thought to have a much greater capacity to reach down to the local, grassroots level. Many bilateral and multilateral aid programmes now seek to claim their political neutrality and altruism by linking with NGOs to spend huge amount and resources on their behalf. In the mid-1990s, for example, the US amazed observers by asserting that it intended to channel half its aid through NGOs (Todaro, 1977). It is very interesting to note that many organizations calling themselves NGOs are in fact largely funded by governments or from official state resources. For example, Norwegian Church Aid (NCA) is mostly funded by the Norwegian State. The government ministries have established a number of Japanese NGOs. Zimbabwe follows the same path. The NGOs generally call them either as philanthropic organization or as humanitarian agencies. One can raise the issue that NGOs act as the agents of the globalization initiators and maintain a parallel form of private development agency. Not only may that one argue that NGOs make the global mindset of the distressed people in the Third World. The NGOs are working on environmental protection, health condition, famine and hunger, the protection of human rights and making lobby within and outside the country. In some countries of the Third World their development action sometimes crosses the border of limit as determined by the state/country development rate. So, their actions and development promotions are more functional than the structural globalization. They have direct access to the distressed rural and tribal people, they run localized projects of development and day by day NGOs are amplifying the canvas of their actions and activities—their voice is sometimes very much accountable to policy makers and they advocate both national and international levels. They have a history of metamorphosis. They are now moving on to the promotion of small-scale self-reliance and to a 'third generation strategy' of sustainable systems development involving "facilitating development by other organizations" (Korten, 1990). The development experts have pointed out that the impact of development NGOs is highly localized and often transitory. It is now being called as the initiator of local developmentalism. The number of NGOs with counselling status with the United Nations Economic and Social Council (ECOSOC) has increased from about 200 in 1950 to 1,500 in 1995. Since the late 1980s, over 4,000 development NGOs based in OECD countries have been spending out six billion dollars annually for relief and development work. It is estimated that there are now over 2,00,000 grassroots NGOs in Asia, Africa and Latin America. Lester Salamon quotes, "A veritable associational revolution now seems underway at the global way that may constitute as significant a social and political development of the latter twentieth century as the rise of the nation-state was of the nineteenth century" (Edwards and Hulme, 1995).

Edwards and Hulme (1995) comment, "In the New Policy Agenda which combines market economies and liberal democratic politics, NGOs are simultaneously viewed as market-based actors and placed in a central position as components of civil society". At present, NGOs are influential social force and they play a big role in stimulating public awareness. They frequently acted as 'watch dogs' (Yearly, 1996) and sometimes seek publicity to shame those governments and companies which are perceived to be 'bad performers'. But, the reality tells another story. Despite their altruistic efforts, they are living behind the screen of globalization process. The concept of capitalism is perhaps unfamiliar to them. Poverty is viewed by them as the product of 'errors' which could be 'corrected'

(Amin, 1997). But global malady particularly in the Third World countries opened the door of a new vision. Their disenchantment with the global development project created an alternative forum, i.e., the other voices of the planet representing growing network of NGOs that now challenge developmentalism (McMichael, 1996). This shift in thinking expressed by NGOs is not simply of scale—from global to local—but also of subsistence. So this alternative forum is seen highly acceptable to the deprived majorities in the Third World countries. But side by side, being funded by the developed countries, the NGOs, in the guise of alternative forum, attempt to spread the message of globalization awareness. It is very interesting to note that the NGOs having enormous amount of 'hype' that is generated by governments and state funding agencies for empowering the poor but in practice they are more accountable to their donors than to their beneficiaries and ultimately they do not keep in mind to change the world. And their aidocracy sometimes echoes. "The development set is bright and noble/our thoughts are deep and our vision global/although we move with the better classes/our thoughts are always with the masses …" (Goggins, 'The Development Set', Africa, 1978). But the real aidocracy means: (a) do not harm; (b) cooperation is an external support to an internal dynamism; and (c) effort with what they have, not with what they lack.

Foreign investment has clearly been a major factor in invigorating economic growth and development in recent times. In 1996 Hirst and Thompson (1995) have estimated that in the early 1900s around 28 per cent of the world's population received 91 per cent of global FDI and so around 72 per cent of the population received 8 per cent of global FDI (pp. 67–68). These figures are based at the level of nation-states rather than people in nation-states. In the real world, not all people within a country will benefit from investment—indeed, many of the major recipients of FDI (First as well as the Third World) have high rates of unemployment. These figures ultimately show the pattern of the diversification of the Third World. Thus, it is evident that economic ties are strengthening in global era but the global hierarchies still exist and are actually intensifying (pp. 49–55; cited in Kiely, 1998: 49). Truman argued that there was a need for the countries of the modern world to solve the problem of the underdeveloped areas. "More than half of the people of the world are living in conditions approaching misery. Their food is inadequate, they are victims of disease. Their economic life is primitive and stagnant. Their poverty is a handicap and a threat both to them and to more prosperous areas..." (cited in Escober, 1995: 3). Truman's version, for the first time in world history, gave birth to a concept of 'underdeveloped' areas in juxtaposition with the 'developed' ones. It also revealed that there was a yawning gap between the poor and the rich. In spite of his honest effort to remove it through democratic fair dealings, the gap is mounting from the early 1990s. In 1990s richest country was richer by eight times than the poorest one, which was increased to thirty-six times in 1980s (Freeman, 1991: 155). In 1992 Human Development Report determined that from 1960 to 1989 those countries with the richest 20 per cent of world's population saw their share of global output (income) rise from 70.2 to 82.7 per cent while the share of those with the poorest 20 per cent shrank from 2.3 per cent to 1.4 per cent. The ratio of incomes of rich to poor income earners therefore increased from 30:1 to 59:1 in this period (New Internationalist, 1996: 19). Hirst and Thompson proved in 1995 that in this ambiguous international system the problem for the relatively poorer countries is not imperial domination, it is sheer neglect and exclusion. Joseph Stiglitz (2002) has commented about how and whose interests structural adjustment policies were advanced and the effects that they have had on the economies of the Third World. He says, "Despite repeated promises of poverty reduction made over the last decade of the 20th century, the actual number of people living in poverty has actually increased by almost 100 millions. This occurred at the same time that total world income actually increased by an average of 2.5 per cent annually". In his analysis of how the structural adjustment or the globalization programme has damaged the economies of the developing world and the Russia, Stiglitz lays much of the blame on the IMF's insistent on rapid privatization and capital market deregulation. Stiglitz (2002) also says, "Perhaps the most serious concern with privatization, as it has often been practiced, is corruption which he jokingly calls *'Briberization'.*"

Space is Shrinking, Not Economy

Globalization is not just a stylish buzzword, but also a set of policies involving the promotion of a free market economy, trade liberalization, Americanization or Europeanization, the Internet revolution, communication boom, global integration, satellite capitalism and cultural consumerism. And side-by-side, the process of alteration in humanity's knowledge of space and time is undermining the importance of local and even national boundaries in many fields of human endeavour. The space is shrinking but not the economy. A German Jewish poet Heinrich Heine notes, "Space is killed by the railways. I feel as if the mountains and forests of all countries were advancing on Paris. Even now, I can smell the German linden trees; the North Sea's breakers are rolling against my door". But, on the contrary, I say, economy is not killed by equality and distributive social justice. I do not feel as if the globalizer's capital were advancing on India, Bangladesh, Argentina, Peru, Bolivia or Brazil. Even now, I can strongly smell the poverty; the wave of disparity, dejection, environmental catastrophe, war, hunger and cry of the deprived majorities are rolling against my door (Dasgupta, 2006).

Let me recall the hymn of our great poet Rabindra Nath Tagore: "The current of the world has its boundaries, otherwise it could have no existence, but its purpose is not shown in the boundaries which restrain it, but in its movement, which is toward perfection. The wonder is not that there should be obstacles and sufferings in this world, but that there should be law and order, beauty and joy, goodness and love. The emancipation of our physical nature is in attaining health, of our social being in attaining goodness, and of our self in attaining love. The fish in the water is silent, the animal on the earth is noisy, the bird in the air is singing. But man has in him the silence of the sea, the noise of the earth and the music of the air. The fundamental desire of life is the desire to exist. The greed of gain has no time or limit to its capaciousness. Its one object is to produce and consume. It has pity neither for beautiful nature nor for living human beings. It is ruthlessly ready without a moment's hesitation to crush beauty and life out of them, moulding them into money".

The Fate of the Depressed Majorities

In terms of the human face of globalization, a few are champions and the great majorities are losers. Because, the Third World countries have not yet been escaped from excessive population increase, missing institutions, lack of capital formation, ill entrepreneurship, debt burden, vicious cycle of poverty, infrastructure deficit and different endowment conditions. We are in the midst of an anti-democratic counter-revolution in which super-citizens, the TNCs, are using globalization and its imperatives to weaken popular and elected authority in favour of a system of domination. This process disseminates the kernels of its own destruction, as it serves a small global minority, damages the majority, brings financial volatility and exacerbates the environmental crisis. Its destructive tendencies are likely to produce an explosion if the process is not contained and democracy is not reformed. The history tells that integrated capitalist or the ruler of global economy and their industrial strength were continuously trying to exploit and destroy the economic bases of the Third World countries. This process affected economic, cultural, social, political and religious spheres of the Third World countries. For example, in cultural sphere, the Internet, video and digital communication system have engulfed the tradition that may be called 'cultural imperialism'. The day will come when the pedigree of traditional cultural activities will completely lose its identity. These are the prime symptoms of globalization phobia now people are facing with its clashes and contradiction.

4 Politics of Capitalists

Our Great poet Rabindra Nath Tagore appositely remarked, "There are men whose idea of life is tactic, who desire for its continuation after death only because of their wish for permanence and not perfection; they love to imagine that the things to which they are accustomed will persist for ever. They completely identify themselves in their minds with their fixed surroundings and with whatever they have gathered, and to have to leave these is death for them. They forget that the true meaning of living is outliving, it is ever growing out of itself. There is a moral law in this world which has its application both to individuals and organized bodies of men. You cannot go on violating these laws in the name of your nation, yet enjoy their advantage as individuals. We may forget truth for our convenience, but truth does not forget us. Prosperity cannot save itself without moral foundation. Until man can see the gaping chasm between his full storehouse and his humanity, until he can feel the unity of mankind, the kind of barbarism which you call civilization will exist". Tagore's version indicates those tactic and greedy men as the capitalists whose lust of money making destroys our planet's bright future and kills humanity. The global players invite that barbaric social organization in the guise of globalization. They have tactically defy the truth that the ultimate end of man, to find the "one which is in him, which is his truth, which is his soul, the key with which he opens the gate of the spiritual life, the heavenly kingdom".

Globalization principally benefits people who can play the capitalist game, but does little for the people who are resourceless, illiterate, and making a living through traditional and folk production activities. Some globalization specialists talk about the different faces of the future and list few changes such as nation-states to networks, traditions to options, export-led to consumer-driven, farms to super cities, labour-intensive to high-tech, male dominance to emerging women, West to East, etc. These are the world trends, and they are affecting Asia very much, especially the people of India. The social scientists also suggest certain challenges for the future. The challenges are education for the people, planning for better urbanization, fighting against anarchy and crime, removal of disparity between increasing wealth of the minorities and pennilessness of the majorities. For example, modern India has its stark contrasts and its own share of contradictions. With its living democracy and fascinating liberalization policies and market restructure, India is emerging as a world leader in indigenous-built communications satellites and technologies. Yet it is one of the poorest countries in the world, with a population boom, illiteracy, health hazards, environmental risks, political corruption, caste and communal violence, religious bigotry and know-how hazards. And, in an age when globalization and new technology are bringing up till now unbelievable bonanzas to one part of humankind, it is disgraceful and improper that another part—and by most estimating the larger part—remains excluded from those benefits, subjected to a life of pulverizing poverty accompanied by illiteracy, unsafe drinking water, health hazards, eco-disaster, malnutrition and disease.

For billions of the world's people, the recent trend of globalization means uprooting traditional ways of life and threatening livelihoods, lifestyle pattern, social and moral values and cultures. The global social justice movement, itself a result of globalization, proposes an alternative path, more responsive to public needs. Intense political disputes will continue over globalization's meaning and its future direction. Globalization is also a very powerful tool of capitalism, which comes dripping from every pore from head to foot of ordinary people in the Third World with blood and dirt. Nobody should be hurt if the unobtrusive and deadening condition of globalization is seen from the viewpoint of pessimism. The reality depicts that globalization is not necessarily one that reaches out and touches all parts of the globe. And, the spatial and organizational dilemma creates 'globalization gloom'. It is now both an exciting opportunity and a formidable threat. Besides its bright promises and potentials the globalization forces accentuate inequitable opportunities and benefits across present generations of the Third World countries and future generations. Some say globalization as salvation of the present generation and some call it damnation. The global arena constitutes the individual self, the national society, the international system of societies and humanity (Robertson, 1992), which results in social processes of globalization. In terms of its applied sense the prescriptive version of globalization creates a strange interlude. If we assess globalization in terms of change of world economy, world culture, world society and world polity, the progress of the rich appears alongside the misery of the poor. So, as the one-world vision of the global initiators, the tactic of liberalization becomes an economic social, cultural and human nightmare for the deprived majorities. Alan Greenspan (1997) argues that the expansion of efficient global financial markets is largely beneficial but also presents new risks. What are those risks? It is disparity and dejection. It is inequality. It is cross-border terrorism and ethnic riots. It is the clash of culture and East-West confrontation and disequilibrium. It is capitalistic implosion. And, we are on the verge of the 'end of civilization'. Secretary General of UNIS (2000) states in his report a target of reducing poverty by half, before the year 2015, the proportion of people in the world living on one dollar a day or less. Some people think that is wildly unrealistic. Others deplore its timidity, since even if we achieve it there would still be 600 million people living in abject poverty.

In truth, this is an optimistic objective. In sub-Saharan Africa, for example, it could be achieved only with an economic growth rate of between 7 and 10 per cent in each of the next 15 years—far above any that the region has managed so far. And yet, the policies needed for it to happen are pretty clear. They must be policies that will lead to sustained growth, because all the evidence shows a strong correlation between economic growth and the incomes of the poor.

Capitalism builds up by way of predicament. Capitalism had only just matured to become capitalism at all when it began to reveal its crisis-generating nature. And it was this forerunner of all subsequent crises that demonstrated for the entire world to see the main genetic feature of cyclical crises (Dadayan, 1988). It is undeniable to comment that globalization means a revised version of capitalism. Capitalism destroyed the economic structure of the colonies and adjusted it to the requirements of the self-expansion of growth of capital. World trade had never developed as quickly as it did in the 19th century. In 1770 the ratio of the per capita product in the developed countries to that in the underdeveloped countries stood at about 1.2:1. By the start of World War I, the gap stood at 11.3:1 and by the year 2000 this gap was 14:1 (Dadayan, 1985: 105) and now it is steadily increasing. It is certainly for the manifestation of capitalism. Dadayan (1985: 105) views, "The saturation of the domestic market, the exacerbation of the contradiction between production and accumulation, reflected the conflict between the limited purchasing power of the population and the tendency for capital to expand without any limits, caused capital, with its unquenchable thirst for surplus value, to set out in search of new markets".

Globalization: Fair or Fairy

The world was divided into the West and the East. The capitalism of the West was disposed to the people in the East. A new type of capitalism (flexible or managerial) in the guise of globalization got its doorway. The word 'globalization' as a concept ultimately turned into a process. It got its room among the academics and developed with rhetoric branches of knowledge. Is it then a reality or merely a knowledge economy? Alvin Toffler (1993: 318) states, "Few words are more loosely thrown about today than the term 'global'. Ecology is said to be a 'global' problem. The media are said to be creating a 'global' village. Companies proudly announce that they are 'globalizing'. Economists speak of 'global' growth or recession. And, the politician, UN official or media pundit do not exist who is not prepared to lecture us about the global system. There is, of course, a global system. But it is not what most people imagine it to be".

It is irrefutable that the 21st century strategic thinking begins with the mapping of the global system. And, the mapping system began with the end of the cold war, which has still an impact on globalization. Primarily, the fall of Berlin Wall and secondarily, the break up of Soviet Union are the prime causes of such a system change. And now Toffler (1993: 319) notes, "We are witnessing, instead, the sudden eruption of a new civilization on the planet, carrying with it a knowledge-intensive way of creating wealth that is trisecting and transforming the entire global system. Everything in that system is now mutating, from its basic components... to the way they interrelate... to the speed of their interactions ... to the interest over which countries contend ... to the kinds of wars that may result and which need to be prevented". So, if one claims that globalization is just a fashionable buzzword, he will do mistake. It is now very much prescriptive for free market economy, trade liberalization, Americanization or Europeanization, Internet upheaval, communication explosion, global solidarity, satellite capitalism and cultural consumerism. And, side by side, the process of alterations in humanity's knowledge of space and time are undermining the importance of local and even national boundaries in many fields of human endeavour. Beck (1992: 20) observes, "In the welfare state of the west a double process is taking place now. On the one hand, the struggle for one's 'daily bread' has lost its urgency as a cardinal problem overshadowing everything else, compared to material subsistence in the first half of this century, and to a third world menaced by hunger".

Practically, globalization catches the aspects like compression of space using new and hyper-technology, communication and information technologies, abolition of distance, free trade, cultural consumerism, acceleration at all levels of human organization, extension of the scope of 'virtual reality' (Heidegger, 1971) and finally interconnectedness and dialogue among civilizations. But, the gap between winners and losers has become doubled. The ethical version of globalization was something different. The speedy "globalizing and extra-territorial economy being freed from localization and political constraint is known to produce the ever deepening wealth-and-income gaps between the better off and the worse off sections of the world population ..." (Bauman, 2001: 114). But, in terms of the human face of globalization, a few are frontrunners and the great majorities are trashes. Because, the Third World countries have not yet been escaped from extreme population increase, missing institutions, lack of capital formation, ill entrepreneurship, debt burden, vicious cycle of poverty, infrastructural deficit and different endowment conditions (Siebert, 1999).

Globalization is, at present, facing the problem of impasse. One may lift the question: Is globalization an ideology or a practice? Petras and Veltmayer (2001) view that globalization is both a description and a prescription, and as such it serves as both an explanation—a poor one, it has to be said—and an ideology that currently dominates thinking, policy making and policy practice. "As a description, 'globalization' refers to the widening and deepening of the international flows of trade, capital, technology and information within a single integrated global market ... as a prescription, 'globalization' involves the liberalization of national and global markets in the belief that free flows of trade, capital and information will produce the best outcome for growth and human welfare" (Petras and Veltmayer,

2001: 11). As an ideology, I see it as academic and intangible enigma and as prescription it is a half-finished project. Because, advocates of globalization have not yet been succeeded to identify and solve the increase in global social and economic inequalities. And, therefore, global advocates are seriously thinking about the reasons of such unfinished or half finished project and they have been engaged in debates over the significance of the changes in the capitalist economy and its real implication.

One may raise a basic question: Is globalization an opportunity or threat? Some, of course, view it as a process that is beneficial—a key to future world economic development—and also inevitable and irretrievable. Picco (2001: 21) notes: "Market economy, democratic polity, civil society and individual rights as characteristics of modernization have assumed global significance; at the same time the strength of traditions in shaping the modern world compel us to move beyond the simple mentality of 'either-or'. They have just imagined the philosophy of global village as virtual reality and indication of integration and harmony. DG Mike Moore (2000) says, "Few topics are as controversial as globalization. It is bringing distant markets and people across the world closer together is a huge change that affects everyone, whether they are peasants in India, students in London or bankers in New York.... We need to reassure people that globalization in generally a force for good ... In the first half of the 20th century the globalization of the 19th century was rolled back. We cannot rely on people's grudging acceptance of the perceived inevitability of globalization. We must not shrink from making our case ... when people say globalization lacks a human face, they may also mean that it does not benefit ordinary people. But this is simply not true". It is fact that people in India talk on mobile phones, use Japanese cameras, drive German cars, drink foreign scotch, eat American pizza, and communicate with people in USA and UK through Internet. It is also true that a great number of programmers of Indian call centres sell their services to American companies. But they are a very few in number and they do not reside on the ground with sky above and mud below.

The US hegemony, which has existed for more than half a century, is screening new features at the turn of the century. In the wake of the Cold War, the United States, soaring in the face of the world trend which errands peace and development, has taken the way of military expansion, triggering a new round of tension as the world comes out from the dark cloud of the war. In the year 1945 the United States was hegemonic in the true sense of the term. The US was the strongest, it had an economic potential so far ahead of anybody else in the world. It had a military strength that was supreme. As a consequence, it had a power to create dreadful alliances, NATO, the US-Japan Defense Pact and so on. At the same time, as the hegemonic power, it became economically, politically and culturally the nucleus of the world. Ray Kiely (2005) reveals the weaknesses of globalization theory, and argues that we can only approach a proper understanding of the contemporary world order by linking globalization to debates on capitalism, imperialism, neo-liberalism and universal human rights. He explores US hegemony in the light of these issues, showing how 'liberal internationalism' cannot be separated from capitalism, neo-liberalism and US empire-building.

For at least half a century, the global theatre has had one dominating actor—the United States of America. Patrick Fitzsimons (2002) notes, "The American presence in the world economy and culture remains authoritative economically: a $7 trillion plus economy; the home base of the majority of the transnational corporations, who scour the world for markets and profits; the overseer of the many facades of international decision-making—the UN, NATO, the International Monetary Fund (IMF), the World Trade Organization, the World Bank and others; the cultural-electronic Goliath of the universe". Rodrigo de Rato (2006) gives rather a positive version of 21st century globalization. He argues, "The global economy remains strong. The Fund projects that the global growth will be closed to 5 per cent in both 2006 and 2007. We expect some slowing in growth in the United States from the over 5 per cent rate of the first quarter, but there has been some pick up in growth in the euro area, and the Japanese recovery remains on track. However, downside risks have increased, as evidenced by increased financial market concerns. Asia remains a leader in world growth. We have recently increased our projection for growth in the region to 7 per cent, about the same as in 2005. In part, this growth is driven by an increase in demand for the region's exports, but in many countries it also reflects rising domestic demand—a welcome trend". Globalization is the latest hegemonic expression of capitalism. It can be explained in terms of economic, political, intellectual and cultural hegemony of the global players. We can argue that at present, globalization has completely been merged with neo-capitalism and the features of capitalism have already been exposed from the murky situation of archaic type of capitalism such as market capitalism and monopoly capitalism. It has now been reinstated by flexible or managerial or corporate type of capitalism. And if someone looks back, he can easily perceive the return of the Empire which is ruling over the earth with its all possible modernized and hyper-hegemonic power and motivation of domination. The global capitalists even achieved great success penetrating the mind and political culture of the communist pockets in the Third World countries. Mostly, a great majority of the deprived are in favour of globalization and most of the countries, finding no other alternatives, are accepting the capital from the multinational companies and global players posing politically 'anti' words and 'anti' slogans. The today's 'Empires' are really hegemons.

Petras (2001) writes, "One of the fundamental issues facing critical intellectuals today is the consumption of political language, the obfuscation of capitalism as it presently exists through the use of euphemisms and concepts… ." The total globalization is a remote controlled process. The protagonists, of course, are not agreed to such black-hole-game of the process. Ulrich Beck (1992) has called the attack on the World Trade Center "the Chernobyl of globalization" exposing "the false promise of neo-liberalism". Joseph Stiglitz (2004) writes, "The war on terrorism and in Iraq has distracted much of the world's attention from the pressing issue of how globalization should be managed so that it benefits everyone. A new report, issued by the International Labour Organization's Commission on the Social Dimensions of Globalization, reminds us how far the Bush administration is out of line with the global consensus... this very heterogeneous group was able to crystallize the emerging consensus, that globalization—despite its positive potential—has not only failed to live up to that potential, but has actually contributed to social distress".

In recent years debates about the positives and negatives of capitalism have been overtaken by debates about the positives and negatives of globalization. Globalization is a relatively new idea in the social sciences, though some argue that while the term is new, what the term denotes is not a novel set of phenomena (Waters, 2001). What most scholars agree about, however, is that the term has many meanings and that the debates around these meanings are often confused. Much of the confusion derives from an untheorized identification of globalization with what we can term 'capitalist globalization'. The idea of capitalist globalization implies, of course, that there are other types of globalization. It is important at the outset to establish a generic concept of globalization without losing sight of the fact that the dominant form of globalization today is literally unthinkable without actually existing capitalism.

Generic globalization takes to be a relatively new (post-1960) phenomenon defined by four fundamental characteristics. The first criterion of generic globalization is the widely discussed electronic revolution vital to what Castells (1996) famously dubbed the information age. The second is the post-colonial revolution; the third is the creation of transnational social spaces. Finally, the electronic transformation has made possible qualitatively new forms of cosmopolitanism, where relations between the national and the international can be increasingly re-conceptualized in terms of relations between the local and the global. While the electronic revolution and this embryonic new cosmopolitanism both emerged historically in a time of rapidly globalizing capitalism, neither is necessarily a capitalist institution and both could exist and prosper—albeit in different ways—in a non-capitalist world. These four characteristics of generic globalization are, in my view, irreversible in the long run, but this does not mean that capitalist globalization is irreversible. The failure to grasp this idea has led to confusion in the ranks of the so-called 'anti-globalization' movement. But this is not the only source of bewilderment about globalization. Different, even contradictory, approaches to globalization have created a situation where the term is widely used but little understood.

Leslie Sklair (2000), while analyzing global system theory and its linkage with global capitalism, argues, "Analytically, transnational practices operate in three spheres: the economic, the political and the cultural-ideological. The whole is what I mean by 'the global system'. Today, the global system is not identical with global capitalism, but the dominant forces of global capitalism are the dominant forces in the global system". Sklair's argument is that "individuals, groups, institutions and even whole communities, local, national or transnational, can exist, perhaps even thrive, as they have always done outside the orbit of the global capitalist system, but that this is becoming increasingly more difficult".

There is little question that capitalism has undergone profound changes in its global forms of development in its post-World War II period. Petras and Veltmeyer (2001) note that "in the post-World War II context of an east-west division of the world, the hegemony of the US within the world economic system, a major decolonization process and the resolve (at Bretton Woods) to impose a liberal world economic order created the framework of twenty five to thirty years of continuously rapid rates of economic growth and capitalist development—the "Golden Age of Capitalism"."

But, the billions of people are as yet totally faceless, die in hunger, vend their blood for having food for a day, live in slum pockets, and became the sufferers of health hazards, environmental pollution and illiteracy. To them globalization lacks human face. We should not forget that hunger allows no choice between a citizen and elite. But, the global initiators, in the name of globalization, are playing game with the deprived majorities. It is true that in general living standards in poor countries are not catching up with richest one. It is still a tragedy that 1.2 billion people—a quarter of the world's population—survive on less than a dollar a day and that a further 1.6 billion—another third of the world's population—make do with between one and two dollars a day (Moore, 2000). It is obvious that the progress is not evenly dispersed. The gap between rich and poor countries and rich and poor people within countries has grown. The report of the IMF staff (2002) says, "The richest quarter of the world's population saw its per capita GDP increase nearly six-fold during the century, while the poorest quarter experienced less than a three-fold increase". It is also evident from the world development reports that the rich countries have experienced a steady growth in their share of the global GNP, while the poorest countries have experienced with a very sad decline in the share of world GNP (Dasgupta, 2004). Between 1960 and 1991, the richest fifth of all nations had its share of world income rise from 70 per cent to 85 per cent, while the poorest fifth of all nations had its share fall from 2.3 per cent to 1.4 per cent (UNDP, 1994). The following tables yield such devastating happenings:

Table 1

Worldwide Income Inequality Increase, 1989

Chart of nations (%)	*(%) share of world GNP*	*(%) share of world trade*	*(%) share of world investment*	*(%) share of world savings*
Richest 20	82.7	81.23	80.56	80.51
Fourth 20	11.7	13.94	12.65	13.39
Third 20	2.3	2.53	2.95	2.59
Second 20	1.9	1.35	2.62	2.53
Poorest 20	1.4	0.95	1.25	0.98

Table 2
Global Income Disparity, 1960–91

Year	*Poorest 20% of nations (percentage of world GNP)*	*Richest 20% of nations*	*Richest to poorest ratio*	*Gini coefficient*
1960	2.3	70.2	30 to 1	0.69
1970	2.3	73.9	32 to 1	0.71
1980	1.7	76.3	45 to 1	0.79
1989	1.4	82.7	59 to 1	0.87
1991	1.4	84.7	61 to 1	—

Source: UNDP (1992, 1994).

This increased disparity makes good globalization gloomy and it is more difficult to address in the future. In the ambiguous global system, problems for the relatively poorer countries are not empirical domination but sheer rejection and exclusion. Secondly, the globalization feathered by technology and communication network in the postmodern society is also not equally available for everybody (Dasgupta and Chattopadhaya, 2004).

It is evident from the available documents that only one-fourth of the US families with incomes below $ 30,000 have personal computers while 80 per cent of these with incomes exceeding $1,00,000 possess it. Access to the Internet is 20 times greater in families with incomes of $75,000 and above than those having lower incomes; and the former category is nine times more likely to own PC than the latter. But the number of PC and Internet users in low-income countries is statistically negligible (see Table 3).

The World Bank, in its report, could not justify the greatness of good globalization. It is undeniable that in the past 20 years the global economy has become increasingly integrated. International financial flows have grown. More people are on the move. And countries are exchanging more goods and services. In 2002 trade in goods and services as a share of world output reached 54 per cent—up from 31 per cent in 1980.

Table 3
Technological Disparity, 1996–97

Countries	*Personal computers per 1,000 persons*	*Internet hosts per 10,000 persons*
High Income Countries		
Finland	182.10	635.60
Germany	233.20	107.70
Japan	128.00	75.80
Switzerland	408.50	208.00
USA	362.40	442.10
Middle Income Countries		
Algeria	3.40	0.01
Brazil	18.40	4.20
Mexico	29.00	3.70
Russia	23.70	5.50
South Africa	37.70	30.70
Low Income Countries		
China	3.00	0.21
Ivory-Coast	1.40	0.17
India	1.50	0.05
Kenya	1.50	0.16
Uganda	0.50	0.01

Source: World Bank, 1998.

The Betrayal of the Promise

The idea of a global world was predicated on the promises of a pervasive prosperity of economic globalization, and the further belief that this prosperity went hand in hand with distributing the fruits of liberal democracy. The betrayal of these promises, however, is evident in growing inequalities and increased poverty. It may now be argued that the globalization paradigm is no longer functioning because its libratory potential was never realized. Some see the events of 9/11 in USA and 26/11 in India as the symbols of the failure of globalization and the triumph of the frustrations that it engendered. Indeed, the ecstatic ideal of global freedom has been replaced by the very real threats posed by globally unbounded and unrestrained 'others'.

Still there are many impediments to global integration. National policies that protect domestic industries from competition or subsidize their output distort patterns of trade and prevent developing countries from reaching their full potential. Risk and uncertainty also inhibit the flow of finance, while development assistance may be directed more by political considerations than by development opportunities. Not only that the crisis in the Third World countries is severely aggravated by the heavy debt burden, it has also increased enormously in the poor countries. It is not because of the fact, which global capitalists view, that the debt continues to increase because of the inability to service it. It is mainly because of the degree and intensity of dependency caused by capitalist implosion, extension of power of the globalizers from metropolis to satellite, global-local confusion and commercialization of aid-ethics. Humanity is certainly a global phenomenon. But integration and singleness of humanity in the age of economic inequality is rhetoric because economy dominates over humanity. Debt has been used as a stick by the international capitalist institutions such as the IMF and the World Bank for over 30 years to force countries to introduce austerity packages that force up prices and ravage what few services exist. The production of goods for exports has been privileged over the production of what people need to survive. Often this has resulted in ecological degradation as monocultures of cash crops have replaced traditionally mixed agriculture. Poverty, disease and death have inevitably followed. A child dies in a dilapidated Third World country clinic. Another suddenly drops out of school. One's future got tremendous shock in infancy, the other's aspirations and dreams turned into nightmare before they could even begin to unfold. But they have something deeper in common—both are victims of the effects of the crushing debt burden facing the Third World. The debt burden is the only obstacle to development in the Third World—the most powerful tool that the dominating western nations use to keep whole countries in subjugation. The debt burden pervades and perverts the mission of so-called progressive globalization process and it dehumanizes human faces.

Tylor argues that a democracy is always transitory in nature; it just cannot exist as a permanent form of government. A democracy will continue to exist up until the time that voters discover that they can vote themselves open handed offerings from the public treasury. From that moment on, the majority always votes for the candidates who pledge the most advantages from the public treasury, with the result that every democracy will finally collapse due to loose economic policy, which is always followed by a tyranny.

The average age of the world's greatest civilizations, from the beginning of history, has been about 200 years. During those 200 years, these nations always progressed through the following sequence:

- from bondage to spiritual faith;
- from spiritual faith to great courage;
- from courage to liberty;
- from liberty to abundance;
- from abundance to complacency;
- from complacency to apathy;
- from apathy to dependence; and
- from dependence back into bondage.

Tylor was right about the process, but not its outcome. He did not foresee globalization—humanity's complete interconnection. But it is precisely the need to survive, to exist in an interconnected system that will compel humanity to seek a method of curbing every person's individual egoism. And, when we search for a method to correct egoism, we will find that Kabbalah is the only adequate method (Globalization Is the Unexpected Force of Development) posted on 23rd December 2008.

By the beginning of the 1990s most people in sub-Saharan Africa were poorer than they had been thirty years before. Of the population of about 500 million, nearly 300 million are living in absolute poverty (Kiely, 1998). Not only that the crisis in the Third World countries is severely aggravated by the heavy debt burden, it has increased immensely in the poor countries also. It is evident from the report of World Bank that the debt of the developing countries increased by 8 per cent to over $2 trillion in 1995. The Third World debt has grown from $9 billion in 1955 to $217 billion in 1996 (Gelinas, 1998). The motive of discussions held in Paris about Multilateral Agreement on Investment (MAI), in Geneva about WTO, in Cardiff about European Monetary Union (EMU) and in G-8 summit in Birmingham, was just to promote a new global harmony with deregulated and de-authoritarian free trade and capital flows. This was the beginning of neo-liberal economics. But, the hegemonic command remains unchanged. And globalization begins as an offshoot of neo-capitalism. The global players highlighted that "while globalization offers great opportunities, at present, its benefits are very unevenly shared, and its cost unevenly distributed". A few questions are very relevant in this context. Is it possible for globalization to be inclusive and fair? Can globalization reduce the poverty syndrome? Would the dream of the leaders assembled at the Summit affirming their faith in globalization becoming compassionate and caring in which economic and technological progress distributed to unite rather than divide the community is a reality or just plain rhetoric? Most of us want to live better; to give our children more options than we have had and to see them choose as we would have chosen.

Observing the recent experience in India, Yogendra Singh (1973) writes: "As the size of youth in our society has grown, as the magnitude of unemployment both rural and urban has increased, and as the disenchantment of the poorer and weaker sections of society with the national ideology of development has also grown significantly, it has resulted in large-scale de-legitimation of the civic structure of authority and power. The incidence of violence and lawlessness, the growth in protest movements and movements based on violent separatist or alienative ideologies in many parts of the country is indicative of the writing on the wall. In the Third World, of course, for the vast majority of rural residents, it is the urban centre that has become the equivalent 'positional good' as large numbers migrate to towns in search of greater economic security."

Neo-Liberalism in the 20th and 21st Centuries

Neo-liberalism is deeply rooted in the works of Adam Smith, David Ricardo and Herbert Spencer. Neo-liberal ideas stride into the applied world in the late 1970s as being supported by some prime factors of economic depression like inflation, high unemployment etc. Making a strong ground for the return to free market policies of the past, the neo-liberalists drew on the neo-classical *laissez-faire* economic theories. Some British advocates called it 'second coming of capitalism' or 'turbo-capitalism' (Steger, 2002). "By the late 1980s", Steger notes, "British Prime Minister Margaret Thatcher and US President Ronald Reagan were both revered and reviled as the founding figures of a new market paradigm. Since then, their ideological heirs have marshaled their considerable resources to expand the neo-liberal project into a full-blown globalist ideology" (p. 11). The market liberalization now creates 'new market ideology' which bequeathed globalization as the new economic reform of the old capitalists. But, the impact of neo-liberalization in a Third World country mostly appears as depressing as smog. The ground was not ready to accept either time-space compression or free trade and market orientation. Not only that, the Third World country fails to blend its own development modus operandi from the world economy and compels to be the part of imposed neo-liberal economy of the West, which results in complete socio-economic and socio-cultural stagnation. The globalization hegemony of the West might be real or rhetoric or abstract but in some sense, very limited which fails to honour the importance of local and thus intensifies the uneven development. "And that, therefore, globalization is differently and unequally experienced in the world today" (Kiely, 1998: 17). Setting aside the good and altruistic words of and about globalization, I say, and majority feel, that the triumph of globalization today is the triumph of capitalism of a certain new kind with certain human-tuned specific discourse. And it has been unmasked to the people with the naked exposure of Third World crisis.

Patnaik (1995: 193) notes, "In a Third World context, the correlation between the pursuit of liberal economic policies and the imposition of political authoritarianism is quite strong. The countries, usually cited by the advocates of World Bank-style 'liberalization' as success stories to emulate, have all had authoritarian regimes or military dictatorship presiding over such 'liberalization'. But the very narrowing of the class base opens up the possibility of mobilizing broad section of the population against the imposition of World Bank-style liberalization". The neo-liberal capitalism historically emerges through three successive stages of power of the US, i.e., industrial power, military power and hegemonic power. Wallerstein (2003) writes, "In terms of the world class struggle, the weakening of the anti-systematic movements—old and new—allowed establishment forces to launch a counter offensive of considerable magnitude initially took the form of the neo-liberal regimes in Britain and the US; the rise of the 'Washington Consensus' which buried the ideal of developmentalism and replaced it with globalization; and the vigorous expansion of the role and activities of the IMF, World Bank and newly formed World Trade Organization, all of which sought to curtail the ability of peripheral states to interfere with the free flow of goods and, above all, of capital." This neo-liberal capitalism thus compels the people in the Third World to become de-localized, de-traditionalized, disempowered and helpless. The newly introduced 'free market' gospel thus resists the ethics (imaginative or motivated!) of globalization, which deface common humanity. The protest movement thus begins from the dilemma of 'revolutions of rising expectations (globalization mission) and 'revolutions of rising frustrations' (inequalization) (Dasgupta, 2004).

The failure of mainstream globalization was a sudden ordeal to the global initiators. The ever-increasing economic gap between the West and the rest, the global-local cultural conflict, the upsurge of ethnic violence, the vibrant intensity of cross-border terrorism, fundamentalism, religious bigotry and inequality within and between nations threaten the ethos and ethics of globalization process. The crisis in the emerging markets has made it evident that globalization opportunities come with high risk. Hunger and poverty dominate over technology and communication. The 'World Economic Outlook', in its report (2004), shows that the distribution of income among countries (42 countries representing 90% of world population) has become more unequal than at the beginning of the century. Pieterse (2001: 165) notes, "We inhabit a global theatre of the absurd, a winner takes—all world in which the wealthiest billionaires own as much as approximately half the world population". So, the neo-globalization initiators change the track and coined the words like civil society, good governance, uncorrupted privatization, government's transparency etc. Joseph Stiglitz (2002: ix-x) argues, "... I saw first hand, the devastating effect that globalization can have on developing countries, and especially the poor within those countries. I believe that globalization—the removal of barriers to free trade and the closer integration of national economies—can be a force for good and that it has the potential to enrich everyone in the world, particularly the poor. But I also believe that if this is to be the case, the way globalization has been managed, including the international trade agreements that have played such a large role in removing those barriers and the policies that have been imposed on developing countries in the process of globalization, need to be radically rethought". Stiglitz (2002) further emphasizes on the issue of privatization with the motive of strong competition policies. He insists on 'reinventing government', which would be responsive and efficient. The proposal is certainly good but I do feel, is very much difficult in terms of globality. Because most of the governments of the rest are very much nationally tuned, regionally unique and locally very traditional. The feature is also true in politics, which sometimes seems ethnic-oriented, caste-based and even religiously-moulded. Here, time-space compression or policies of global initiators or Washington Consensus cannot enter deeply into the political temperament of the local space.

Stiglitz (2002: xiv-xv) views: "The backlash against globalization draws its force not only from the perceived damage done to developing countries by policies driven by ideology but also from the inequities in the global trading system. Today, few apart from those with vested interests who benefit from keeping out the goods produced by the poor countries defend the hypocrisy of pretending to help developing countries by forcing them to open up their markets to the goods of the advanced industrial countries while keeping their own markets protected, policies that make the rich richer and the poor more impoverished—and increasingly angry". It is the reality that if IMF, World Bank, WTO and other associate global funding organizations could develop the models of development of local countries without improving direct authoritative intervention of the countries of the East, could develop their own paradigms of development models accordingly. But soil connection has totally been ignored by the global initiators. "A half century after its founding, it is clear that IMF has failed in its mission. It has not done what it was supposed to do— provide funds for countries facing an economic downturn, to enable the country to restore itself to close to full employment. In spite of the fact that our understanding of economic process has increased enormously during the last fifty years, and in spite of IMF efforts during the past quarter century, crises around the world have been more frequent. Worse, many of the policies that IMF pushed, in particular, premature capital market liberalization, have contributed to global instability" (Stiglitz, 2002: 15). The policies would not be a misnomer if there was the room for the Third World countries to participate and to express their voices in the policy making. The gap between policy makers and policy takers thus creates unfair globalization and indicates the sign of capitalistic game. Someone calls it oppressive globalization (Wiseman, 2000), someone, globalization anarchy (Wallerstein, 2003), and someone, globalization gloom or bad globalization. But I call it capitalist globalization. When it has become unmasked (and it took a very prolonged time to perceive the black hidden of such rosy dawn of globalization), the initiators innovated another journey of implementing revised or neo-globalization. The recognition of the link between actions, at different levels of space and governance, and "to think and act at a range of levels without losing our grounding in the particularity of our own home place" (Wiseman, 2000: 214). Theoretically speaking, the neo-globalization action follows the concept of 'particularism' where 'universalism' has no room. Does neo-globalism indicate the sense of localism? This is a new theoretical dilemma. This neo-globalization process put pressure on the importance of thinking of global, national and local communities, based on cooperation rather than consumerism, the creation of neo-global market which will be democratically and ecologically sustainable in terms of economic relationship, intervention of new forms of transnational governance, development of transnational civil society, globalization from down to earth, democratization of local economic relationships etc. (Wiseman, 2000). But all these neo-globalization thinking remains rhetoric and the cry of the hungry people shatters such an imagination and economic romanticism.

The ideology that has emerged at the end of the 20th century to justify this unhappy state of affairs is neo-liberalism. Neo-liberalism can be defined as the belief that the unregulated free market is the essential precondition for the fair distribution of wealth and for political democracy. Thus, neo-liberals oppose just about any policy or activity that might interfere with the untrammeled operation of market forces.

Pieterse (2006) argues, "Studies generally explain the onset of neo-liberalism as the confluence of the economic ideas of the Chicago school and the policies of Ronald Reagan and Margaret Thatcher. A further strand is the Washington consensus, the economic orthodoxy that guided the IMF and World Bank in their policies through the 1990s and turned neo-liberalism into global policy". Pieterse further notes, "The Washington consensus that took shape in the late 1980s as a set of economic prescriptions for developing countries echoes the core claim of cold war ideology: the free market and democracy go together. The main tenets of the Washington consensus are monetarism, reduction of government spending and regulation, privatization, liberalization of trade and financial markets, and the promotion of export-led growth".

Tickel and Peck (2003) discuss the development of neo-liberalism in three phases: *proto-neo-liberalism* from the 1940s to the 1970s; a phase of *roll-back neo-liberalism* in the 1980s when it became government policy in the US and UK; and *crush neo-liberalism* in the 1990s when it became hegemonic in multifaceted institutions. Kiely (2006) is convinced that globalization was undoubtedly central to political debate in the 1990s. This was true in the academic social sciences, but equally in mainstream (and alternative) political discourse. He argues that the alternative account focuses on the continued centrality of a hierarchical nation-state system and the uneven outcomes of capitalist, neo-liberal globalization.

But a big wheel is turning. It brings new, different problems which are very difficult to analyze through the 20th century/1990s analytics of neo-liberal globalization. We have moved on to a different station. This is controversial and one can question and disagree but cannot gloss over it. On the contrary, we think this power shift is crucial to the politics of globalization. This neo-liberal globalization has been and continues to be like a storm, argues Martinez (1997) "that is sweeping over the planet, affecting all countries to a greater or lesser extent, creating economies and societies increasingly exclusive and polarized".

Neo-liberal ideas in recent decades have seen a tremendous resurrection and have displaced the state-domineering economic theories of the inter-war and post-World War II periods to become the reigning ideology of our time. Neo-liberalism emerged as a full force in the 1980s with the right-wing Reagan and Thatcher régimes. "Its influence has since extended across the political range to include not only central political parties but also even much of the traditional social-democratic left. In the 1990s, neo-liberal hegemony over the global politics and culture has become so overpowering that it is becoming difficult to even rationally discuss what neo-liberalism is" (Fitzsimons, 2002).

The spreading out of liberal democracy across the world is vital to neo-liberal narratives of economic globalization; free trade, free markets and free elections, it is regularly asserted, go together to produce market democracies. The desirability and necessity of liberal democracy is endorsed and imposed through global institutions. The global extension of liberal democratic polities is thus connected staunchly to the ongoing development of "capitalism to new spaces and the growth of world markets and multinational or transnational corporations to service them. The dominant discourse of globalization is overwhelmingly corporate or neo-liberal globalization and the celebration of liberal democracy is part of it" (Lafley and Weldes, 2005).

It is the common usage that globalization panoramically refers to the extension and expansion of global linkages, the organization and institution of social living on a global parameter and the growth of a global consciousness, hence to the consolidation of world society. This virtual definition is not enough to explore the real meaning of globalization. I will not do any mistake if I mean globalization as a very powerful tool of capitalism in its plural forms, which comes dripping from every pore from head to foot of ordinary people in the Third World with blood and dirt.

5 Ecology and Humanity

Humanity creates its own life through labour as a cognisant social activity. Humanity does not just develop biologically, but also itself through history. It passes through different modes of production; it changes its relationship with the environment and modifies the environment itself. That is called species-oriented impact on the environment. The nature of our impact is not destined in advance. Sometimes more progress does not automatically entail more environmental destruction. But, mostly, progress invited ecological destruction and loss of biodiversity. The bond between human development and the environment is dialectical. We have options. Development does not necessary mean material and quantitative growth. We can build up our network of human resources while protecting the environment. Disregarding history and the concrete mode of production in a discussion of humanity and nature can only lead to a seemingly trite but very dangerous conclusion: that, other things being equal, the more human beings there are on earth, the more ecological problems we create (Tanuro, 2008). Will globalization and the new global market be the demise of humanity? Many believe so and if we do not slow down the industrialization of the earth, the death of our planet will occur soon. Many countries across the world desire to be the giant players in a global economy. However, we must remember that there is not adequate reserve for everyone to be the big brother. The world is so focused on globalization that it is forgetting reality. The reality is that we are spending the world's resources at a rate that surpasses the planet's natural capacity to recuperate. Furthermore, we are introducing ten times the amount of waste and pollution we did ten years ago and the earth is just not able to digest all of this waste into its natural cycle. We are pushing humanity to the threshold. It is stated (www.voteswagon.com, 2007) that if we do not decelerate the rate of globalization of the world, we will be fighting over just the basics such as wheat and water in the matter of twenty to thirty years. We will also have gigantic holes in the ozone as well as flooding throughout Asia and the Pacific. The more we globalize our economy and industrialize the world, the faster we are approaching toward the obliteration of humanity. The earth is not noticeably large and this means that we cannot substantially continue to keep mounting our industrialization of the world. Our planet can only take in so much man-made created waste and then it reaches a tilting point where it can do nothing but give up. Development means people. People are the starters and end products of development. Humanity is closely linked with development. Humanity means love for ecology which is now overshadowed with the concept of ecological exploitation and man-made savagery to have more economic potentials. Capitalism robs nature, but in a very varied way: capitalist pillaging intends to obtain and sell exchange values, not to please requirements, so it causes more environmental poverty than traditional societies.

The capitalist ecological crisis mainly ensued from overproduction and the consequential overconsumption. It also does so by developing environmentally hazardous technologies. "Each capitalist tries to get surplus profit, also called technological rent, by replacing human labour with machines, chemicals, etc., to improve productivity. Among other problems, this race for more productivity, this permanent revolution in production, leads to the development and use of new technologies like nuclear power, new molecules like DDT or PCB, and even new genetically modified organisms" (Tanuro, 2008). Climate change must be seen within that framework. The IPCC reports that the global warming is not an effect of human activity in general, but specifically of capitalist human activity. Indeed global warming is the purest and more ideal example of a capitalist environmental catastrophe: it is a direct result of overproduction. Tanuro (2008) notes: "Climate change is the global inheritance of 250 years of capitalist accumulation."

While there is no global agreement on how best to fight environmental degradation, most people today recognize that humankind is on an untenable path. It is reported by Pew Center on Climate Change that from 1850 to 2000, the United States was responsible for nearly 30 per cent of global carbon dioxide emissions—making it the world's top emitter. The European Union's 25 member-states together were responsible for more than 27 per cent of global carbon dioxide emissions—making them the world's second-biggest emitter. From 1850 to 2000, China accounted for 7.3 per cent of cumulative carbon dioxide emissions, fifth-most in the world. By comparison, India was responsible for only 2 per cent of global carbon dioxide emissions—making it the world's 12th biggest emitter. Among developing countries, emissions are expected to increase 70 per cent for India and 124 per cent for Mexico. China's emissions will grow by 118 per cent, surpassing those of the United States—and making China the world's largest emitter by 2025. It is evident from the report of US Energy Information Administration that the emissions are very high in the United States because it currently uses 20.3 million barrels of oil a day—as much as China (6.6 million barrels), Japan (5 million), the former Soviet Union (3.9 million), Germany (2.5 million) and Canada (2.3 million) combined. Under the Kyoto Protocol, Canada is required to cut greenhouse gas emissions down to 6 per cent below 1990 levels by 2012. However, Canada's overall emissions are about 20 per cent above 1990 levels as of 2005 (Kidney, 2005). Under the Kyoto Protocol, the European Union (EU) is supposed to cut global warming emissions to 8 per cent below 1990 levels by 2012. To meet that goal, the EU should have cut emissions by 4.8 per cent in 2002—when, in effect, its members only cut by 2.9 per cent (Kidney, 2005). Japan pledged to cut greenhouse gas emissions by 6 per cent from 1990 levels over the period from 2008 to 2012. However, as of 2002, Japan's emissions were 7.6 per cent above 1990 levels— and are expected to increase to 8 per cent (Kidney, 2005).

So, the new millennium of our planet is pricked with unprecedented environmental catastrophes such as earthquake, flood, drought, tsunami, hurricane, tornado, tidal waves, volcanic eruptions and global warming. Other ecological vulnerabilities like ozone depletion, loss of biodiversity, waste dumping, excessive use of chemicals, bio-chemical warfare, pollution, health hazards and effect of greenhouses gases etc., are menacing our planet. For example, flood in Bangladesh and China, earthquake in Japan, Cambodia and California, volcanic eruptions in Philippines, tsunami in India, Sri Lanka and Taiwan, hurricane in New Orleans and Texas, to name a few of the recent environmental tragedies. These cause severe social, economic and human damages. Particularly the marginalized and the poor are the worst victims. Instead of making a very harmonious relation with the nature, man has inhumanely extracted all the potentials from nature. And, according to the Newtonian Third Law of Motion, now, this is the turn of the nature to retaliate. The globalization is indeed a multidimensional and often self-contradictory process. The topics covered include much that is familiar, but our main aim is to examine previously unexplored aspects of globalization and its impacts. This has produced a wide-ranging approach that blends ecology and environment, culture and economy (Dasgupta, 2008).

The social and ecological effects of a new, global capitalist climate policy could be dreadful indeed. Hundreds of millions of people, mostly underprivileged people in poor countries, will face more coastal floods, more malaria and more food shortages. Billions of people face water shortages. In case of Katrina hurricane in New Orleans most of the 1,500 casualties were marginalized people, black people, women and children who died because money that could have strengthened was spent on the war in Iraq, and because the city, state and federal authorities did not evacuate the poor. Katrina may offer a glance of the catastrophes we will face in the future (Tanuro, 2008).

These will not be natural catastrophes but capitalist catastrophes. As James Hansen, NASA's chief climatologist, said to the US Congress: "Special interests have blocked transition to our renewable energy future. Instead of moving heavily into renewable energies, fossil companies choose to spread doubt about global warming, as tobacco companies discredited the smoking-cancer link. CEOs of fossil energy companies know what they are doing and are aware of long-term consequences of continued business as usual. In my opinion, these CEOs should be tried for high crimes against humanity and nature."

The spatial aspects of globality/locality correspond to cultural particularism on one hand, and the creation of new cultural rooms on the other. This perception of the world as a single place (Robertson, 1992) foresees the globe as a natural body. Sociologists often view society as a set of nations, but this concept needs to be harmonized with an unequivocally environmental perception. It is implicit that bio-physical reality forms social reality, which ultimately produces a diverse bio-network. Thus, it is not easy to deem all nations as part of a single global system (Yearley, 1996). The differences between warm and cold climates and natural topographical and climatological differentiation come into view to refute the vista of globalization. The ecologically-linked impression of time and space has been transformed into another neo-ecological facet of late modernism. It is the only source of globalization in disagreement. Environmental disequilibrium, as a universal phenomenon, comes into sights to refute the leeway of international culture and humanism. Human race on this planet has fallen casualty to social, economic and ethical insanity. And now the war industry is threatening to our civilization and to the ecological balance. The bloodshed in the war for gaining more and more power invites environmental threat and ecological disbalance. As for the level of development, a few countries remain on the top with the crown of modernized industrialism, stylish technological achievements and material wealth. The vast majority of the countries are on the sine qua non with hardship, illiteracy, filth, diseases and environmental hazards. The capitalist countries concentrate their views not only on the issues of education, health, safe drinking water or easily available cheap life-saving drugs and healthy environment but also on the issue of store pilling of thermonuclear weapons and war machineries for the obliterations of life on earth. We have, as yet, faced two world wars, civil wars, Gulf wars and war menacing and we are not yet ready to combat with such a development error. The invention of neutron, chemical, biological and laser weapons not only produces uncontrollable upsurge of over-heated confrontation in a global war, these also produce environmental catastrophe and directly affect human organs and human health. Eventually, war industries sternly impinge on the protection and development of environment and invite ecological adversity. It can be argued that the reality situations of hostility against hostility, threat against threat, war against war, blood against blood and homicide against homicide are the major causes of global environment menace. The argument reveals that environment hazards, the result of war industry and uncontrolled technological advance, are the creation of the capitalists. According to J.V.B. Foster (1999), "There is an irreversible environment crisis within global capitalist society".

Our world is now divided into 'we' and 'they'. The use of excessive energy for industrial development, the spreading out of war industry, the all-embracing movement of motor vehicles, and the lifestyle pattern of consumer society cause severe pollution problems across the globe. It is established and acknowledged that the member-states of OECD (Organization for Economic Corporation and Development) release 45 per cent of carbon dioxide, 40 per cent of sulfur dioxide, and 50 per cent of NO_2. These countries produce 60 per cent of the total global wastes and use 52 per cent of the total energy resources. The percentage of fossil fuel used by these countries is nearly 50 per cent and for mineral oil it is 56 per cent.

USA itself is liable for 17.6 per cent gas emission. The developed countries are mostly responsible for greenhouse consequences. These states are highly industrialized and they also put pressure on the Third World countries to sell their carbon dioxide emission right. The toxic dissipates of the war industries, chemical and electronic industries impinge on the environment of Third World countries. The shift and dumping of the toxic wastes from North to South invite grave ecological suffering. The multinational countries already initiated to dump iron, copper, lead, metallic wastes, plastic and injurious nuclear wastes from developed countries to the Third World countries. India imports lead wastes, electronics and plastic wastes. It also imports monthly 10 million tons of such wastes as mobile phones, typewriters, telephones, PVC wires and rejected parts of computers from USA. According to a report, nearly one lakh tons of hazardous wastes enter into India which damage our environment scenario. Australia, Canada, UK and USA export plastic wastes, lead and other metal wastes, copper and tin wastes to India regularly and freely. Holland exports 'Envirodung' (cow and pig's dung), a deadly wastes, which pollutes the fertility of soil and underground water resources. India now becomes a dumping ground of the capitalists (Dasgupta, 2008). And, such a slow poisoning not only signifies the negative motivation of the global players, but such a process of dumping a load of toxic wastes in the Third World country is never impeccable. The environmentalists should raise their voice of dissent with the expressions of Fiedel. Castro: "Tomorrow will be too late to do what we should have a long time ago?"

One might refute the fact that our bodies are constrained in time and space. This vista is related to the decisive issue of global warming. Many social scientists who fear threats to the global environment (e.g., Archer, 1991) seek a global identity in relation to environmental issues. Yet, little has been done to explore ecological problems in most contemporary work on globalization. An exception to this trend is Robertson (1992), who stresses the need to study globalization-ecological problems in terms of species threatening phenomena. Sing C. Chew

(2004) observes the tie between culture and nature, a relationship that has been interjected by periods of ecological crisis. These crisis moments or Dark Ages exhibit conditions of ecological degradation, climatic changes, and reorganization of socio-economic and political structures. M. Tolba and El-Kholy (1992) identify a number of major premises as symptoms of a global ecological crisis. These include climate change, biodiversity loss, population growth, fresh water pollution, contamination, air pollution, the greenhouse effect, deforestation, land ruin and desertification. Globalization connoisseurs promote technological inputs as the saviour from global ecological degradation. However, the introduction of technology and electronics, from the kitchen to the bedroom, not only conserves human energy, it also creates environmental hazards. Meadows (cited in Dadayan, 1988) identifies the major factors that are likely to present insurmountable barriers to future economic growth. These include the limited volume of food production and constraints on the extraction of non-replenishable natural resources, together with the pollution of the environment resulting from technology (Dadayan, 1988).

The ecology and globalization offer an exclusive discernment. Many within the environmentalist movement recognize that uncertain globalization is no longer possible, and instead, have focused on revision of the ongoing process of globalization. Institutionalists have documented that environmental resilience is required and they speak to environmental concerns more honestly. While the lines between the different factions have become blurred, recent events, such as the Kyoto Protocol talks at the Hague, demonstrate that the discussion continues between the environmentalists and institutionalists as to what is the proper way to ensure environmental reform. Some global scientists being the victims of eco-disaster fear attempted to think over the issue of nature and began talking about sociological parameters of global environment. And, there are strong grounds for talking about environmental degradation that "threatens the globe" (Yearley, 1996). The global sociologists are now speaking of and writing on the issues related to ozone depletion, dumping of the wastes on the land and in the sea, pollution rate and ratio, resource depletion and loss of biodiversity, eco-disbalance, global warming, green talks, eco justice, environment movements, disaster management, economy-ecology dilemma and environment consciousness. Yearley (1996: 140) notes, "There is growing awareness of the Earth as a cultural reference point with widely accepted connotations. Furthermore, specialized discourses, such as that of sustainable development, are emerging in relation to the putative policy requirements of the globe". According to Todd Sandler (1997: xiii), "We live in an era during which the side effects of these activities (economic) have surpassed limits, beyond which stresses placed on the planet's ecosystems lead to permanent deteriorations". We may claim that the maximum utilization of natural resources and terrible exploitation of eco-wealth for accumulation of more and more capital in the name of industrial development using maximum technological gadgets have degraded our planet, its biosphere, its stratosphere, oceans, seas, lands, forests and hills which result in maximum heat and temperature. Nature has its own limit to bear the burden. It is not possible for a mother to give births hundreds of babies. Like wise, it is not possible to shoulder the overpressure of technology and inhuman extraction of natural resources. So, we see ozone hole, acid rain, nuclear meltdown, chemical hazards, excessive toxicity, desertification, loss of biodiversity and global warming (Sandler, 1997).

There are some living and perceivable enemies like poverty, disparity, economic inequality, population explosion, terrorism, religious bigotry, fanaticism, global-local dilemma and war threatening exacerbate environmental problems. In the 1994 the global population stood at 5.6 billion with 1.2 billion in the developed countries and 4.4 billion in the Third World (UN Population Fund, 1994). The earth is overstraining to take the load of such huge population on its surface. This population-land ratio causes ecological disequilibrium. Secondly, the poverty appears as a human species-threatening phenomenon. It is the reality that climate change is not just an environmental issue but also a major human issue that global players must respond to. To earn the livelihood, the poor people in the Third World countries have to depend on some illegal wood smuggling activities. The unregistered and unofficial deforestation accounts a huge amount which expedites the process of deforestation in general. Then come war, ethnic violence and terrorism in which different weapons including bombshell, gas, biological and chemical substances are used in a very sporadic but large scale manner, which cause severe eco-damage. If we look at the terrorist attack on Mumbai, the war in Iraq and Afghanistan, the nuclear test in USA, China, India, Pakistan and other countries, we may allege that the issue and saying of 'New World Order' is at stake. These make air terribly polluted. "Technology has become a two-edged sword in which beneficial aspects are often associated with potentially negative consequences that are tied to some of the global contingencies", says Todd Sandler (1997: 7). Technologies that use in cultivation have also unfavourable effect on environment. 'The green talk' of farming meant the upward jump of crops and yields but at the cost of menacing pollutants. The use of pesticides, chemical fertilizers and insecticides in agricultural production harmfully affects the health of the planet. It causes soil contagion and health hazards among the human beings. So, profiting drives of the agricultural and industrial big brothers make environment obscure. This attitude makes all the agreements/conferences starting from Antarctic Treaty (1959), Convention of Climate Change (1993) to Kyoto Protocol (1997) obsolete. Traders' ravenousness, deprives' hunger, rulers' cruel and demoralizing grip to acquire land of others, multinationals' frantic challenge of taking over the planet and the capitalists' impervious attitude to accumulate more capital by surveillance and regimentalism, and the escalation of local, global and cross-border terrorism invited environmental disaster (Dasgupta, 2008). Globalization can both be used as a way of procuring environmental safeguards and creating environment risks and eco-disasters. Our environment is a single whole and with the raison d'être of one planet and one human race we should walk around the global environmental scenario so that one could comfortably identify the concealed of eco-disasters and nature threatening.

The environment is the only talk of this age. When we are very loud to reach the intense point of technological progress and postmodern culture, the world is also ringing the bell of ruin and environmental tragedy. It has already signalled the death knell of our civilization which is now nearly to our door. Global warming is the indicator of such destruction. Globalization has given anxieties, poverty, inequality, hunger, disease, health hazards, malnutrition, illiteracy and uncertainties to the Third World countries. Not only humanity or global environmental peace, but the accumulation of nuclear weapons, the making of hi-tech biological and technological weapons, and panic of nuclear catastrophe have also globalized. Ulrich Beck (1995), in his excellent work, *Risk Society* (1995), examines the impact of dominant global economic forces and postmodern culture. According to him, these will lead to uncertainty and loss of control. Beck observes that "forests have also been dying for some centuries now—first through being transformed into fields, then through reckless overcutting. But, the death of forests today occurs globally, as the implicit consequence of industrialization ... It is nevertheless striking that hazards in those [early] days assaulted the nose or the eyes and were thus perceptible to the senses, while the risks of civilization today typically escape perception and are localized in the sphere of physical and chemical formulas ... In the past, the hazards could be traced back to an undersupply of hygienic technology. Today, they have their basis in industrial overproduction. The risks and hazards of today thus differ in an essential way from the apparently similar ones in the middle ages through the global nature of their threat". These are the risks of modernization. This is the sad story of the blow of globalization on the environment. In the past, the people survived with environmental vulnerabilities and were at menace. But, today, the influence of globalization has also threatened their natural safety. The transformation of premodern to modern social risks has led to a total lack of control over our destinies. Beck's thesis thus underscores some serious queries concerning what type of 'development' developing countries should pursue (Salih, 2001).

In view of the current concern about the current global environmental crisis and its impact on socio-cultural change, Sing Chew (2004) analyzes that the past can help us understand likely possible futures. He examines the past trends of environment, such as deforestation, soil erosion, pollution, trade and economic disruptions, de-urbanization, political regime and climatological changes during the Dark Ages. These, he argues, provide insights into the conditions that give rise to system transformations, and the possibility that we might be about to experience another Dark Age phase. Sociology plays a vital role in understanding the links between man and environment. With the appearance of globalization environment study builds around several interrelated aspects like ecology, economy, culture and politics. So, it is now irrefutable that environment studies wrap all the aspects of bio-sociological dimensions. The spatial facet of global-locality links to culture oneness and the creation of new cultural spaces. The philosophy of thinking the world as a single place (Robertson, 1992) makes the planet as a natural entity. Sociologists often view society as a set of nations, but this concept needs to be complemented with an explicitly ecological perspective. It is assumed that bio-physical reality shapes social reality, which ultimately creates a diverse ecosystem (Dasgupta, 2004).

Steven Yearley (1996) argues that it is difficult to consider all countries as part of a 'global village'. The climatic differences and natural, topographical and climatological segregation appear to deny the prospect of globalization. The ecologically linked notion of time and space has been transformed into another neo-ecological dimension of late modernism, which is a source of globalization in conflict. Ecological disequilibrium as a universal phenomenon appears to deny the possibility of global culture and humanism (Dasgupta, 2004). Robertson (1992) views the need to study globalization-ecological continuum in terms of species threatening phenomena. Globalization specialists support technological inputs as the saviour from global ecological degradation. However, the introduction of technology and electronics, from the kitchen to the bedroom, not only conserves human energy, but also creates environmental hazards. It is undeniable that globalization has given to the human race of this planet the bonanza of hi-tech weapons and nuclear power. The gifts that we received from the initiators of globalization are worries, psycho-physical trauma, fear of poverty and inequality, hunger and disease, value erosion and illiteracy. As stated earlier "the preservation and development of the environment are continually being sacrificed in the name of ecological modernization" (Dasgupta, 2004). This is the gloomy effect of globalization on the environment. In the past, the people lived with environmental hazards and were at risk. But, today, the influence of globalization has also threatened their biological security. The change of premodern to modern social hazards has led to a total lack of control over our destinies. In considering the current concern about ongoing global environmental crisis and its impact on socio-cultural change, In a word, we may claim that environmental problems are escalating rapidly with the ever-accelerating pace of globalization. Therefore, environmentalists' concerns are now an accepted matter of discourse not for theoretical jugglery but for saving our planet.

Menace, developing from technological or industrial accidents, dangerous procedures, infrastructure failures or certain human activities, may cause the loss of life or injury, property damage, social and economic disruption or environmental degradation. Industrial pollution, nuclear activities and radioactivity, toxicity, industrial and chemical wastes, dam failures, transport, industrial or technological accidents such as explosions, fires, spills are the different forms of natural and man-made hazards. Natural abnormalities that crop up in the biosphere also cause environmental damage. The environment hazard begins with the appearance of industrial revolutions. Air, water and soil pollutions have given fertile grounds to swallow up human fortune with the emergence of industry. It is noticed that the worst victims live mostly near the vicinities of factories, and slum pockets. This causes another dimension of social discrimination. Industrialization is always invited and it is now the last expression of development in the era of globalization. But it has also some side and unpleasant effects. Industry is developed and expanded in the affluent countries. The Third World countries account for only 14.2 per cent of the world's industry and least developed countries in Africa and Latin America share just 0.21 per cent of the industry of the world. The industrialized nations are responsible for creating problems like global warming, ozone depletion and acid rain etc. The major problems of pollution are being produced by the global players. The ecosystem dangled from the emergence of globalization and the eco-disequilibrium create environmental marginality. The deforestation venture, which is a prerequisite for creating industrial sectors, leads to eco-lessening and environment risks. So, we may claim that there might be a possibility of creating a 'risk society'. The risk of regional or local warming is mainly due to vanishing trend of green nature, natural rainfall, climatic set-up and soil erosion. The erection of heavy machine shops and landuse for such eco-disaster reveals a much cemented relationship between man and nature. The mutual reciprocity between man and environment shapes and makes the ecological balance. We can claim that the crisis of humanity invited environmental hazard on the one hand and eco-crisis and eco-disaster bring destruction of human living on the other. In this context, the concept of sustainable development comes into the fore to the developmentalists with economy-ecology balance. The idea of sustainable development implies harmonizing environmental security with the generation of increased opportunities for employment and improved livelihood. The role of the environmentalists as the sustainers and developers is not only to look after the health of environment but also to eliminate social inequality of the victims of environment hazards. It is undeniable that poverty is the prime cause of eco-stress. From an estimation of World Bank it may be cited that every year more than two million people in the Third World countries die from the diseases caused by water pollution and billions of people fall ill from water-borne diseases. The population whose life expectancy varies from 45 to 50 years suffers from acute skin complaint and eye troubles due to extreme sun-heat exposure caused by exhaustion of the ozone layer. Industrialization is the symbol of modernization as well as development. But industrial development changes the thermal balance of the earth increasingly affecting the moisture turnover and the natural processes associated with it (Gerasimor et al., 1975). Sky-high apartments, pressure of heavy vehicles, excessive carbon emission, drainage and storage of chemical garbage, dumping of scraps etc., are the negative versions of industrialization, which create environmental hazards. Monitoring and systemic protection management could only lower down the degree of hazard. The World Disasters Report (2003) divides disasters into natural and unnatural. We may have a sense from the following structural paradigm of the sources of environmental risks.

Industrial wastes enter coastal waters from earthly activities. Industries waste is disposed of in two ways: while the liquid waste is flown through wastewater systems whereas is solid waste is buried under the ground. It is evident from various studies that the quantity and quality of industrial wastewater depend on the type of industry. Industrial waste recurrently goes down the same sewers as domestic and commercial non-industrial waste, sewage often contains high levels of industrial chemicals and heavy metals. In coastal areas, some industries discharge their wastes directly to the ocean. Industrial chemicals can harmfully affect the growth, reproduction and development of many marine animals. In addition to the environmental and ecological issues, there is budding concern over the human health impacts in indigenous communities whose residents depend on fish and aquatic mammals for daily breads. Some half-hearted regulatory measures have adopted to control such a hazard caused due to industrial wastes but it is still a serious cause of human sufferings. In general, ecological vulnerabilities refer to natural disasters such as earthquake, cyclone, flood, volcano, global warming, tsunami, hurricane, drought, etc. While humans have been exposed to hazards for centuries, risk is considered more of a 20th century phenomenon. Initial sociological work on risk dates from the mid-1980s. Though studies on natural disasters have a longer history within the field, they have been very much concentrated on 'emergency adjustments' instead of adjustments of humans to their physical environments (Dasgupta, 2008).

The hazards that people terribly face include chemical-prone risks, and arising out of explosions like application of dynamite etc., fire of the machine oven and boiler plant, fire arising from melting mechanism of steel industries, leakage from gas plants, toxicity due to use of some materials and minerals and radiation that comes from thermal power plants, high power welding machines, iron melting shop etc. According to Madhusree Mukerjee (1995) in Bhopal, Methyl Isocyanides (MIC) gas spread over 75 square kilometres, causing an estimated 6,00,000 people to suffer from choking and burning eyes and skin, and killing many in distant fields. The official death toll was 2,500 but estimates based on the sale of shrouds and wood for cremations range from 7,000 to 8,000. According to the 1991 census of India, out of the total population of 838.6 million, 403.4 million were women. Approximately, 23 per cent of women work outside the home. Of these, 34.6 per cent work in cultivation, 44.2 per cent in agricultural labour, 5.9 per cent in household industries and 15.3 per cent in other professions. According to the Indian Ministry of Labour, in 1994, about 4,97,000 women worked in factories, 56,000 in mines and 5,58,000 in plantation industries. The Indian women working in major small-scale industries face the occupational hazards and suffer from respiratory ailments conjunctivitis, occupational dermatitis, tuberculosis, lung cancer, gynecological problems, fungal infection, and skin diseases.

All such hazards need protection. The global initiators are very energized to make their network of capitalist implosion bigger at the cost of human lives and environmental distress. The fly ashes that come from the chimneys of different power plants and wrap the sky like the dark cloud and shadow the kitchens, bedrooms and drawing rooms of the people engender environment. No one would be hurt if the inconspicuous and deadening condition of environment is analyzed from the viewpoint of pessimism. The information demonstrates that the environmental pollution on a global scale has grown to a perilous level. Quite a large number of cases have been reported of disease and deaths among residents of industrial pockets as a result of ejection of toxic substances by industrial sectors, machine shops and vehicles. In the words of L.S. Abramov (1975), "The Earth's atmosphere continues to be contaminated with dust, carbon dioxide, sulphurous compounds, lead, nitrogen oxides, soot, and pesticides. The carbon dioxide levels in the atmosphere are rapidly growing, which is likely to lead to great and even catastrophic changes in the Earth's climate." And, it grew appallingly. It causes global warming, climatic change, topographical worsening, eco-disbalance and ambiguity of human living. As yet the eco-danger is beyond to measure. These all are the results of natural and mostly man-made catastrophes. It is undeniable that modernization has given us speed and bonanza of technologies but it has also destroyed nature and environment exploiting its resources and potentials. Perhaps so environment roars in anger and desperation. So, we face earthquake, tsunami, hurricane, twister, flood, volcano and drought. The citation of David Lyon (2002) appears very interesting in this context. He states in his preface to the second edition of his book *Post Modernity*: "Reality refers to go away, even when the air is thickly postmodern. I curled in front of a long fire by candlelight to work on this preface, but not by romantic choice. A freak ice storm had brought down trees and power lines in eastern Ontario and Quebec, wreaking havoc with modern conveniences. No power, no phone, no Internet. No radio or TV either ... our situation was already a media event elsewhere that was a postmodern twist". Globalization thus follows Newtonian law that "every action has its opposite and equal reaction". It is mainly due to the heavy pressure of modernization/globalization on environment and nature.

Interaction between man and nature began through the consecutive stages of biological progression. Man, for his survival, began to exploit land and ecological reserves. The degree and intensity of eco-exploitation reached to its culminating point today. The population of the world is increasing very steadily and rapidly and side by side the use of eco-resources is also growing accordingly. The global space is becoming narrower day by day in terms of residential, industrial, commercial transport and recreational land use. So it is undeniable that space and nature on the earth's surface is facing tremendous pressure and it is now beyond its capacity intake. The development of capitalism and extension (of is sphere) of its domination were marked by competition for profits, which are the major stimulus to economic advance in the social systems (Gerasimor et al., 1975). E. Fedosov (1980) observes that over the past 50 years (I say 76 years), radiation from the planet in the radio frequency range has increased hundreds of time. Secondly, the limits of satisfaction of human needs become so limitless that human being invites environmental vulnerability and eco-destruction.

It is now very difficult to control population and provide human beings with balanced spatial accommodation; it is impractical to make attempt to stop and check the speed of rapid industrialization. It is next to the impossible for the capitalist countries and initiators of globalization to stop endeavour of establishing multinational industrial sectors and novelty of technological know-how. We may claim that destruction—the opposite face of creation—has not been perceived by the human beings. We are now crossing winter. But we should remember: "if winter comes can spring be far behind". It will be possible to avoid the crisis of environment, if an over all long-term plan of action for the whole of humanity is drawn up now and measures are taken on a global scale to prevent eruption of the crisis.

U. Thant (1969: 8), the former UN Secretary General, states, "the deterioration of the human environment may be related to three basic causes; accelerated population growth, increased urbanization, and an expanded and efficient new technology, with their associated increase in demands for space, food and natural resources .... The efforts to accommodate population, to integrate technology into complex environments, to plan and control industrialization and urbanization, and to properly manage land and resources, have fallen far short of those required".

Globalization is compounded with war economy and therefore any examination of the relationship between economic globalization and environmental destruction is more accurate when expanded to include militarism. Military activities are liable for resource exhaustion and environmental extermination. Militarism is recognized as a major threat to the environment in our universal future. Militaries are the prime threat to the global environment. Environmental devastation attributable to militarism includes not only the more obvious impacts of conventional war, weapons of mass destruction and troop and tank activities, but also those created by the presence and wastes of military personnel and their bases, and the fuel consumption of the military vehicles, ships and planes, especially jet planes. Michael Renner states that nearly one quarter of all the jet fuel in the world, about 42 million tons per year, is used for military purposes. Bandarage reports that the Pentagon is considered to be one of the biggest users of oil in the US and perhaps the world. She also notes that although little work has been done to calculate the military contribution to global warming and ozone depletion, some sources estimate that total military-related carbon emissions could be as high as 10 per cent of emissions worldwide. Militarism is leading the world down a path towards ecological catastrophe and global insecurity (cited in 'Introduction' in Dasgupta and Kiely, (eds) 2006).

The term 'weapons of mass destruction' is related to nuclear, biological and chemical weapons. Italians used chemical weapons during the war 1935–36 in Ethiopia, the Japanese in China during World War II (1938–42), and these were used also in Yemen (1966–67). Various new chemicals were developed for use in weapons. *Sarin, Soman* and *VX* followed *Tabun*, the first nerve gas, invented in 1936. During the Vietnam war (1961–1973), the US used "lachrymatory agents and heavy doses of herbicides (defoliants) in much the same manner as chemical weapons. Some international organizations consider Napalm, its trade name, to be a chemical weapon; others put it on equal level with flame throwers, and consequently not falling under any of the articles of the CWC".

It is reported that Saddam Hussein used chemical weapons against Iraqi civilians as well as against Iranian soldiers between 1980 and 1988. And, approximately 27,000 Iranians exposed to Iraqi mustard gas. Over the entire period of war, several reports state that Iraqi chemical weapons killed 5,000 Iranians. This constituted less than one per cent of the 6,00,000 Iranians who died from all causes during the war. The easiest—say cheapest—way to eliminate chemical weapons in the aftermath of World War II appeared to dump them into ocean. There had been a worry that, after their defeat in 1945, Germans could be tempted to use part of their arsenal, which totalled 2,96,103 tons. Therefore, the weapons were captured and dumped into the sea. There were more than 100 dumpings of chemical weapons that took place from 1945 to 1970 in every ocean except the Arctic. About 46,000 tons were dumped in the Baltic areas known as the Gotland Deep, Bornholm Deep, and the Little Belt. According to the Continental Committee on Dumping, the total was shared by 93,995 tons from the US, 9,250 tons from France, 1,22,508 tons from Britain, and 70,500 tons from Russia. The US dumped German chemical weapons in the Scandinavian region, totalling between 30,000 and 40,000 tons. The Russians alone have dumped 30,000 tons in an area, 2,000 square kilometres in size. Between 1945 and 1949, the British dumped 34 shiploads carrying 1,27,000 tons of chemical (containing 40,000 tons mustard gas) and conventional weapons in the Norwegian trench at 700 metres depth. The chemical weapons at the bottom of the Baltic Sea (mean depth of the Baltic Sea is 51 metres) and the North Sea represent a serious danger for the aquatic life. The US is responsible for 60 sea dumping totalling about 1,00,000 tons (equal to 39 filled railroad box cars), of chemical weapons filled with toxic materials in the Gulf of Mexico, off the coast of New Jersey, California, Florida, and South Carolina, and near India, Italy, Norway, Denmark, Japan, and Australia (cited in Dasgupta, 2008).

It is evident from Danielle Knight's writing (2002) that massive quantities of scrap electronics are being exported from the United States to China, Pakistan and India, where the dispel is causing environmental and health problems. Up to 80 per cent of all electronic waste collected for recycling in the United States actually ends up on container ships bound for Asia. Tons of electronic waste bearing labels and identification tags from the United States are dumped along rivers, in open fields, and in irrigation canals. They call this recycling but it is really dumping. According to a report, India is becoming the largest dumping ground for e-waste, especially used computers, from the US, Singapore and South Korea.

Thousands of small-scale and even some bigger industrial units simply dump their waste, more often toxic and hazardous, in open spaces and nearby water sources. Asha Krishnakumar (2003) notes that India is increasingly becoming a dumping ground for toxic industrial wastes from developed countries, which can pose serious threats to public health and the environment. Over the last three decades, many cases of serious and everlasting damage to environment by these industries have come to the fore (Sule, 2007). India generates around 7 million tonnes of harmful wastes every year, most of which is concentrated in four states: Andhra Pradesh, Bihar, Uttar Pradesh and Tamil Nadu. Household wastes are also very hazardous that include old shoes, bottles and strips of medicine, old bags and luggages, daily garbage, used sanitary pads, cotton and bandages, old batteries, shoe polish, paint tins, etc. Hospital wastes in India like solid waste, disposables, anatomical waste, cultures, discarded medicines, chemical and wastes metals such as formaldehyde and phenols, mercury etc., create severe health hazards and ultimately ecological crisis. The dumping of electronic gadgets like mouse of computers, defective key boards, tape recorders, tapes of the cassettes, polythene and plastic buckets and tubs, especially the toys that contain dangerous elements and parts, are the added household wastes that create environment hazards in the families. Not only households but hospitals are also the producers of hazardous wastes. And it is true that most hospitals in India do not have proper removal facilities for these hazardous wastes. Other hospital wastes that can be mentioned are disposable syringes, swabs, bandages, body fluids, human excreta, etc. It has been roughly estimated that of the 4 kg of waste generated in a hospital at least 1 kg would be infected.

In the era of globalization hotel industry has flourished in a very large scale. To catch the world under the grip becomes a very easy process. The spatial and geographical mobility has become very high. It is mainly because of the time-space compression and the speed of time over space. The people who nests in the hotels starting from five-star to the ordinaries are facing awful health hazards. The deluxe infrastructures are there, the rooms are equipped with all sorts of modern technological and electronic gadgets, the food may be hygienic but touching the used remote control or other electronic gadgets may create severe contamination. The hotel workers will change your linen, your pillow, mattress etc., but they will not clean and disinfected the technological and electronic gadgets. During the 1950s, the United States initiated an ambitious nerve gas programme, manufacturing what would eventually total 4,00,000 M-55 rockets that play deadly game with the human race. This is something amusing that we claim ourselves as the architect of new civilization or as the designer of a global village with homogeny and humane concord but we are silently killing our pride, our making and remaking of new society, our knowledge and skill. So fear and fear is everywhere. We are now waiting for a doomsday where mass killing agents will dominate over green leaves, blue sky and lovely flowers.

It is reported by several environment organizations that global warming causes 1,60,000 deaths every year from diseases and hunger, following extreme weather conditions such as droughts and floods. For example, the Environment News Service calls on Russia to promptly ratify the Kyoto Protocol, which could contribute to halting climate change. With the Millennium Development Goals, the United Nations has devoted itself to halve the proportion of people suffering from chronic malnutrition by 2015. We can feel the magnitude of recognizing the links between food anxiety, poverty and bio-loss of diversity, and it is true that biodiversity loss is a root cause of hunger and socio-economic inequality. UN Population Fund calls for total education, health care and reproductive rights for women to fight poverty and extreme population escalation. The report states that by 2050, 4.2 billion people will be living in hunger, out of a total projected world population of 9.3 billion. Thirty-four countries are now experiencing droughts and food shortages, and their number could increase. Droughts could become semi-permanent if climate change persists, increasing global food shortages. Scientists predict that global warming will cause the dunes of the Kalahari desert to spread, shifting sand across huge tracts of Botswana, Angola, Zimbabwe and western Zambia.

Exposure to environmental health risks can be traced to historical and contemporary economic, spatial, ecological and social situation of inequality which structures and determines where people reside, which groups have the political and economic power to construct and maintain secured and healthy environments and which groups lack the power to influence the quality of their residential environment. The heightened health risks which people of ethnic disadvantaged groups and low-income people are subjected to as a result of disproportionate exposure to toxins, and the lower aesthetic quality of their communities, are the result of economic and social arrangements of power and the inequitable distribution of resources in our society. It is our experience that the affected people of environmental hazards and natural disasters are the economically and politically marginalized groups who are in the majority.

Amartya Sen (2002) rightly states, "I won't leave it to the WTO to save the world from an environmental point of view because that's not where they come from, they come from a very different part of the economy, they are very concerned with, you know, running the economy, the financial balance and you know we are grateful to them, that's part of the job too, but we need more and the environmental concerns have to be represented through other ways". So, globalization of environment is an impossible concept. It might be possible when the Noah with his Ark will return to a lost world to give mankind a fresh beginning. It is very much true for the human race of this planet that are going plunged into an era of uncertainty and a new unpredictable geological stage where perhaps there would be no human race as such and now we feel such a fear of global warming. We should wake up from a dead sleep. If we still sit back and say, "There is nothing we can do", then environmental disasters not only heat on 'big brothers' but also wipe out the rest. We are now on the doorstep of environmental destruction. Now, we should be bold and beautiful like nature. Now, one may raise a basic question: What do we invite? Green landscape gives us life. And factory chimneys give us bread and livelihood. I do feel both are the integral part of social and economic development. We can only uphold a equilibrium between green and grey, i.e., between ecology and economy. We could detect the environment culprits who are exploiting nature with their inhumane motivations. We should remake the environment policies without any political bias. We should worship our nature offering our traditional cultural bearings. Economy is the love of life and nature is the love of heart. So, the blending of life with heart or otherwise life with livelihood is a contextual phenomenon now. Time rotates with the wave of globalization. Time is running over space. People are saying, "Run Lola run". In this competitive world, in this arena of rat race, the only talk is development and money-making. We are very much worried and concerned with head, not heart. So environment is showing us its ugly face. And, we are terrifying. Now, the global initiators feel that the ugly face of nature is more deadly than any horror film. Nature is very much related to culture and it satisfies the need of human race but the greed and motive of profiting more and more invited eco-disaster that we are facing now. But, we should not tolerate our Mother's (Nature) sufferings at the cost of anything such as technological advance, modernization, industrialization or globalization. Another most important consequence of ecological depression is global burden of disease. Globally, 70 million people suffer from alcohol addiction. About 50 million have epilepsy; another 24 million have schizophrenia. A million of global people commit suicide every year. Between 10 and 20 million people attempt it. Rare is the family that will be free from an encounter with psychological disarrays. The loss of mental and physical health in the Third World countries, which is the result of high alacrity and velocity of globalization, communication technology, media blaze, excessive and total dependence on computer and networking system, overuse of domestic and commercial technological gadgets, regular use of banned medicines, overuse of poisonous pesticides and fertilizers and lastly the sorrow of the looser, projects a vicious circle of globalization risk which results in the incidence of psychosomatic disease like depression, dementia, anxiety, chronic stress, bronchial spasm, heart problems, hypertension, neurotic expressions, psychosis, alienation, violence, alcoholism, schizophrenia and suicide. And, thus, the future of our global society, particularly the Third World countries, is more horrible. The incidence of AIDS in India is steadily rising amidst concerns that the nation feels the prospect of an AID epidemic. According to the 2006 report on Global AIDS Epidemic, India had 5.7 million cases of HIV, by the end of 2005, as against about 5.5 million people infected in South Africa. The emotional disorders also affect 59 million people across the world and top the list of disabilities.

The impact of globalization on life-saving drugs depicts a very sordid picture. Multinational pharmaceutical companies bring benefits not to the humanity across the world. They feel interest to have more and more profits. The life-saving drugs of the tropical disease are not profitable to them because most people with such diseases are too poor to afford cures. Not only that addressing the excessive quest for profits, poverty should be overlooked. This is really inhuman globalization where the lives, humanity and right to live are not included in their moral agenda. These pharmaceutical industries talk capitalist corridors of power. Ken Silverste (1999) says, "Millions for Viagra. Pennies for Diseases of the Poor". The multinational corporations sell viagra across the world mainly because of the serving the people who are very much addicted to sex pleasure. It is getting more importance in the era of globalization because most people in the Third World countries have to depend on sex selling to satisfy the cravings for absolute hunger. They desire their long life span but cannot afford costly life-saving medicines. The global pharmaceutical corporations sell products in developing countries that are banned in the West; sell their products by persuasive and misleading advertising and promotion; cause the poor to divert money away from essential items, such as foodstuffs, to paying for expensive, patented medicines, thereby adding to problems of malnutrition; sell products such as appetite stimulants which are totally inappropriate; promote antibiotics for relatively trivial illnesses; charge more for products in developing countries than they do in the West. This is certainly the violation of global human rights.

6 The Cultural and Moral Dimensions of Globalization

Environmental problems are increasing rapidly with the ever-accelerating pace of globalization. Environmentalist concerns are now an accepted matter of discourse (Yearly, 1996). Yet, the linkage between environmental consciousness and 'species consciousness' remains problematic. To some extent, the people of the world share a global culture (here defined as 'communicable intelligence'). But it is a culture in conflict, as opposed to a universal consensus, because of the confusion between globally local and locally global phenomena. Some critics note that globalization in its current phase is thus a product of 'triadic cultural hegemony'. The cultural homogenization model does not fit the Third World countries, mainly for economic reasons. Economy and culture are intimately interrelated. Our age of cultural realism is tied with the current stage of market capitalism. Monopoly capitalism links cultural modernism; and postmodern cultural phenomena constitute the denominator of managerial capitalism. Thus, capitalist hegemony continues. Those who promote globalization conceal questions of economic particularism domination behind their programmes of global culture. "[T]here is a significant political link between culture and economy which proves very difficult to analyze... ." (Tomlinson, 1999). The issue of universalism has an intimate connection with globalization. For, it promises to create global homogeneity. But, for Gray (1997), both the social processes of globalization and the cultural and political norms of universalism are negative. Universalism is "one of the least useful and indeed most dangerous aspects of the western intellectual tradition... the metaphysical faith that local western values are authoritative for all cultures and people" (Gray, 1997). Such 'progressive individualism' (another name for universalism) aims to make the rest of the world—the rejected world—de-traditionalized and disenchanted. Cultural globalization is also malignant in the form of the ever-expanding electronic culture and the ever-proliferating fast food outlets—the process that George Ritzer refers to as *McDonaldization*. Ritzer (2002) notes that these restaurants are the new 'cathedrals of consumer culture'. The result is, thus, a conflict between new cultural spaces and traditional cultural spaces.

A binary cultural fusion arises from this imposition. Yan Yunxiang (2002) writes, "During the 1999 student demonstrations against the NATO bombing of the Chinese embassy in Belgrade ... many young protestors were drinking Coca Cola as they chanted 'down with American imperialism' in front of the US embassy in Beijing. The irony goes much further, when some young activists sent messages over the Internet calling for a resistance movement to the invasion of Western Culture ... Others went to eat at a KFC outlet immediately after parting anti-McDonald's slogans on the streets.... This observation reveals the phenomenon of 'Managed Globalization'.

Older explanatory schemes, such as Talcott Parsons' pattern variables, fail entirely to account for such dual cultural functions. Particularism, according to Parsons, is a cultural emphasis on familiar and familial values, i.e., loyalty to one's society. Universalism, on the other hand, emphasizes the organization of interaction according to general, cosmopolitan standards, i.e., loyalty to humanity as a whole. Whether such universalism is harmful or not is a matter of debate. But, a metamorphosis of the universal into the particular has occurred, and with it the transformation of emotion into a disciplined cultural reality. Immanuel Wallerstein (1974) emphasizes that the term 'globalization' emerged with the end of Cold War, and a new concept of culture became part of international discourse. Wallerstein analyzes multiculturalism in terms of the interplay of universalism, particularism, and time. The result of this interplay is a clash between 'we' and 'others' that, according to Wallerstein, turns benign cultures malignant.

A fundamental reorganization of our epistemologies may help us understand this multiple universalism. A multicultural society is one made up of people belonging to different cultures. Under such circumstances, culture clash is likely if those who share 'their own' values and standards unintentionally accept the culture of the 'others'. At the extreme, this can result in genocide, holocaust, and ethnic cleansing. Globalization creates a distance between particular and universal cultures. Slavoj Zizek (1997) notes, "Multiculturalism is a disavowed, inverted, self-referential form of racism, a racism, with a distance—it respects the other's identity, conceiving the other as a self-enclosed 'authentic' community towards which he, the multiculturist, maintains a distance rendered possible by his privileged universal position. The multiculturalist respect for the other's specificity is the very form of asserting one's own superiority". In this context, conflict can also occur between 'privileged universality' and 'shared universality' (Bharucha, 1999). In other words, it is a clash between multiculturalism and interculturalism. Whereas multiculturalism works within the "cultural logic of multinational capitalism" (Zizek, 1997), interculturalism opposes such a logic (Bharucha, 1999). True universality can occur when, in a socially constructed world, 'we' are the constructors. This is perhaps the true form of benign global culture.

Most promoters of globalization, according to Wallerstein, favour hierarchies because they will benefit from the wealth and power thereby accumulated. They attempt to command intelligence and knowledge; that is, they seek hegemony. But these groups represent the numerical minority of the world's populations. Their quest for control is largely unpopular. Their victory is not guaranteed. The cultures and ethnicities of most people in the world are viewed as subordinate by the globalizers. This leads to confusion, but also to a kind of solidarity among the majority and its representatives. In this context, the clash of cultures follows two tracks: (a) multicultural particularism in conflict; and (b) conflict between multiple universalisms and multiple particularisms. Wallerstein refers to the blend or synthesis as a 'rainbow coalition'. No doubt, the creation of such a global coalition is a formidable political task. But, the increasing rate of economic disparity between the minority and the majority renders a dialogue of inclusion increasingly unlikely.

The colossal use of the word 'globalization' helps it to achieve a global status, in which culture positions itself at the centre. In practice, culture is a set of palpable and impalpable elements, including beliefs, values, norms, material objects, rituals, technologies etc., which shapes and adds meaning to the daily lives of a particular group of people. It plays a pivotal role in any society since it designs the pattern of social action without which the members of a society would be unable to understand each other at all. Through interactions among people, social action changes its form and thus culture is also changed. Earlier, colonialism, trade, migration, missionary activities, technological changes (particularly, the advancement of production and communication system) incorporation of tribals into states and large-scale systems of exchange were the principal factors behind cultural diffusion that resulted in cultural imperialism or globalization of culture (Eriksen, 1995: 278).

Presently, for the modern communication system, space can no longer be said to create a clear buffer between cultures. Newspaper, radio, TV and the last of all—the Internet—have linked up different cultures, making broad avenues for cultural exchange or cultural fusion to proceed and thus initiated new cultural forms, ideas and objects. "Tradition and old assumptions about community based on geographic location are rubbing up against the realities of a networked, changing world. The strain is accompanied by violent conflict in some places (like Serbia and Indonesia), social repression in other places (like Afghanistan), and denunciation of globalization virtually everywhere" (Healey, 2001: 141).

Due to the spread of global culture, today, many societies are facing cultural lags. The reason is that the material culture diffuses and changes quite quickly than its non-material counterpart (Ogburn, 1964). Present-day TNCs and other foreign agencies, by means of state-of-the-art technology, introduce us to the new, newer and newest 'materials' or 'cultural products', which we are yet to think of. And that is not all. Through their advertisements they claim that if you do not buy their products you will lose something—they try to hammer this idea into our (consumers') minds; side by side, 'intellectuals and cultural elites' function "as both the commentators and practitioners of cultural globalization" (Yan, 2002: 35). Though, in non-material aspect of culture, their influence is limited and so is less impressive than that of the TNCs in the material field. The values, beliefs, ideas, ethics and artifacts of the occidental culture sneak into the territory of the Orient through different media and thereby produce cultural hybridization. Socialization, a life-long process by which, one adopts the non-material elements of a particular culture and familiarizes himself with its material components, plays an important role in permanent coalescence of many cultures. Children are socialized into a set of sub-cultural ambiences rather than a single cultural environment. Interactively, socialization helps children to adopt their culture. It is noteworthy that during the adoption "they are also re-inventing or creating new meaning for aspects of it" (Corsaro, 1997: 18). Adolescence culture distinguishably influences the larger one. The youths are the main vectors of the global culture. They are the most loyal and zealous customers of the alien culture too. For them Coke, pop CDs, denims, the ingredients of the imported culture, are 'prestige commodities'—the rate of acceptance being very high. In addition to that, abundant portrayal of violence and sex in TV has degraded their normal behaviour pattern. Hence, the mushrooming youth cultures—representatives of the globe at the globules—are starkly different from the traditional ones that were once prevalent there. So, the younger members of the society are not only subjected to the process of socialization but also are forming their own culture, which is often based on blind aping of the western one.

At the same time, a good number of youths, mostly in the Third World countries, rear a negative version about the global high-hatting of the US in different issues. So, beneath the external flow of global culture, there is also an undercurrent of political nationalism among the youths, which invokes a sense of patriotism and self-identity in their minds under certain circumstances. Earlier, we have mentioned that media act as vehicles of 'web lifestyle'. Actually, there exist some forms of an authority which—in order to secure their interests—advocate the global spread of a particular culture. And, to achieve this, they are actively trying to take over the control of the world media and manipulate it according to their need—which in short can be termed as 'media imperialism' (Giddens, 1989: 559). However, to explain the thing, practical examples will prove more effective rather than theoretical jargons.

A multitude of the peripheries who were almost untouched by the widespread western consumerist culture, even a few days ago, are now going to be acquainted with it. These people were not under the direct influence of cable TV network. Hence, they were not so much exposed to the global cultural trends and the culture that they maintained was almost pristine. But, now, foreign investment is being permitted in the print media, these people will soon succumb to the West—culturally. In India, the previous ban on foreign investment in print media, imposed by Nehru's cabinet in 1955, has been lifted and 26 per cent FDI in newspapers and 74 per cent in specialized magazines has been granted initially. Actually, the Indian government was pressurized by the foreign governments (particularly the US and the UK) and the TNCs to take the decision. From their previous experience of investment in the electronic media, the TNCs have realized that until they could grab the control over the press they will not be totally successful in motivating people to buy their products and capturing the vast and unexplored market of the Third World thereby. Hence, the decision will prove fruitful for them in monetary terms and side by side it will also speed up the cultural hybridization that is taking place round the globe. Moreover, a logical speculation says that manifolds in the near future resulting in the 'de-Indianization' of the 'still-new-Indian' media will multiply the percentage of FDI. Noam Chomsky bequeaths two responsibilities on media as the democracy custodian of the society—first, it "must report the news fairly, completely, and without bias" and second, it "must function as a watchdog for the public against abuses of power"—which are sure to be shirked under the aegis of foreign participation (Cogswell, 1996: 69). The anticipation will not be irrational that the press will be a mere campaigner of the TNCs in the coming days, "transmit biased information instead of news, and do their masters' bidding without even being asked" (ibid.: 82). To put it simply, they will be engaged in publishing the recent news about the Hollywood chartbusters, gossips of Bollywood and advertisements for Coke, Ford, McDonald and other corporate houses etc., rather than depicting the misery of the native people.

Earlier, we have hinted at the ramified media network and showed how it imports alien culture and thus alters the interpretations of the cultural elements. The process leads towards cultural creolization. However, we should not forget the other function of the media that is providing its investors with better access to information of even the farthest corner of the world. Mass media, in Chomskian view, is just a "public relation industry for the rich and powerful" (ibid.: 69). Well, whatever that may be, I am now interested in writing a few words on the term 'cultural creolization'. According to Eriksen (1995: 284), "cultural 'creolization' or 'hybridization' refers to the intermingling and mutual influencing of two or several bodies of cultural flow (or 'tradition')". In his book on postmodernism, Powel

(1998: 2) presents us with its true picture—"the entire world's culture, rituals, races, data banks, myths and musical motifs are intermixing like a smorgasbord in an earthquake". We further clarify it by culling the example of contemporary style of the world music, which is a meeting place of different cultural influences.

The postmodern world music has a kaleidoscopic flavour. It has tinges of different regional music in it. By just switching on the TV one can hear a music band is singing "a blend of Irish love song, Indian raga, heavy-metal anthem, Mongolian Buddhist chant—and all to the tune of peyote drums, gamelans, didgeridoos, panpipes, nose flutes, alpenhorns, sitars and tambourines. And all these sounds may be produced not by the original instrument but electronically, to a danceable reggae or hip-hop beat, and broadcast worldwide via satellite to millions of viewers" (Powel, 1998: 1). In essence, the postmodern artists, like the ancient explorers, simply dive into the unknown and strive to showcase it through their creations. I can cite example of Indian pop singer Daler Mehndi for a better elucidation. He sings Punjabi folk songs punched with preludes and interludes on piano, guitar, keyboard or saxophone and uses beats on octapad, thumba, bongo or congo and makes an international business on this hodge-podge. And, one thing to note, he need not has to pay any royalty for this. However, it must be admitted that he has bestowed a global status to a local culture. But, in doing so, he did make some compromises. He did commodify and commercialize the original folk music deliberately, which denotes a sheer loss of originality and authenticity.

Again, in sharp contrast, we have seen Uday Shankar enthrolles the audiences in Europe and America with his dance shows in 1940s. These shows were mainly based on Hindu mythological stories, which were generously applauded. At present, Tagore and his works are immensely popular in the western countries. I can also mention the name of the sitar maestro Ravi Shankar, who has considerably contributed in globalizing the Indian classical music. Today, American students are crowding his music schools in the US. All these facts indicate a single thing, that is, the local culture also has the capability to influence the influential global culture or to say it differently, the local culture can get globalized. Such reciprocal influences are the basic traits of cultural hybridization.

In the postmodern era of globalization, when occidental consumerist culture strangulates the rural culture, pop, rap and the hegemony of the Hollywood reaches the remotest nook of the world and jeopardizes the cultural heritages there—still then some local cultures are fighting valiantly to safeguard their own identity and sovereignty allowing some minor changes and thus positioning the wolves as the final fortress before the onslaught of 'Americanization'. A proposition by Levi-Strauss, every culture must give out its 'creative potential' by choosing the perfect equilibrium between 'isolation' and 'contact' with surroundings, further supports it. Thus local culture but local customs assimilate some features of extraneous culture and conventional lifestyle continues to be very much active. In the last decade, for instance, urban peoples of India, China (and other Third World countries) accepted some characteristics of western culture—entrepreneurship, individualism and consumerism. But, the rural people of these countries even now are very much less enthusiastic in this regard.

Today western culture seeps more and more into the far-flung and the remote places on the earth, which poses a threat to all the local cultures, resulting in a slow and gradual change in them, and some weaker culture may pale out in this process. As we write in English although it is not our vernacular, to air our thoughts globally. However, hitherto, local culture advocates its identity in its own way. Depending on Healey's position, the reasons behind the co-existence of local and global cultures can be pointed out as under:

First, culture creates a sense of 'we-feeling' through standardized behaviour among the people of a territorial community. Their connection with others, from different geographic locations, of 'similar interests and concerns', which creates a 'shared meaning' about life, does not hamper their links with those from the same geographic location.

Second, local culture is 'surprisingly resilient and durable' to survive under pressure. Actually, values, norms, customs and other non-material components of culture remain so deeply embedded in their minds that it is tough for a global culture to eradicate there. Third, global culture has to rely on local culture to reach the local people, that is, because global messages are most effective when they are put via local languages. For instance, Christian church services in Africa have endeared local customs, dance, music and languages. Hence, the global culture, till now, is incomplete without the local, which means the co-existence of the first and the second, at least at present. Fourth, we have stated earlier that children are socialized into a mosaic of cultures. Therefore, we have an innate inclination towards cultural diversity and so it will be ridiculous to think that peoples around the globe will accept a 'single global super-culture'. Finally, there are many people who value the old customs and ideas that contain 'deep personal meanings'. They refuse cultural homogenization by cultivating the traditional things.

The Moral Dimension: Creative Altruism

A prime item on the political agenda of the majority is the reconstruction of our ethical and knowledge systems. Until this is undertaken, it will be difficult if not impossible to confront such phenomena as multiple temporalities, multiple universalisms and multiple particularism. Fortunately, this project is already underway. It is part of current reflections on the vision of our common humanity and the search for universal dialogue (Annan, 2001). It is related to the expanding search for altruism and a sense of humanity that can dissolve the 'either/or' mind set and the 'us' and 'them' mentality. A new knowledge system, informed by an altruistic sense of humanity, can help produce a global ethic that provides a new and revised sense of belonging.

Based on the practice of 'aidocracy' (rule through helping others), such a global ethic would begin and end with humanity. For, "we appeal as human beings to human beings to remember your humanity and forget the rest. If you can do so, the way lies open to a new paradise" (Russell and Einstein, 1955). An inventory of the effects of globalization on the 'other' world reveals disparity, dejection, faceless universalism, hegemonic control and monopolistic behaviour, ethnocentric bigotry, religious exclusivism and cultural chauvinism (Picco, 2001). Thus, Joseph Stiglitz, in his excellent work *Globalization and Its Discontents* (2002) makes the following observation: "[T]he way globalization has been managed, including the international trade agreements that have played such a large role in removing those barriers and the policies that have been imported on developing countries in this process of globalization, need to be radically rethought .... Decisions were made on the basis of what seemed a curious blend of ideology and bad economics, dogma that sometimes seemed to be thinly veiling special interests ... Rarely did I see forecasts about what the policies would do to poverty.... We are a global community, and like all communities have to follow some rules so that we can live together". What are these rules to which Stiglitz refers? Are they merely a few lines on economic conduct or policy resolution? These are hardly adequate. No, they must be principles of conduct for a common humanity, for an unprecedented and authentic form of altruism. Learning to be humane is a profoundly meaningful challenge in the contemporary world. For true altruism—perceived inclusively and holistically—is applicable to every person under all circumstances. Reciprocity and altruistic love underlie the Golden Rule. Positively stated, it directs one to "do unto others what you would want others to do unto you". In its negative form, it warns, "do not do unto others what you would not want others to do unto you".

The Golden Rule, like *The Gita* in Hindu philosophy, identifies all the altruistic and humane qualities that result in awareness, recognition, inclusion, and love. This is called the 'species consciousness' (Weinstein and Elvira del Pozo, 2004), Weinstein and del Pozo argue that the most complete and effective realization of a truly global socio-cultural system involves the coming to species consciousness by all of humanity (much as Karl Marx stressed that meaningful social change could not occur without the workers coming to true class consciousness). Marxist humanism is founded on such principles. Labour, according to Marx, is the main ingredient in the humanization of nature and humanity itself. In *The German Ideology* (1844) Marx noted, "Above all we must avoid postulating 'society' as an obstruction vis-à-vis the individual. The individual is the social being. His manifestations of life ... an expression and confirmation of social life".

Our adaptive possibilities have increased substantially through the use of technology and the resulting 'artificial intellect'. Will these alter our species nature? Will 'Simulacra' replace Homo sapiens? For, our species consciousness is inherent in the mind, and is not a matter of biological determinacy. The Dutch philosopher Spinoza (1677) states, "every definition of man is a negation, a negation of its own, inevitably limitedness, abstractness and one-sidedness". Spinoza further emphasizes that human action is determined by interactions with fellow humans, guided by reason. Others who have stressed the need for altruism as a prerequisite for authentic globalization include Auguste Comte, Emile Durkheim, James Ozinga (1999), and Pitirim Sorokin (1950). Jay Weinstein and his associates (2004) also connect an altruistic social order with the prospects of a common humanity. Dasgupta (2004) declares social altruism as the prime agenda in our quest for true and humane globalization. Analyzing Indian society in terms of Vedic thought we may define the centre of the global village as the universal self. The philosophy of altruism, according to Dasgupta, can lead to a world in which trade in love is a sin. In this context, Dasgupta seeks out the roots of sociology of humanity and its impact on the process of globalization. Adoption of a global policy of benign altruism, he argues, can help to solve the problems of religious dualism—between peace and violence and between tolerance and aggressiveness. Globalism involves sublimation and compassion. The synthesis represents the true nature of *Karma* (deed), which ultimately leads to *Moksha* (salvation). In assessing the prospects for a common humanity, Weinstein and del Pozo reflect on why altruism is considered deviant behaviour in modern and postmodern cultures. This assessment is deeply rooted in the two worldviews. Modernists focus on variables such as capitalism, industrialism, surveillance capacity, and rise of military power (Giddens, 1990). All of these are faceless and represent only a shadow of human interaction. The postmodernists perceive the cultural logic as a metamorphosis of form into anti-form, purpose into play, design into chance, hierarchy into anarchy, presence into absence, genre into text, and root into rhizome or surface (Hassan, 1982). In the postmodern age, there is no linguistic normality, only 'pastiche'. In this context, it is important to note Baudrillard's (1970; 1980) comments. In his *Vanishing Point*, he defines postmodernism as "the death of meaning, the death of reality, the death of the social and political and the death of sexuality".

These are hyper-rational (Ritzer, 1996) or hyper-real expressions; that is, the "irrationality of rationality". The inclusion of mind, culture, civilization, reality, and the whole, on the one hand, and repression of body, nature, tradition, appearance, and the part, on the other, signifies the state of uncertainty that Ulrich Beck (1992) referred to as 'risk society'. Modern and postmodern cultures, each in their own way, thus reject the possibility of species consciousness. True altruism is excluded from the discourse of both because both attend to the surface of the road to the future, not to the underlying foundation of humanity on which the road is constructed. Thus, the obsession with our 'body' and the denial of our 'mind' render as deviant the very act of *being* a human.

7 Gender Inequality and Global Humanity

The impact of globalization on gender relations is far-reaching. Increasingly involved in the world's production and consumption processes, women have been affected by globalization in the most diverse aspects of their lives and in the farthest reaches of the world (Afshar and Barrientos, 1999). Women's lifestyles have been dramatically affected, as have their decision-making power and their decision-implementing roles in the family. In principle, globalization also does—or ought to—challenge the traditional subordinate status of women virtually everywhere. But, the potential empowerment of women is contradicted by the realities of continuing male domination of the major social institutions. Thus, it is necessary to review and rethink the extent to which women today have authentic 'bio-power', economic power, cultural power, and power in making and implementing political decisions.

More than a century ago, the early feminist, Elizabeth Cady Stanton and associates observed that the actual size of the movement for gender equality (in her case, suffrage) is readily underestimated. "[T]he number is larger than appears on the surface, for the fear of public ridicule, and the loss of private favors from those who shelter, feed, and clothe them, withholds many from declaring their opinions and demanding their rights"

(Stanton et al., 1881). Because men have power, notes Dorothy Smith (1978), they have the power to keep it. These and related issues indicate a continuing and underlying dilemma between the reality and ideology of empowerment. In one sense, empowerment refers to the capacity of women to become more self-reliant and to increase their internal strength. This entails the right to determine life choices and to influence the direction of change through control over material and non-material resources. Yet, women still have subordinate social positions. They suffer from extensive abuse, psychosocial stress, and somatic complaints. Poor women especially, who comprise 70 per cent of all women and have the greatest responsibility for child rearing, suffer from the consequent overwork, and experience more domestic violence and sexual mistreatment. Much of this is traditional, but much can also be traced to the colonial experience.

In 1989, a United Nations Report observed that "economic progress for women has virtually stopped, social progress has slowed and social well-being in many cases has deteriorated". Citing Indian cases Jean Dreze and Amartya Sen (1995) identify four main dimensions of gender inequality:

(i) Extraordinarily high levels of gender inequality and female deprivation persist.
(ii) Gender inequality does not diminish automatically with economic growth.
(iii) Gender inequality is not merely a social problem in itself; it also leads to other social problems.
(iv) The agency of women as a force for change is one of the most neglected aspects of the development literature.

Globalization has had pessimistic allusions for the women in the Third World countries. Their plights show the inhuman side of globalization. The women in these countries are suffering extremely due to this spreading out of business empires. Tomlinson states, "Women work two-thirds of the world's working hours, produce half of the world's food, but earn only 10 per cent of the world's income, and own less than one per cent of the world's property". Vandana Shiva (2002) argues that, globalization, with the support of the World Bank and the IMF, has created slave wages. While globalization has brought jobs to rural, developing areas such as India where there was previously no employment, these jobs seem to be wolves in sheep's clothing. In the era of globalization the work available to women is always underpaid, mentally and physically detrimental, humiliating, and insecure. According to Merlin A. Taber and Sushma Batra, "development for poor women has meant the migration of men to cities, higher prices for commodities and poorer job opportunities. The fusion of flexible capitalism and Mac culture models is dissolving family and community social controls as observed by domestic violence, rape, divorce, and family breakdown". Women are still struggling for equal treatment in the Third World countries. Whether it is health care, education, the labour market or political rights, women often obtain less of a share than men. And yet, women make vital contributions to society were men often take no part. The shamefully atrocious customs are still practised in some countries like India and Bangladesh. It is reported that even though dowry has been illegal in India since 1961, every year about 6,000 women are killed—often doused with kerosene and set on fire in staged 'kitchen accidents'—by husbands and in-laws angered by unmet dowry demands. As of 2004, young women comprised 75 per cent of those between the ages of 15 and 24 who are infected with HIV globally (US National Intelligence Council). The emergence of feminism as an international movement has introduced the prospect of change. With it has come an alternative conception of the role of women in the process of socio-economic development (McMichael, 1994). The first UN World Conference on Women, held in Mexico City in 1975, focused specifically on the connections between empowerment and development. Attention thus shifted from an 'integrationist' to an agenda-setting approach. In terms of globalization ethic the women should not be suppressed from social, economic and political life. In these terms, real empowerment means growing awareness—emancipation in the true sense.

Robyn Bateman Driskell (2004) analyzes the concept of women's empowerment in terms of economic development. Recent research indicates that the nutritional well-being of children, as reflected negatively in low body weight, wasting and stunting, improves with betterment in economic conditions. All members of a society are ultimately benefited when the economy grows: economic growth leads to an increase in wages, which in turn are spent on more and higher quality food. Thus, Driskell (2004) notes, empowerment of women in development planning involves the linkage between improvement in the lives of women and in the health of their children. Unfortunately, the economic status of Third World women remains extremely low. Questions of gender have long been ignored within mainstream economics. And, the few studies that have considered the issue have not been very powerful in shaping the discipline's theoretical treatment of gender (Grapard, 2001). The inclusion of gender issues in formal economics practically began with the emergence of globalization. Yet, early in the 20th century, Charlotte Perkins Gilman (1966) challenged accepted gender roles and domestic relations. In response to criticism of her work as 'socialist' and 'feminist', she countered, "The anti-suffrage masses had blankly marked me 'suffragist', while the suffragists thought me a doubtful, if not dangerous, ally on account of my theory of the need of economic independence of women". In another passage, Gilman writes: "Without the economic dependence of the females, the male would still be merely the hunter and fighter, the killer, the destroyer; and she would continue to be the industrious mother without change or progress". Gilman's evolutionary concepts reveal the consequences of women's subordination. The twin struggle for gender equality and economic justice has for generations brought together the women's movement and the labour movement (Grapard, 2001). Women are naturally the bearers of children and to some extent necessarily involved in their care. Since time immemorial and in every conceivable cultural context, it has been argued that women who are economically independent can be neither good housekeepers nor ideal mothers. It is fact that women, at least in the industrialized nations, are becoming economically independent. But it remains to be shown that this is at the cost of their child care or household work. In this light, Driskell (2004) explores a new concept of feminism. Empowerment, according to Driskell, means living autonomously, freedom from male entrapment, and the achievement of self-esteem and productive roles. Her empirical analysis, using data from the World Bank, reveals some significant relationships among empowerment and development variables. The study also indicates that women's empowerment has a somewhat more significant impact on children's nutritional well-being than economic development.

Many women's campaigners recognize that globalization affects women in different ways, creates new standards for the treatment of women, and helps women's groups to mobilize. In situations where women have been historically repressed or discriminated under a patriarchal division of labour, some features of globalization may have liberating consequences (Dasgupta, 2006). Globalization presents opportunities to some women but causes marginalization of many others; it advocates, 'mainstreaming' as the way to achieve gender equality. Women play a distinct role in globalization, experience more harmful effects, and become a constituency for anti-systemic movements. Dasgupta (2006: 148) notes, "The philosophy of globalization process is to promote gender disparity and the empowerment of women as efficient ways to combat poverty, hunger and disease and to stimulate development that is truly sustainable, and also to combat all forms of violence and assault against women. But the recent trend shows a rather sordid picture of gender exploitation and a nexus between the increase in workplace based sexual harassment claims and the proliferation of work-based email and Internet use is quite visible now". We can view how Internet technologies are implicated in sexual pestering and consider some of the reasons why these technologies have goaded nuisance claims. This is of course the dark side of globalization, which is very perilous for the identity of womanhood or motherhood. It is evident from the facts and figures that 98 per cent of wealth on earth is in the hands of men, and only 2 per cent belongs to women. The 225 richest persons in the world, who are men, own the same capital as the 2,500 million poorest people. Of these 2,500 million poorest people, 80 per cent are women. It is also disheartening to note that $7,80,000 million are spent on armaments worldwide compared to $12,000 million spent on women's reproductive health. In terms of child prostitution, 90 per cent are girls and 100 per cent of the beneficiaries are men. This is the inconspicuous and sedating condition of women in this era.

Amartya Sen's work on gender inequality (2001) is of decisive importance. His work on the theory of the household represents the household not as an undifferentiated unit, but as a unit of cooperation as well as of inequality and internal discrimination. He has worked on problems of discrimination against women in the development process, on survivorship discrepancies between men and women under conditions of social unfairness against women, and on women's agency in the process of social development. Sen also proposes and popularizes the concept of 'missing women'—estimated to exceed 100 million round the world—which has given us a new way of understanding and mapping the problem. Indian women's empowerment is still a long way ahead if the World Economic Forum's report, which has put the country among the bottom 10 is considered when it comes to their participation in the economic agenda in any unit. In gender gap index the Forum has ranked India at 114th position after taking into account economic, political education and health positions among a total 128 countries

The current wave of globalization has greatly improved the lives of women worldwide, particularly in the developing world. Nevertheless, women remain disadvantaged in many areas of life. For example, the Centre for Global Development estimates that 43 million primary age girls are not enrolled in schools. In only 18 countries in the world do women hold even one-third of seats in the legislatures. Five hundred thousand women die in pregnancy or childbirth each year. An African woman, for instance, faces a 1 in 16 chances of dying in childbirth in her lifetime, while in the industrialized world, the chance is 1 in 2,800. Almost half of the adults living with AIDS and HIV are women. The number of women and girls infected with HIV has increased in every corners of the globe with high rates in Europe, Asia, Latin America and sub-Saharan Africa. In India women account for around one million out of 2.5 million estimated number of people living with HIV/AIDS. Their heightened vulnerability has both biological and socio-economic reasons. Early marriage, violence and sexual abuse against women are the major socio-economic reasons of their vulnerability to HIV infection. Their biological construct makes them more susceptible to HIV infection in any given heterosexual encounter. The spread of such a disease is mainly due to the powerlessness of women in controlling or negotiating power in their sexual relationships, including marriage. They have pitiable access to information and education,. This is aggravated by deadening poverty among women. Sexual assault, violence, sex selling, prostitution, sex trafficking and overuse of genital organs of the porn stars also expose the women to HIV infection. Violence against women and HIV/AIDS continue to be inextricably linked: rape, incest, assault by males, violence in the course of trafficking or at workplace expose them to HIV infection. Women have poor access to health services as a result of lower priority given to their health and their lack of decision-making powers within the family. Also, women usually have poor mobility, which inhibits their access to information and services. The UN's Millennium Development Goals (MDGs) put stress on the issue of gender equality and especially on empowerment of women. As part of the MDGs, the international community, especially the UN, will monitor indicators of gender equality such as levels of female enrolment at school, participation in the workplace, and representation in decision-making positions.

With the emergence of globalization the objection to such a gender gap or gender discrimination has been sustained and overruled. Because the entire history of women's struggle for self-determination has not been muffled over time and space so it is not the right time for the elite women, who are with the mainstream, to look back in anger. But to the vast bulks of rural people who are the victims of poverty and dejection, to the housewives who obey their husbands as lord or God are disempowered in the sense of reality. To them male power dominates over their existence. Dorothy Smith (1978: 281–96), notes, "Because men have power, they have the power to keep it".

Perhaps Smith speaks of the domination of knowledge as the expression of power of male which "consists of specific, localized relationships which together constitute the social body" (Foucault, 1982). If we analyze male domination over female, then male power seems positive but gender inequality emerges from the act of repressing and controlling nature of patriarchal man. Foucault (1982) notes, "where there is power, there is resistance". But when we speak of male domination in the patriarchal society, the question of resistance emerges from the hide of women. So, we see the women's protest movements in the world. Practically, male power is merely a 'bio-power' that comes from the masculine sex organ which punctures women virgin layer and penetrates into the women's genital organ. This bio-process is the expression of domination. Women, on the other hand, desire to be punctured and remain passive. This is the gender politics in the sense of reality.

Practically in the era of globalization women's empowerment may be interpreted in the context of power relations. The power relations may be social, economic, political, cultural and familial. Shifting of bio-power to institutional power has now being considered as the prime agenda of gender empowerment. And behind such a power play with the women is hidden politics of globalization, Today's women have been drawn into paid labour under corporate capitalism which Marx and Engel expected as gender empowerment. But this is not enough to measure the degree of empowerment. Women are now equipped with modern technologies, they are taking advance academic courses, getting access to the wider world—using computer and Internet in a very large scale, participating in public performances and television programmes, posing nude in the films, theatre, soap operas and advertisements, having abortions very smartly, involving in premarital and extramarital relations, becoming careerists without emotional stimulation, taking part in active politics, protesting half naked and so on. Are these the symbols of disempowerment? Actually, the issue of gender inequality varies from space to space, economy to economy, class to class, individual to individual and family to family. It cannot be a universal phenomenon. It is a problem-specific which depends on the mindset and temperament of man. I must not argue that all men are bad or all women are good; likely I want to say that most of the men in this world are good and a feeble percentage of women are bad. It means both men and women in our global society are good and empowered. The philosophy of empowerment exists in the mind. If a woman feels mentally stable and upright she is empowered in the real sense. No man could make her disempowered. Mind is the only power to get rid of emotional or socialization strain. Pooja Chauhan of Rajkot (India) had that mind power. Perhaps so she had stripped to protest against dowry system. Another makes protesters were a section of women who in Manipur (India) stripped in front of 17 Assam Rifles gate in 2004 against ruthless killing of Manorama. This type of nudity is not the expression of exhibitionism; rather it expresses the women's empowerment which develops from the mind power. They have expressed their voice of pre-test against social anarchy and gender oppression.

Postmodernists' Views

A section of the postmodernists view neo-classical economics as a sexually specific subject positions (Hewitson, 2001).

Female body as defined by the neo-classical economists is 'constituted as the excluded other', i.e., 'the other' (women) ... outside the fence of neo-classical economists. Cornell (1991) notes that woman 'is' only in language, which means that her 'reality' can never be separated from the metaphors and fictious in which she is presented. But I argue that women are not either 'the other' or just language but they represent a reality—a reality in the sense of her reproductive power. The male, who claim himself as the symbol of patriarchy, superpower, is totally dependent on female's body. In this point the women, in the ... of biology and divinity, are totally empowered. They are the mothers—the creators of both the sexes who are always regarded as two contending forces like Marx's *proletariat* (female) and *bourgeois* (male).

The human being, as we know and as gender history taught, are the two divided forces like 'we' (men) and 'they' (women). The women should perform multiple roles of housekeeping, motherhood, wife, cook, nurse, rearing and caring of children, cleaning and washing of utensils and so on. In a word, they are compelled to sell their labour and we act as the master, as the feudal lord or as the capitalist to dominate over them. As if women are the satellites and men are the metropolises. And, the capital (labour and plight of women) comes dripping from every pore, from head to feet with blood and dirt. Secondly, in the era of globalization, female bodies are sold as commodities. Surrogated motherhood is increasing day by day, sex crime is crossing its limit, ours 'global village' is very much worried of sex trafficking, wife battering, dowry killing, AIDS contamination and immature deaths caused by unwanted pregnancy. Are women becoming the prime object or commodity in the era of neo-classical economies and globalization? Can we claim that globalization is affecting inequalities between two sexes?

The postmodernization depicts a hyper-knowledge regarding feminism. Most of the viewpoints are mainly concerned with the hyper-language game. Here reality has no room to be occupied. "A feminist post-structuralist takes a quite different view of the relationship between neoclassical economics and women or the feminine ... neoclassical economics is a discourse which actively produces its objects as well as its subjects of knowledge, rather than being a knowledge in relation to which the 'real world' .... Has a separate existence" (Hewitson, 2001: 223). Ulrich Beck (1992) argues that the omni-dimensionality of gender inequality began to change in western countries over the past decade or two. He notes, "Epochal changes have occurred especially in the area of sexuality, law and education" (ibid.: 103). Did these changes exist on paper? This is the point of contradiction that should be noted by the gender sociologists. A section of social scientists and development experts argues that globalization has a direct impact on such a change which they claim is not rhetoric but real. But the clash of the sexes and the violence of intimacy do not support such a view. The blending of traditional conditions of women with the new consciousness is becoming very explosive. Beck's (1992: 104) statement was straightforward: "Men have practiced a rhetoric of equality, without matching their words with deeds ... the contradictions between female expectation of equality and the reality of inequality, and between male slogans of mutual responsibility and the retention of the old role assignments, are sharpening and will determine the future development in the thoroughly contradictory variety of their expressions in politics and in private".

Modernization, a bi-product of industrialization, has already divided the biological-self. The degree of inequality between two sexes increased very promptly. Beck (1992: 104) states, "The image of the bourgeois industrial society is bared on an incomplete or more precisely, a divided commercialization of human labour power". On the basis of such a theoretical paradigm we can speak that gender inequality is the product of globalization where we notice the mechanism of multinationals to take over the world with the motive of capitalist implosion by the process of technological revolution. So, Beck rightly states, "Industrial society is dependent upon the unequal positions of men and women" (ibid.). Secondly, the rise and dominance of individualism also created gender inequality which has diluted the gender reciprocity, gender cohesiveness and personality make up. In the era of globalization the rise and dominance of 'I' feeling has created a situation of confusion regarding gender roles, gender empowerment and sexed body versions. The celebrity women in the global era are very much loud of saying, "I am I". The males are also high sounding in this context. Now, the clash between two 'I's is creating empowerment-disempowerment dilemma. On July 4, 2007 one Indian woman, Pooja Chauhan (22 years old) walked down the streets of Rajkot in her undergarments to protest the inhuman treatment by her husband for delivering a baby girl which had created a sensation nationwide but in course of time the matter was settled. Here, Pooja's attitude may be referred to as *"I am I"*. Otherwise, such a case of rebel may have a wider impact nationwide.

Sunny Leone, a pornographic star in the West with Indian background, who once shared off her public hair to protest against George Bush's Presidentship in 2004 (Gimmick?), is in favour of the economics of sexed, body. In an interview with PDG (*Times of India*, April 23, 2007), she says, "I look at it this way that I am extremely happy with my life and decisions I have made… . I idolize women who have stepped forward in life and stepped pass boundaries that the world has set for us". Sunny Leone has thus the view of *"I am I"*. A very interesting view of wifehood has recently been noticed across the globe. Like motherhood, the concept of wifehood in the era of globalization is taking shape among both working men and women. Joyce Lustbader, a research scientist at Columbia University, says, "The thing I most want in life is a wife. I am not kidding …. I work all day, sometimes seven days a week, and still have to go home and make dinner and have all those things to do around the house" (cited in Boss, 2007: 10). Economic emancipation as the sole searching deduction of women empowerment again diluted with the old axiom of traditional role performance of the women. Wifehood, the neo-feminists will certainly confuse, is redefined as old fashioned standards of household management and housekeeping. Women in this globalization era occupy a major per cent of managerial, professional and clerical positions.

Shira Boss (2007) notes, "Having children is, overall, an impediment". Not only that working woman with children gets penalty—paid less than working woman without children. If globalization opens the economic, cultural, political and social doors to the women, then why such a penalty? Motherhood is the most beautiful and aesthetic truth of the planet. If it is so, can we claim that globalization is playing politics with women empowerment?

I can mention another to incident which contradicts with the notion, rationale and philosophy of globalization. Very recently, one Indian woman, Amrit Lalji, aged 40, who had been working in the Catering Services of British Airways, was suddenly dismissed from her service on account of wearing Indian traditional nose pin. Wearing of such a nose pin is obligatory for any woman as the symbol of marriage in Gujarat (India). In the age of globalization when we utter a very high sounding words like 'global communication', 'free trade', 'borderless education and interaction', 'local-global continuum' etc., how could it be possible to impose such a restriction? Is this the philosophy of multiculturalism?

In fact, it is an incident of 'local-global' clash. Of course, Ken Livingstone, the Mayor of London, condemned such an incident. He said, "I unreservedly condemn the sacking of Amrit Lalji for wearing a Hindu nose stud. It is an attack on her right to freely express her religion and an attack as a woman to dress as she wishes" (cited in *Times of India*, September 25, 2007).

We can cite thousands of such cases which tell the impact of the dark side of globalization. A number of conventions have been held on the issue of women empowerment—a great number of laws have been enacted for the safeguard of the global women. But the reality depicts sometimes a very sordid picture, sometimes makes confusion and mostly creates a dilemma. Since the Fourth World Conference on the Women in 1995 in Beijing, more than sixty countries have changed their laws that discriminate against women. It is undeniable that women are getting education, job opportunities, political power and sex freedom. But these gifts of globalization do not identify gender inequality. Multicultural feminists argue that as yet a number of contributing factors reinforce gender discrimination such as race, caste, class, age, religion, sexism and biological disability (Tuna and Tong, 1995: 242).

Secondly, I can argue that the women who live in urban elite areas, who are celebrities, and who always speak of empowerment and women's liberation movement, are very much empowered. The indicators of such empowerment are high education level, high job status, political power holding, culture-specific style of living, good earnings, spatial-elitist lifestyle pattern and sex-freedom lovers. But a vast bulk of the total global women populace is still deprived of having such privileges and empowered status. They earn less money, receive less education and subjected to domestic violence and male atrocity. Worldwide 70 per cent of women still live in poverty. They are still unable to walk, talk and interact like men.

Globalization makes women sexy and uses them as the sex commodities. The sexed body of woman is now on the Internet—on television screen and is used as enchanting bonanza of global tourist economy. A newly married girl says, "He watches porn every night and then wants me to try those facts. I find it absolutely abhorrent". So globalization accelerates the rate of breakdown of traditional marriage system. Only sex dominates over sanctified marriage system. And now bad sex is everywhere. Bad sex or sexual freedom should not be the only symbol of women empowerment. It is reported that 30 per cent women twist to porn films and playboys, sexy lingerie, sex toys and lubricants to spice up their sex lives.

Under the shadow of globalization women empowerment is measured as sex consumerism which has been clouded the global sky. Different adult sites, increasing sex crime, expansion and growth of sex-tour trade across the globe, the uncontrolled global sex traffickings, sex selling of the distressed women in the Third World, free sex trade and so on identify female body as the global sex commodity. Is this the image of women empowerment? Bradshaw et al. (2001: 277) note, "Western marketing around the world not only communicates information about products but conveys implicit messages about the kinds of people who consume the products, messages about their modernity and their desirability". The global players by the process of marketing put sexuality in service of selling goods. Global consumer culture, we can claim, promotes the 'sexualization of consumption' and the 'consumption of sexuality'. Here 'bio-power' converts into 'sex commodity'. And selling of sexed body makes the women disempowered in the real sense.

The women who enter into such a hell are subjected to the paralysis of hopelessness and helplessness. This is the hidden coma of women empowerment. The ultimate result is death either by AIDS or by the diseases caused by the excessive and wrong use of genital organs. The global tourist centres, fast food centres and private rooms, which are the creations of the capitalists, use distressed women as the capital of their trade growth. Women as the 'subjects of desire' become the subjects of consumer culture. Now, the women begin to suffer from identity crisis. In the era of globalization, as a human being they have become designified and in the sense of sex subject became highly significant. The metamorphosis from gender neutrality to gender differentiation becomes a regendering phenomenon in regard to empowerment, which ignores gender pluralism.

If we look at the sex tourism, the other side of globalization comes into the fore. Thailand is regarded as the turning point of notorious sex industry, which serves the desire of mainly Japanese and western tourists. In 1967 Thailand made an agreement with the US government to provide 'rest and recreation' services to the militaries during Vietnam war. It is reported that that Korean and Philippines women are tricked, raped and forced to work as prostitutes. During the past decade Cuba has become a haven for international sex tourists. In Thailand, for instance, travel brochures promote "sun, sea and sex". They build on the patriarchal and racist fantasies of European, Japanese, American and Australian men by touting the exotic, erotic subservience of Asian women.

"They [sex tours] offer meetings with the most beautiful and young Eastern creatures (age 16 to 24 years) in a soft and sexy surrounding and in the seductive and tropic night of the exotic paradise. You get the feeling that taking a girl here is as easy as buying a pack of cigarettes" (excerpts from a Dutch tourist pamphlet on sex tours in Thailand; cited in Judith Mirkinson, 1994).

The war in Vietnam brought a military build-up in Asia that ironically proved fortuitous to many countries' economies. Korea, Vietnam, Thailand, the Philippines and Okinawa built up a burgeoning sex industry outside the bases. Rest and recreation actually created new cities and added much-needed capital to the overall economy of each nation. It is estimated that by the mid-eighties sex industries around the bases in the Philippines had generated more than $500 million. At the end of the war in Vietnam, Saigon had 5,00,000 prostituted women—this is equal to the total population of Saigon before the war.

Here are some estimated figures (excluding the US and Canada):

- 75,000 prostituted women in Japan
- 50,000 maids in Singapore
- 50,000 domestics/prostituted women in Hong Kong
- 75,000 domestics in England
- 50,000 domestics in Spain
- 75,000 domestics in Italy
- 50,000 in Germany
- 1,50,000 in the Middle East

Source: Judith Mirkinson (1994), Red Light, Green Light: The Global Trafficking of Women (http://www.armory.com/~leavitt/women.html).

So it can be argued that women disempowerment is very much related to the expansion of war and regimentation. The slogans like 'sex for military' shatter the noble sentiments of the slogans like 'food for hungry'. The question thus may arise: Are the women food for war people? This also represents the negative version of globalization. This is a deadly game of globalization with the women which results in capitalist implosion. This represents another kind of modernity which symbolizes a newly shaped holocaust. It is not the burning of human flesh which occurred during the fascist colonialism. It is more cruel, more horrible and more inhumane.

In the 2000, in a *New York Times* report (International Trafficking in Women to the United States: A Contemporary Manifestation of Slavery) the number of women and children trafficked to the United States for sexual slavery to be as high as 50,000 per year. Not only they are forced to satisfy the desire of the males, but they are also forced to dance nude, and serve sometimes as domestic servants and sometimes as sex sellers. A section of globalization narratives of new-liberals speaks of 'rape scripts' which are based on the assumption that men and women play out fixed gender roles of aggressors and victims (Marchand and Runyan, 2001). So, we see such a capitalistic penetration (masculinity) into non-capitalist system (feminity).

The sex industry has come to occupy a strategic and central position in the development of international capitalism. For this reason the sex trade is increasingly taking on the guise of an ordinary sector of the economy. This particular aspect of globalization involves an entire range of issues crucial to understanding the world we live in. These include such processes as economic exploitation, sexual oppression, capital accumulation, international migration and unequal development, and such related conditions as racism and poverty.

Capitalist globalization today involves an unprecedented 'commodification' of human beings. The fast-growing sex trade has been extremely 'industrialized' worldwide. Millions of women around the world are victimized by traffickers each year. Women and girls are particularly susceptible to the trafficking industry. Some are abducted; some are deceived by offers of job opportunities in another country; some are sold by their distressed parents or are themselves driven by vicious poverty into the lure of traffickers who prey on their distraction. It is reported that regardless of how they are propelled into the multi-billion dollar industry of sexual exploitation whether through force, deception, coercion or simply through desperate poverty, these women and girls suffer unimaginable human rights violations as commodities of the trade in human beings by third-party profiteers. The process of industrialization produces profits amounting to billions of dollars. It creates a market of sexual exchanges in which millions of women are converted into sexual commodities. This sex market has been generated through the massive operation of prostitution.

The industrialization of the sex trade has involved the mass production of sexual goods and services structured around a regional and international division of labour. These 'goods' are human beings who sell sexual services. Prostitution and related sexual industries—bars, dancing clubs, massage parlours, pornography producers etc. depend on a massive unfathomable economy controlled by pimps connected to crime. Businesses such as international hotel chains, airline companies and the tourist industry benefit greatly from the sex industry. The International Labour Organization (ILO) estimated that prostitution represented between 2 and 14 per cent of the economic activities of Thailand, Indonesia, Malaysia and the Philippines (Jeffreys, 1999). According to a study conducted by Ryan Bishop and Lilian Robinson (1998), the tourist industry brings four billion dollars a year to Thailand. Over ten years, 2,00,000 Bangladeshi women and girls were the object of trafficking to Pakistan, and we find that 20,000 to 30,000 Thai prostitutes are from Burma. A good part of the migratory stream makes its way towards industrialized countries.

UNICEF (2001/2003) estimates that a million children are brought into the sex industry every year. The industry of child prostitution exploits 4,00,000 children in India, 1,00,000 children in the Philippines, between 2,00,000 and 3,00,000 in Thailand, 1,00,000 in Taiwan and in Nepal, 5,00,000 children in Latin America, and from 2,44,000 to 3,25,000 children in the United States. If one includes children in all the sex industries, the US figures climb to 2.4 million. In the People's Republic of China, there are between 2,00,000 and 5,00,000 prostituted children. In Brazil, estimates vary between 5,00,000 and 2 million. About 35 per cent of the prostitutes in Cambodia are less than 17 years old (Coalition Against Trafficking of Women, CATW). The growth of sexual tourism over the last 30 years has entailed the 'prostitutionalization' of the societies involved. In Thailand, with 5.1 million sexual tourists a year, 4,50,000 local customers buy sex every day (Barry, 1995). The now massive South East Asian sex industry began with the Vietnam war. The US government stationed servicemen not only in Vietnam, but also in Thailand and the Philippines (Jeffreys, 1999); these last two countries serving as rear bases in the fight against the Vietminh. The resulting increase in local prostitution established the infrastructure necessary for the development of sexual tourism. The presence of the military created an available workforce.

Looking at the growth and profits of the sex industry, it is easy to overlook the human cost. The profits of the sex industry are based on sexual exploitation, which first has to be acted out on real women and girls. Sexual exploitation traumatizes and scars women and girls for life.

Many critics fear that globalization in the sense of integration of a country into world society will exacerbate gender inequality. It may harm women economically, through discrimination in favour of male workers, marginalization of women in unpaid or informal labour, exploitation of women in low-wage sweatshop settings, and/or impoverishment though loss of traditional sources of income; politically, through exclusion from the domestic political process and loss of control to global pressures; and culturally, through loss of identity and autonomy to a hegemonic global culture.

Women and Media

Women are portrayed negatively by the media even when it takes up the cause of women. To give one example, the media, from time to time, tries to expose what is described as flesh trade. However, there is little attempt on the part of the media to thoroughly expose the men involved in the trade.

Women are glorified by the media only in advertisements. The female figure, often scantily clad, is used to advertise all kinds of products ranging from tooth paste to automobiles. The wide use of the female figure in advertisements has only further degraded the image of women. Unfortunately, the people in the media, mostly men, have not given any thought to bringing in some semblance of decency in the advertisements.

The past few months have seen much discussion, heated debates and controversies, pertaining to whether television has been appealing to the baser instincts of the viewers, in order to keep them attuned to the television sets. The issue that has claimed much attention and protests relates to the portrayal of women on television. There have been persistent questions arising from several quarters, as to whether there is an increasing distortion, an unfair and unrealistic projection of women on the media.

The portrayal of women in advertisements reinforces and creates impression of their being as mere sex symbol. Advertisements use beautiful woman to sell the products to both male and female consumers by virtue of two-dimensional roles as housewife, mother and daughter and as a decorative sexual object. Woman's entire being is reduced to physical appearances only. Advertisers exploit woman's sex appeal by vulgar exposures of her body. There are many advertisements which show half dressed young seductive looking woman in suggestive and revealing poses advertising for motorbikes, cars, radios, beer, cigarettes, machinery and all such products (e.g., male condoms) which have no relation whatsoever to her figure as shown in the advertisement. Both in their content and presentation such advertisements are only aimed at attracting male consumers. Such a distorted portrayal of women is not only humiliating and dehumanizing, it also reinforces male sexist attitude towards women as playthings. Despite media's aim of raising the general awareness in regard to the status and problems of women these advertisements reinforce stereotype and thereby project contradictory images of woman. An advertisement depicts that there is some special joy derived by women from washing clothes with a particular brand of detergent. Women are seen lovingly feeding their families with food cooked in a particular oil. To treat household consumers as only feminine concerns is yet attempts to reinforce a stereotype image of women. Use of a particular soap is essential to get married and win husband's heart. This again projects the male superiority over the female.

Globalization and Internet Sex

Feminist movement should be associated with the philosophy of to be free from mental bondage such as freedom of speech, freedom of mindset, freedom of taking decision and above all attainment of economic emancipation and emancipation of soul.

The mission of rhetoric globalization was to promote gender equality and the empowerment of women as effective ways to combat poverty, hunger and disease and to stimulate development that is truly sustainable, and also to combat all forms of violence and assault against women. But, the recent trend shows a rather sordid picture of gender exploitation and a nexus between the increase in workplace sexual harassment and the proliferation of work-based Internet use is quite visible now. We can look at how Internet technologies especially e-mailing, are implicated in sexual harassment and considers, some of the reasons why these technologies have provoked harassment claims. This is of course the negative and other side of globalization, which is very dangerous for the identity of womanhood or motherhood in future.

Many urban and rural women are forced into prostitution in the cities. Sex trafficking of women and children is increasing due to the wide network of multinational corporations in the industrial and rural areas.

The incidents of sexual assault, which I strongly consider, are the impact of digital globalization and deregulated cultural and moral freedom. The young generation is adversely affected and influenced by globalization of media, travels, fashions, McDonaldization and economic changes.

The Internet, as a communications medium, would exist without the sex industry, but the Internet industry would not be growing and expanding at its present rate without the sex industry. The Internet industry does not like to admit how much it is being supported by the sex industry, but a few indicators are revealing:

- The sex industry is among the top five groups buying state-of-the-art computer equipment.
- Sex industry businesses were the first to buy and use expensive T3 phone lines that transmit compressed, high-resolution images.
- One of the largest Internet companies in the world, Digex, whose largest customer is Microsoft Corporation, has a sex industry site as its second largest customer.

- One of the website designers who works at a large sex industry website, described his work as a 'dream job' because any new technology was available for the asking.
- In 1998, US$ 1 billion were spent online on 'adult content,' 69 per cent of the total Internet content sales (Hughes, 2000).

Most of the owners of sex industry sites with live sex shows moved to the Internet from phone sex operations. One advantage they had was money for the capital investment. For example, the Internet Entertainment Group (IEG), owned by Seth Warshavsky, who had a phone sex business, invested US$ 3 million in computers and communications equipment to start up his website. The Internet industry flourishes on the sex industry and technicians from the Internet sex industry have developed new techniques to deliver high quality multimedia (Rose, 1997).

Pornography—both printed and video—is a divisive issue among feminists. Women who call themselves feminists view pornography in two very different ways. First, as an exploitative industry that reaps large profits of the degradation of women. An industry that sends a message to society at large that women are nothing more than sex objects, merely existing as both amusement and jack-off material for men. Secondly, as the ultimate empowerment of woman—the true test of said woman's independence. The idea that a woman can do and be anything she wants to be—even if Daddy doesn't like it or it makes you squirm. These examples may be extremes, yes. Just as with all issues, there are shades of gray. But which side leans closer to the truth? (Hagood, 2007).

The fast growth of the global Internet sex industry has deepened the injury to the victims, and globalized women's victimization and exploitation. Two components of globalization—rapid development and operation of information technology and the industrialized commodification of women and children—have become linked to expand and truly internationalize sexual exploitation. The lack of regulation of the Internet and prevailing uncritical views on the sex industry are contributing to the escalation of the global sexual exploitation of women and children through global advertising of prostitution tours and online bids for virginity. The global players have created such an enchanting disneyland of industries, but their impact is felt all over the world, especially by women.

At its fortieth session, in 1996, the Commission on the Status of Women considered the poverty among woman as the critical area of concern within the context of reviewing the implementation of the Beijing Platform for Action. The deliberations resulted in the adoption of a resolution, which emphasized that the empowerment and autonomy of women, along with the improvement of women's social, economic and political status are essential for the eradication of poverty among woman. "The empowerment and autonomy of women, and the improvement of their political, social, economic and health status, constitute an important end in themselves and one that is essential for achieving sustainable development. There should be full participation and partnership of both women and men in productive and reproductive life, including shared responsibilities for the care and nurturing of children and maintenance of the household."

Women Empowerment and Globalization

Our world witnesses the clash between globalization-politics of uniqueness/singleness and politics of disparity. On the one hand, the women in the global era suffer very badly from identity crisis, which results in desperate sex selling, entering into porn world, enjoyment of over-freedom, destruction of traditional, ethical and aesthetic sense, bohemian style of living, deregulated cultural and moral freedom, identifying celebrity in terms of sex power, unnatural, morbid and grimy exposure before male audiences, adult sites and so on. On the other hand, the women in the Third World countries are becoming the victims of politics of difference. In this critical juncture one can argue that changes in the global political economy since the 1980s have had a dramatic effect on the lives of women. They have already entered into the arena of global production and consumption processes.

And, the effect of globalization on women seems "contradictory, inclusionary and exclusionary" (Afshar and Barrientos, 1999: 1). Shifting of women from local to global space for sharing political, economic and cultural opportunities has accelerated the degree of gender disparity. It is a never-ending story like a refrain that is played again and again. Through the decades, in so many survey reports, conference proceedings, books and newspaper articles, both in developed and developing countries, feminists have documented and belittled commercial media's treatment of women and stories that have perpetrated violence against them. It seems that their battles have not yet been won. A few lines of a poem written by Kaplan tell such a heartbreaking narrative of empowerment:

> Today another woman died/and not on a foreign field/and not with a rifle strapped to her back, and not with a large defense of tanks rumbling and rolling behind her.../the target was simply her face, her back, her pregnant belly/the target was her precious flesh that was once composed like music in her mother's body and sung in the anthem of birth.
>
> Another woman died today./not far from where you live; Just there, next door where the tall light falls across the pavement./Just there, a few steps away/where you've often heard shouting, Another woman died today.
>
> She was the same girl/her mother used to kiss; the same child you dreamed beside in school./The same baby her parents walked in the night with and listened and listened and listened/For her cries even while they slept. And someone has confused his rage with this woman's only life.

Rabindranath Tagore writes, "Man gathers round him rubbish women comes and constantly cleanses is a way". But Tagore's idea appears at epitomic to us. Because, the sublime image of women has been distorted by the influence of consumer culture in the era of globalization.

Is this the hidden politics of globalization that the global players are playing with the enchanting word 'empowerment'?

Can we argue that globalization has perpetuated under-discrimination and women discrimination?

But women, the beauty of nature and symbol of love and divinity, who can bear the pain of creation, can also give pain to the so called first sex as the *stree shakti* (woman power). In Hindu cult, *Devi Durga* (Goddess of power and strength) slayed *Ashura* (the demon). The women should be proud of themselves because they are the source of the creation of human being of this planet and they also should be proud of their twin X chromosomes (Priyanka Dasgupta, 2006).

> "Women, you are blessed!"
> You have your home your household work.
> In the midst of it you keep a little gap
> Through which you hear the cry of the weak.
> You bring your offering of service
> *And pour out your love*" (Rabindranath Tagore).

8 Promise and Betrayal of Humane Globalization

In the unending debates that are raging about globalization, it is often found that people are taking extreme views, like the end points of a pendulum. One side is totally in its close and ready to swallow its hook, line and sinker. The other side is equally ardent to reject it viewing it like an ogre, ready to swallow the poor countries. It is quite a tough task for a sociologist to find out the exact point along the swinging track of the pendulum. Contemporary segmented realities, nevertheless, suggest that the spirit of 'we-ness' and the process of globalization as such represent a myth; it is perhaps, a tragedy that the spirit so much endowed with the promise of reconstructing the world had to express symptoms of uncertainty, dissonance, fundamentalism, threat, exclusion and identity crisis. It demands rethinking of the globalization discourse. Social scientists and altruists are divided over how globalization promotes homogeneity, integration and co-existence on the one hand and disparity, dejection, differences, dissonance and unevenness, on the other. It has become the focal point of attention in the social sciences since the late 1980s and has appeared as a paradigmatic concept in analyzing economic, social, political, environmental, ecological and cultural metamorphoses occurring in major parts of the modern world. The currency that the concept reflects the agenda that the world is now interconnected and interdependent mainly as a result of changes in the global economy and the rapid changes in communication and in information technology, which have a great impact on the cultural, social and political shift. Globalization is used to describe the process by which the world is transformed into a single arena. At the heart of this is the contention that the concept of globalization *per se* should be applied to the concrete structuration of the world as a whole. It is not simply an economic phenomenon; rather, it covers all the aspects of modern life: the economic, the cultural, the political, the humanitarian, the social and the ecological. In relation to these aspects the social scientists increasingly turn their attention to global phenomena. Simply, globalization can be defined as a process, which denotes a transformation in the spatial organization of social relations and transactions. The prime features of this process are associated with historical trajectories, i.e., the universal adoption of state system, globally interdependent economic, political, cultural, technological and communication system. But, side by side, it also tends to be associated with the feeling of powerlessness and economic depression in that the speed and scale of current global socio-economic change appears to overwhelm political leaders, planners, policy makers, altruists and academics. The unevenness of globalization compounds such dejection and strong are becoming stronger and the weak, weaker. So, we may claim that globalization is an uneven process, which divides winners and losers. For the most affluent it entails a shrinking world but it is very deceptive for the destinies of the deprived majorities. The interconnection between globalization and inequalization sheds a head-spinning glimpse of alien future because we are confronted with two contradictory forces: emergence of a single civilization and clash of civilization on the one hand and progress and misery, on the other. So, it seems very unpractical to go beyond the world of 'us' and 'them'. As the 20th century came to a close we all felt the incredible and positive changes of mindset among people and nations on the one hand and tales of tragedies, fear of identity and uncertainty on the other. As we move beyond the dichotomies of globalization and localization, developed and rejected, we become an increasingly interconnected global village. We are afraid of thinking the future of such a global village. What would be its identity? What would be its nature of interaction? What would its economy, culture, environment and polity? Unification is not an averaging out. If some values become universal, for instance, all people the world over equally value peace and hate violence, then we would welcome such unification and we do not see in what way it can contradict such concepts as individuality or personal freedom.

The term 'global' is an indicator of the change. In the year 1960s this came to be used to mean "belonging to the world" or "world wide". Marshall McLuhan (1962) uses the term 'the global village' capturing a property of modern culture like the possibility of global communication and suggests that the instant reception of far-off lights and voices changed the concept and content of culture. His idea focuses on the worldwide network of communication as a key organ of transforming local life of equal significance to the impact of capitalist markets. The advent of the global village as an imagined community is a sign of not only integration and coexistence but it indicates differences and dissonance.

The ideal type 'global village' was created with the imagination of opening discourse of integration, interaction and harmony that can triumph over discord, differences, demarcation, discrimination and dissonance of local villages. But, the people in the Third World have been misled into believing that the world has changed and globalization means homogenization. The hegemonies and domination of the globalists indicate the black hole of exclusion and threats. It is mostly because of the crisis of human values. It is undeniable that there is a set of common values that humanity has shared over centuries and it is only the gateway to the ideal globalization discourse. The humanity is always in favour of accepting the necessity and significance of global dialogue and the rejection of force, the promotion of understanding in the cultural, economic and political arena and the strengthening of the foundation of freedom, rationality and human rights. If humanity devote all its efforts to institutionalizing the dialogue, replacing enmity and conflict with discourse and understanding, it will leave an invaluable legacy for the benefit of future generation (Khatami, 1998). The west and the rest dichotomy makes our world not compressed but divided. The horror of contrast between winners and losers, between lions and foxes at all levels of human existence feeds a pervasive mood of uncertainty that creates a situation of 'either-or' mentality and exclusion-inclusion fear psychosis. The result is the expression of fundamentalism, religious bigotry, ethnic cleansing, separatism, genocide, crossborder terrorism and struggle for food and shelter. It appears that the notion of globalization sounds with the lines of Dante's 'Inferno': "the motto on the gate of hell was: abandon all hopes yea, who enter herein". It means present-day globalization is becoming a misnomer mostly because of the threat of exclusion and the crisis of new global ethic. Is it true that the danger of nuclear catastrophe has already been removed? Can we say that the risk of proliferation of weapons of mass murder is out of our imagination? So, we have to say, "We appeal as human beings to remember your humanity and forget the rest. If you can do so, the way lies upon to a new paradise" (Russell and Einstein, 1995). The makers of globalization have failed to move to world vision of inclusion, of participation, of humanizing the differences, discrimination and dissonance. The commonalties that unite the people of 'the rest' might have been possible if they were not dejected. The globalizers have created a 'global gloom' where we can see a dichotomy of 'revolutions of rising expectations' and 'revolutions of rising frustrations'. If we talk about humanity, it is always with us. We are not born fundamentalist or born terrorist. The threat of global exclusion creates such an identity crisis of humanity. Let me cite an illustration:

> On July 20, 2000, on the shores of Lake Tiberias, two young families were enjoying a summer day, strangers to each other. A young boy decided to swim in the waters of a lake that touches three countries. A few minutes into joyful swim, panic or fatigue overwhelmed him, and he gasped for air. From the shore, the first two notices were a young man, father of the other young family. Instinctively, he dove into the waters and within minutes he rescued the young boy, who managed with a bit of help to regain the shore and the safety of the sands. Unfortunately, the young man who saved the boy was physically overcome and drowned. What history recorded of that day on Lake Tiberias is that the young boy who was saved was of the Jewish faith and the young father who helped him was of the Muslim faith. Under the new paradigm, one father had saved the life of a young boy who was not his own, as any parent would do, no matter when, no matter where, even at the cost of his own life (based on widespread news reports, July 2000 and quoted from G. Picco, ed., *Crossing the Divide*, 2001).

The above incident does not indicate that we are becoming increasingly globally interconnected, rather the majority of the states of the world are far from encouraging. The rampant commercialization and commodification of social life threatens the humanitarian fabric of societies of the 'the rest' world. Here, the global ethics like longing and striving for peace, justice, partnership and truth appears as a misnomer code of global conduct. What is clear is that the global-local dichotomy is giving birth to an uncertain globalization where there is no room for humanity. In inner space of the earth we see the tragic events of the division of humanity. Globalization, as a humanity threatening phenomenon, has possessed this beautiful earth. One of my friends, Professor Abbas Mehdi, has expressed in a message the tragic event of the sad demise of his loving younger sister, who became the victim of recent militarization in Iraq. I am taking the liberty of citing that heartbreaking event, which I call globalization gloom:

> This is what Iraq's liberation looks like to me right now: a woman bleeding to death on a public highway, unable to get help because

coalition forces have blocked the road while looking for insurgents. A large room in a hospital where corpses are laid at random on a dirty floor, some of them uncovered, with nothing to identify them, a scene of horror for those trying to find the bodies of their loved ones.

The woman is my younger sister. She was involved in a car accident on the road between Najaf and Baghdad, travelling home after visiting my parents. When she finally reached the hospital in Baghdad after being stuck on the road for more than six hours, no one could do much for her, and no one was able to get in touch with her family. The hospital was overwhelmed and disorganized, and telephone lines were down.

My parents didn't find out what had happened to their daughter until two days after her death. When my other sisters finally got to the hospital, the staff didn't even know exactly where her body was. They were directed to a large room full of corpses.

"Do you remember when we lost our luggage in Jordan?" one of my sisters asks me. "It was like that. The bodies were lying all over the floor like lost baggage"....

I have been working for regime change in Iraq, hoping that Saddam Hussein would fall from power and that peace, democracy and stability would come to my country. Yet I opposed last year's invasion. I feared what the cost might be for the Iraqi people of being subjected to yet another war, weakened as they were by the last Gulf War and the war with Iran, and by protracted economic sanctions. Now that scenario has played itself out and come home to me personally in a way that I never expected, fearful though I was for Iraq and for my family....As I talk with the friends and relations who have gathered for my sister's burial, what I hear most plainly is hopelessness. Hopelessness, frustration and resignation...

"She was lucky," one person says bitterly. "It is as if we are all dead already," someone else says. Yet another is grateful that he has no money—that is why the thieves have left him alone, he says...

> My eldest sister tells of waiting in a long line to buy gas. There was a quarrel, voices were raised, the American soldiers panicked and started to fire their guns, and the result was that six people died before her eyes. When I spoke to my younger sister in Baghdad last year, I could often hear the sound of gunfire in the background.
>
> The Iraqi people I speak to are very frightened by the danger and random deaths they see all around them, at home, at work, in the street. They are also worn down by the hardships of their everyday lives. In this oil-rich nation, people wait in line for five to 10 hours for gas. The supply of electricity is still erratic, and clean water isn't always available. The main reaction of many Americans to the Iraq war and its aftermath may simply be confusion, but for me, and the people of Iraq, it has meant suffering, destruction and pain. In fact, the latest war has been hugely costly to everyone concerned, to Iraq, to the United States and to the rest of the world, in material and non material ways. No one is safe there now, not UN staff, or Paul Bremer, or Paul Wolfowitz. Even when the president of the United States visited Baghdad, he arrived in a darkened plane, in utmost secrecy, and stayed for only a few hours. My sister would not have died from her injuries if she had not been in a country that is unbearably unstable, to the point of anarchy. In this situation, no one is a winner, and no one feels liberated.

This specific case is enough to predict the destiny of the deprived majorities. This globalization hypocrisy and its effect on 'the rest' of the world indicate that we are living in a sorry period. In India Gujarat witnessed one of the deadliest communal riots in our recent memory. Insurgency and sucessionism as the expressions of ethno-political upsurge took roots in Punjab, Kashmir, Nagaland and Manipur, in Tripura, in Assam, Meghalaya and Arunachal Pradesh. In the era of globalization the Indian states are under growing pressure like demands for new states, multi-level government, regionalization of the political forces, secessionist movement, violence, insurgency and terrorism in North-East, caste/class/agrarian violence, growing influence of Hindutva, attacks on the minorities, environmental hazards, Indo-Pakistan conflict, Indo-Bangladesh border problem, nuclearization of South Asia, and so many risk factors. Besides, the severe famine in Somalia, extreme economic genocide in Rwanda, the rise of fundamentalism in India and Pakistan, corruption and economic and political turmoil in Bangladesh, debt burden in Brazil, Argentina and Bolivia and economic disintegration in Peru are the examples of globalization deconstruction. Are these the indicators of altruism and humanity or true spirit of globalization mission? In the era of globalization social scientists are trying to analyze the ideal meaning of altruism which, they argue, mainly stems from the perception of human rationality.

Rational choice theorists believe that decisions are based on rational thought. For the most part, rational decisions are made with the intention of receiving some type of benefit or reward. However, people sometimes make decisions that have no obvious remuneration. From a rational choice theorists' perspective, altruism provides an explanation for decisions in which the rationale is not quite clear. Because selfish acts and decisions with apparent self-benefit clearly demonstrate rational thought, altruism can be thought of as the rationale for selfless decisions.

Howard Margolis divides altruism into two categories: 'goods altruism' and 'participation altruism'. Goods altruism is the idea that we want other people to have things. Therefore, we give to charity and support government decisions that benefit others. Sometimes we gain satisfaction from participating in an activity for non-selfish reasons; an emotion derived from participation altruism. When altruism blends with human rationality and emotion, globalization process becomes a harmonious process. But, when it lacks, the harmony maintains its melody but without uniformity, as it is now.

Global Village: Harmony without Uniformity

We had a pot, made of clay, filled in water. We could see our faces in that water. Once the pot had broken and our faces disappeared. This is the destiny of heated global influence. The water denotes our socio-economic and socio-cultural elements or resources and our faces represent our deep-rooted traditional identities and values. The question arises: Is our existence or identity being the party of globalization at stake? Does globalization intend to reshape and remake us as the new men of new civilization? Once Rabindranath Tagore aptly remarked, "Indian has received all and accepted all".

No one could deny the relevance of human values to the concept of development. It is by and for the people because the people are the starter and end product of development. If someone views techno-economic foundation as the only prime mover in development process, he would not do justice. The process of capital accumulation depends mostly on the quality of natural resources and techno-wealth, which could accelerate the pace of human need and demand. The development of any country identifies the development of collective personalities and self-identities. But, the globalization circle created such an orbit where the faces of humanity merged with the rationality of irrationality. This is the root cause of crisis of globalization.

There is a global village, which we have not yet visited. It is the reality that in the finest film of life on the surface of our globe a vacillating shroud of human activity indistinguishable in the depths of inconceivable never ending space, one finds in constant motion shaking the world to its foundations, progress side by side with hunger, the gift of unimaginable wealth together with the abomination of destitution, the magnificence of achievements and the pain of their destiny.

Behind the architecture of New World Order (benign globalization?) the malignant globalization creates a three-tier structure across national boundaries. The globalists reside in the core of the circle, in the second circle we find the people who labour in insecure forms of employment and thrown into cut-throat competition in the global market and the outer ring represents the excludes. If the world were a global village of 100 people 70 of them would be unable to read, and only one would have a college education. Over 50 would be suffering from malnutrition; over 80 would live in what we call sub standard housing. If the world were a global village of 100 residents, six of them would be American who would have half the village's income; and the other 94 would exist on the other half. How would the wealthy six live "in peace" with their "neighbours"? (Huizer, 2003). To some observers, the process of globalization is linear, unidirectional. But this is a superficial perspective. For, upon reflection, it is clear that inconsistencies and disharmony characterize the process. At root, there are profound contradictions between globalization in progress and globalization in conflict. What seems to be globalization for some appears to be localization for others. Under these circumstances, a key question is whether globalization is bringing people new freedom to act or if it portends an uninvited, unwanted, and cruel fate for the majority of the world's population. For the clash continues between fear, anxiety and uncertainty for the dejected majority and freedom, comfort and happiness for the few elites.

Zygmunt Bauman (1998) notes that being local in a globalized world, is a sign of social deprivation and degradation. The local areas where global inputs exert the most pressure are losing their 'meaning generating' and 'meaning negotiating' capacities. The people in these areas are increasingly dependent on the economic and cultural hegemony of global powers. The gap between the global and the local, although often unobtrusive and dynamic, is potentially explosive. In brief, globalization is now oscillating between global winners and losers. Thus globalization has to be perceived as a process which both includes and excludes peoples and nations. The process is embedded in a hierarchical system of power, exchanges and benefits (Petras, 1999). Can globalization lead us to a brighter world or will it generate more conflicts, poverty and contradictions in our already anxiety-ridden world? Dialogue is the only instrument to understand the present status of globalization. Thus, the need for discourse among the people of different nations has never been more acute than now. And, the present book is a step in this direction.

Until recently, the leading philosophical perspective on globalization emphasized crossing the economic and cultural divide. Ethically and morally, the purpose of globalization was to bring different races, cultures, ethnic groups and socio-economic classes into closer contact with each other. The rationale behind the movement was altruistic: to replace hatred with love, violence with peace, destruction with construction, 'their' culture with 'our' culture, and an 'either' with an 'or' mindset. The elements of this globalization paradigm were the elimination of hostility, the construction of an ideal type civil society, the restructuring of a sick economy, and the integration of all cultures.

Now, however, we fear the injuries that globalization can inflict in each and every facet of our economic, cultural, political and social lives. The concept demands revision, re-assessment, re-evaluation, and re-projection. It also demands reflections on diversity, an open vision of humanity and free discourse. It is a grim fact that many nations and peoples are now confronting reality with what appear to be two mutually contradictory faces: the global and the local. Along with the increasing pace of globalization in science, technology, economy, culture, education, communication, and the empowerment of women, local conflicts are also increasing at an unprecedented pace. This situation weakens the positive potentials of globalization.

According to Martin Albrow (2001), nothing better illustrates the difference between globalization, on one hand, and modernization, on the other, than the debates about the relationship between global and local interests. From Albrow's perspective, the local is always defined in contrast to a specific frame of reference. That is, the local is the neighbourhood in relation to the community; it is the community in relation to the nation-state; and it is the nation-state in relation to the international system. Conflicts emerge with the metamorphosis of localism into globalism. This is the locus of economic, cultural and political marginality, which can easily create a situation of crisis, adoption-rejection conflict, disintegration, chaos and disorder.

It was once believed that the primary mission of globalization was to integrate the parts into whole. But, in fact, the parts have lost their socio-cultural, economic and political identity. The result is severe economic disparity, painful cultural identity crisis, loss of the sense of belonging, ethnic violence, secessionism, and ultimately, civilization shock. The tragedy of globalization is that it began with the aim of restructuring and rebuilding civilizations; yet the mission has produced discord, more separatism, and identity crisis. The 'global village,' once a symbol of integration, unification and harmony, now denotes difference, differentiation, demarcation, discrimination and dissonance. The world, compressed into a single economic, ecological, cultural, electronic and political system, has never been so highly stratified (Picco, 2001). But forty-eight years have passed (since the coinage of the term 'global village' by Marshall McLuhan in 1962), and our society remains as it was. In terms of disparity, we remain parts rather than wholes. In terms of a single humanity, we are divided. In terms of possessions, we are ether rich or we are destitute. From the porthole of a space vehicle high above the earth, it is obvious that the divided and rival peoples comprise only one human race; for the borders that separate nations are not visible from the outer space. But, in the inner space of the earth, we see the tragic division of humanity into hostile groups. Terrorism, sectarianism, bigotry, fundamentalism, and its horrible descendant, fanaticism, have possessed this beautiful planet. They have filled the earth with violence, drenched it often with human blood (Vivekananda, 1893). Does this represent altruism and humanism? Does it indicate the philosophical, idealistic spirit of the globalization mission?

A cosmonaut watched the earth from the porthole of his space vehicle saw the men divided and hostile, comprised one human race. He said, "for the borders that divide countries are not visible from outer space". It means that from the inner space we could keenly feel the tragic events of the division of humanity

Figure 1

Relation between Economy and Globalization

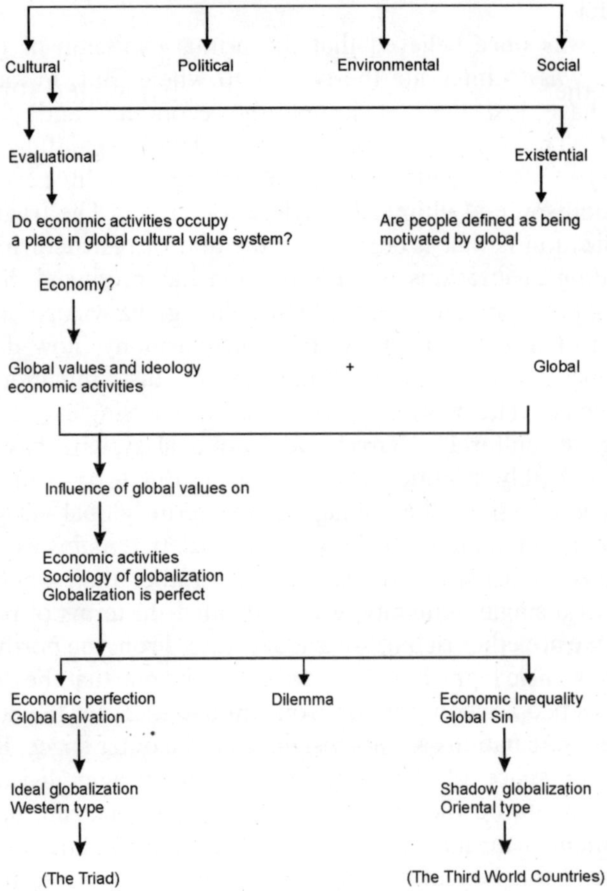

Deduction (i) The triad links the spirit of globalization.

Deduction(ii) The other name of globalization is triadization.

Hypotheseis The triad links the Third World countries with the intention to

(a) remove economic disparity and vulnerability,

(b) eradicate poverty and hopelessness,

(c) make all the corners and parts of this planet as an integrated whole, and

(d) To remove economic ailments and vices and to make an 'ideal type' of global village.

into rival groups. All the countries of the world have not yet risen above their own-ness, 'I'-ness. They have not yet touched the world of 'we'-ness. Peace and social progress, which are the only "sensible and scientifically grounded prospect for humanity" have not yet restored on earth following the balanced and single path.

Growing Disparity

The scars of misery and deprivation mar the face and heart of the world. It presents a "picture of horror and dejection for majority of people who were born to face a slow and agonizing death" (Dadayan, 1988). It is reported in the 'New Times' (1983) that "in the Third World there are now starving over 500 million; life expectancy under 60–1.7 billion; lacking medical care—1.5 billion; living in extreme poverty—over 1 billion; unemployed and underemployed—more than 500 million; annual per capita income—under $150–800 million; illiterate adults—814 million; children having no access to school education and unable to attend school—over 200 billion. Tinbergen (1976) notes, "we have a situation where, in the Third World, millions of people toil under a broiling sun from morning till dusk for miserable rewards and premature death without even discovering the reasons why".

The statistics reveal that since 1960 (the mission of globalization started) income disparity among countries had increased worldwide. It is evident from the World Development Report that the wealthy countries have experienced a steady growth in their share of the world GNP, while the poorest countries have experienced with a tragic decline in their share of world GNP. "Between 1960 and 1991, the richest fifth of all nations had its share of world income rise from 70 per cent to 85 per cent, while the poorest fifth of all nations had its share fall from 2.3 per cent to 1.4 per cent" (UN Development Programme, 1994). This trend towards greater disparity gives a very chronic indication of continuing into the next millennium (Sandler, 1997). Using the model of Max Weber we could evaluate the hidden danger behind globalization.

Debt Burden

Debt burdens have doubled the growing gap between the developed and the developing countries. According to the World Bank, the debt of developing countries rose by 8 per cent to just over $2 trillion in 1995. The steady increases over two decades in the indebtedness of poor countries referred to as heavily indebted poor countries.

The Third World debt has grown from $9 billion in 1955 to $572 billion in 1980, and $2,177 billion in 1996. Its debt service—including interest and principal—is close to $245 billion in 1998 (Gelinas, 1998).

The debt is increasing in percentage of GNP as well. The overall Third World debt GNP ratio reached 27 per cent in 1980 and 38 per cent in 1994. For sub-Saharan Africa, it has reached to 79 per cent. For countries like Madagascar, Cote d'Ivoire and Zambia, it is over 200 per cent. Nicaragua is overburdened with over-indebtedness (801%). In case of Congo it is 454 per cent and for Mozambique it is 450 per cent. Practically, the debt burden in the Third World countries has reached two trillion dollars: entire countries have been destabilized as a consequence of the collapse of national currencies often resulting in the outbreak of social strife, ethnic conflicts and civil war (World Bank, 1994). The global financial system along with the Mexican crisis of 1995, has reached a dangerous crossroads and the declaration of the IMF is very alarming in regard to the fate of other indebted countries: "we will therefore introduce stronger surveillance to be serve that the convalescence goes well...". But, the structural modernization of globalization process which mostly depends on 'deconstructed' economy (!) largely fails to reconstruct and rebuild global economy. The falsification of ideal type model of globalization best suits the Third World countries. It is well known to the social scientists that the year 1998 has been several huge steps forward towards a single global economy and the series of discussions were held in Paris about MAI, in Geneva about WTO, in Cardiff about EMU, in Birmingham for the G8 summit, IMF reforms, APEC etc. The motive of such discussions was to promote a New World Order with deregulated 'free' trade and capital flows. The rationale of such a motive was to create a worldview of neo-liberal economies which by the creation of new markets will stimulate economic development to trickle down to all of society clearing new global consumers to enjoy the status of better living (Technical Centre for Agriculture and Rural Co-operation, 1999). Does it indicate a sign of social altruism? Does the global economic policy agenda geared towards the global poverty eradication and better living? The other face of such a structural model of globalization network is collapsing of purchasing power of the people in the Third World, eruption of food crisis, closure of schools, hospitals and industries, resurgence of diseases like plague, malaria, cholera, anthrax, tuberculosis, hepatitis AID etc., depletion of environment and eviction of millions of people, the demonic spread of localized conflicts, increasing tension regarding cross-border terrorism, religious fundamentalism, regionalism, spread of communal violence, cry of hunger, culture in conflict, loss of national identity, high indebtedness, fear and anxiety for loss of old age security, upward trend of unemployment and adoption rejection problems. The economy of the main players of globalization was firing on all cylinders and beginning to dangerously overheat (Ellwood, 2001). From 1997 to the beginning of the millennium, the 'Jubilee 2000' citizens' movement led a worldwide demonstration to stop the debts of the world's poorest countries. The researchers found that one-third of the Third World debt (approximately $500 billion) is the outcome of loans used to prop up dictators in some 25 different countries. During the period of 1980–1990 the IMF became an enforcer of hard policy conditions on poor countries that were urgent in need of temporary balance-of-payments assistance. The policy of creating fund by IMF was to generate an excessive demand that means there were too many imports and not enough exports. The result was the devaluation of the currency and cutting of the government expenditure. This slowed down the economy, and rate and intensity of domestic demand that results in fewer imports, along with more, and cheaper, exports. Then, the IMF intends the elimination of balance-of-payments. "Countries were more or less forced to adopt these austerity measures if they wanted to get the IMF seal of approval" (Ellwood, 2001). The 1980s were a 'lost decade' for much of the Third World. Growth stagnated and debt doubled to almost $1,500 billion by the decade's end. By 1999 it had reached nearly $3,000 billion. The foreign debts of developing countries are more than two trillion US dollars and still growing. The result is a debt of over $400 for every man, woman and child in the developing world—where average income in the very poorest countries is less than a dollar a day. All these aspects of globalization of poverty (Chossudovsky, 2001) turning our society into an anaemic situation where marginality along with the offshoots of global-local hybrid and winners-losers dichotomy inclined to support anti-globalization protest movement. Chakravarthi Raghavan (1998) rightly points out, "For we are living in dangerous time, with the entire post-war edifice of multilaterlism and cooperation crumbling. The danger today arises on the economic front, and has already spilled over into political and social arena; at the root is the attempt to repeat history, with active neo-mercantilism of the powerful countries lurking behind the rhetoric of neo-liberalism and globalization". In the age of global consumerism and exploitation, it is very difficult to imagine democratic globalization with the sense of humane feeling and altruism. Re-imagination may only be possible if the process of globalization starts newly from the below.

Impact of Globalization on People's Health

In this era of globalization people's health has also been affected adversely. Today, a disease which occurs in a country anywhere in the world, can easily be spread out in the entire world. The swine flu is a recent example of this.

Globalization and Indian Philosophy

Indian society is old and tradition bound. It is estimated that it has covered a span of five thousand years since the period of its first known civilization (Dube, 1990). It is also the symbol of religious and ethnic coexistence. The synthesis is yet to be the issue of debate. Once Cramb aptly remarked, "India is not only the Italy of Asia ... it is not only the land of romance, art and beauty ... India is religion". Most of the major religions of the world—Hinduism, Islam, Christianity, Buddhism, Jainism—are mingled here with their cults, doctrines and ideals and ideas. In a word, India follows a pattern of cultural pluralism.

Indus valley civilization consisting of multi-ethnicism signalized the rosy dawn of Indian society. The term 'Hinduism' draws largely on Brahmanical texts: the Vedas, the Upanishads and the Bhagavad Gita. The normative principles of Hinduism are based on beliefs, ideals and logic of permissiveness, liberalism, being and becoming, creation and destruction, hedonism, utilitarianism and spiritual transcendence (Singh, 1973).

The Vedic thought in India expressed that man is altogether and throughout composed of *kama* (desire). It also believes in unity. Possession of desires gives him second birth but absence of desire makes him one with *Brahma* (the supreme truth God).

Brahma is one and one represents our globe. The concept of globalization was thus inherent in Hindu philosophy. Globalism is very much related to sublimation and the blend represents the true nature of *karma* (deed), which ultimately leads to *moksha* (salvation). So altruism is the basic tenet of the Bhagwat Gita—it is their *dharma* (religion) which makes him *punyabana* (virtuous). The altruistic interaction began to take its liberal shape with the tie of interaction between Indo-Aryans and earlier inhabitants. With the sense of widening the canvas of altruism, Indian society was divided into four groups on the basis of macro-division of labour—the Brahman (priests/twice born), the Kshatriya (the warriors and the aristocrats), Vaishya (cultivators) and Shudra (the servants). This liberal division of labour ultimately made Indian society hierarchic and segregated. This unpredictable outcome of the division of labour created a special 'social category' called caste. A 'clean' or 'pure' caste began to dominate over unclean or impure category. The question of purity and pollution began to disturb the sedate life of Indian society. The polarization of humanity was created with the definitive motive of making politicization of humanity. Ultimately, the divine sense of altruism was converted into rational sense of either purchasable or consumer altruism. The system or process of 'divide and rule' got its easy access. But, the real texture of Indian philosophy says other words. It says about divinity and salvation, about holy and sacred tradition, about global harmony and cosmic rhythm, about spiritual transcendence and morality, irrespective of space, time, labour and human qualities. In traditional Indian society the issue of today's modernism, i.e., space-time linkage or space over time concept was conceived by the philosophers. In terms of humanity the Indian society was in favour of altruistic globalization that we may have from our Brahmanical texts—the Gita, the Vedantic and the Upanishadic thought. The philosophy of Hinduism did never say any single word about sacredness rather it was completely in favour of positive secularism. It did not use as a tool of politics—nor did it preach any message of syndicated Hinduism or Hindu nationalism; rather, it always advocated the doctrine of divinity, eternity and universalism. Let me quote from the chapter of invocation of the Bhagavat Gita, which denotes the philosophy of today's globalism: "Him we salute ... salute to that supreme one who is bodied forth in Brahma." The motive of the initiators of the globalization process is undoubtedly noble but the mechanism they have adopted to redress inequality is shadowed with the interest of capital accumulation. If it would be altruistic and humane which the Bhagavat Gita tells, "the right is to work only; but never to the fruits thereof', then, the defoliation and disparity would not dominate over global economic scenario. In Indian Vedantic philosophy three characters of *Prakriti* (nature) are *Sattva* (equilibrium), *Rajasa (*attraction) and *Tamasa* (inertia), which bind men of our world with *guna*, means a rope. This global tie of humane bondage leads to infinite altruism. An altruistic man should be "he who is everywhere unattached, not pleased at receiving good, nor vexed at evil, his wisdom is fixed" (Gita,

Chapter 2, 1909). The concept of 'species consciousness' (Weinstein, 2002) is derived from the oneness of mind, wisdom of self-realization, love for the global kinsmen path of knowledge and path of work for the active. The anti-concept of 'species consciousness' is called hypocrisy: "He, who restraining the organs of action, sits resolving in the mind, thoughts regarding objects of sense, he, of deluded understanding, is called a hypocrite" (Gita, passage 6). Thus, *Brahma*, having in the beginning created mankind together with the motive of 'good consciousness': "By this shall ye multiply…". Thus, the multiplication, i.e., the global men represent a unit of our 'super organic' surrounding. Today's globalization process itself signifies the work of *yajna*, i.e., sacrifice which is of following types: (a) *Deba Yajna* (offering sacrifice); (b) *Brahma Yajna* (transmission and acquisition of knowledge); (c) *Pitr Yajna* (offering liberation); (d) *Nr. Yajna* (the feeding of the hungry); and (e) *Bhuta Yajna* (the feeding of the animals). This highly philosophic altruistic version of the Gita best suits in the globalization process for a better and higher living. But, the disparity in the Third World countries as an anti-version of globalization slogan, advocates a falsification of altruism which our philosophic text cites: "The man who is devoted to the self, and is satisfied with the self, and content in the self alone, has no obligatory duty" (Gita, version 17). The real altruism in our philosophy means "do thou always perform actions which are obligatory, without attachment, by performing action without attachment, one attains to the highest".

The concept of 'species consciousness' (Weinstein, 2002) is clouded with three types of knowledge: (a) *Sattvika,* i.e., fire enveloped by smoke—the rise of a slight wind of discrimination dispels, the smoke of desire in a *Sattvika* (honest and devoted) heart; (b) *Rajashika* (propertied)—the removal of the dust on a mirror requires a bit of time and preparation; and (c) *Tamasika* (darkness of *Maya* or illusion) takes much time like the release of the embryo from the uterus after birth. So, the absolute *Sattvika* knowledge attains true concentration on 'species consciousness' which is also true for altruism.

In modern society the crisis and disparity arise mainly because of uneven distribution of wealth, comfort and assistance. But our epistemology tells that he attains excellence who looks with equal regard upon well-wishers, friends, foes, neutrals, the hateful, the relatives, the neighbours and upon the righteous and the unrighteous alike. The centre of global village is nothing but the universal self. It would be the 'ideal type' model if all living beings of the globe have their sense of power from the centre. A country like India, which is a complete tradition-bound society in terms of culture and depressed in terms of economy, thought of globalization since the beginning of the Vedic period: "I see Thee boundless form on every side with manifold arms, stomachs, mouths, and eyes; neither the end nor the middle, nor also the beginning of Thee do I see, O Lord of the Universe, O Universal Form ... I cannot distinguish East from the West, nor the North from the South."

I have already mentioned about the epistemological break-up in Indian Vedantic philosophy. The nature of true altruism for better living lies in the seed of *Sattvika,* i.e., knowledge related to sincere desire having no demand of result or fruit. But practising *Rajasika* (motive of gaining honour and ostentation) and *Tamasika* (motive of ruining other to gain something) knowledge does not act as the prime mover in altruistic globalization.

The tradition began to change with the emergence of British rule in India. From the close of 17th century right up to the beginning of the 18th, India had been wading through a bewildering welter of cultural, social, political and economic ideals and ideas. Politically overthrown by the British India had been fast coming under the sway of an exotic civilization. The hypnotic spell of foreign civilization began to recede slowly but steadily with the mighty reform movements.

The first phase of reform movements called for changes in the culture and values of Indian society and the second meant for synthesis of new cultural and valuational ideals and ideas with the traditional forms. The reformers of both movements accepted the ideal-typical cultural context of Indian society. The social thought, which lies embedded in reform movement, was the issue of unity in diversity: assimilation, transmission and transformation of soul from 'I' to 'we'. The 'We'-ness is the only indicator of humanitarian philosophy of Indian society. So, the cult of globalization was in process since the period of inception of Indian philosophical thought. The social thinkers, the poets, patriots and prophets, the reformers were all believers of humanized globalization—globalization in terms of human interaction, in terms of emotional closeness, spiritual transcendentalism and human values.

Rabindranath Tagore, the great poet and social thinker, was the believer of 'string theory': one has to come down from the top stair and share his soul with the souls of the helpless. Here individual self blends with the global selves. Otherwise, the concept of the globalization of economy would be turned into 'globalization of poverty'. The following countries exhibit such a sordid picture:

Table 1

Countrywise Percentage of Population Living below Poverty Line, 1998

Country	*Population*
Brazil	17.4
Vietnam	50.9
Zambia	86.0
Peru	49.0
Mexico	10.1
Pakistan	34.0
Bangladesh	35.6
Indonesia	15.1
India	35.0

Source: World Development Report, 2001.

The percentage of poverty-affected people, as shown in Table 1, is not actual, because the people living in insular poverty pockets are not included in it. It is estimated that near about 80 per cent of the rural people in India are living below the level of subsistence, i.e., below 2,400 calories. The structural adjustment programme more or less failed to achieve its target of removing global economic disparity. It is evident from the report of UN Development Programme (1994) that the earnings of five richest countries of the world from the global market increased from 70 per cent to 85 per cent whereas the earning of the poor countries downed to 1.4 per cent from 2.3 per cent. Besides, the victims of the absolute poverty and hopelessness in most of the Third World countries now beget a new concept of inequalization instead of globalization. The disparity is so acute that free-ride aid and free-riding behaviour cannot even enter into the orbit. Side by side a tripling of trade dependency occurred over a 45 year period (1950–1995), with no sign of slowing down. In the year 1995 the 'tri-polar concentration' has accelerated the speed of globalization process. But stimulated by the aid system, indebtedness has also been globalized. The financial and economic dependence of the underdeveloped countries signify the first seal. Massive modern technology transfers, which have made the undeveloped economies dependent on know-how, they cannot pay for and unable to increase productivity. The result is referred to as second seal. The third seal acted as the mode of reinforcement of the first two seals by IMF and World Bank's structural adjustment programme, where the underdeveloped countries drowned to debt. The Third World, with no control over the mechanisms of the globalization of capital and market, is becoming highly marginalized and depressed. This is the fourth seal. The emergence of a new political class as a true aidocracy becomes the debt system's intermediary forms, which is called the fifth seal. The sixth seal related to the military aid, which is used to repress the progressive social movements. The development ideology when viewed as a virtuous deed or a moral obligation called the seventh seal (Gelinas, 1998).

The above-mentioned seals have sealed the humane rationale of globalization policy and prospects, because the Third World debt has increased from $9 billion in 1955 to $572 billion in 1980 and $2,177 billion in 1996. The formation of

OECD from OEEC in 1961 brought together all the industrialized capitalist countries. In 1977 there were about 190 sovereign economically and geo-politically interdependent countries in the world. Twenty-nine OECD countries are on the top of the stair; the middle stair consists of 23 countries and the rest, i.e., 126 underdeveloped countries are on the last step of the stair. The last step consists of four categories of underdeveloped countries like high income petroleum exporting countries, developing countries, maldeveloped countries (India belongs to this category with per capita GNP of $340) and least developed countries (World Bank, World Development Indicators, 1997; UNDP, Human Development Report, 1997). Development assistance as defined by the agreement, is "the granting of resources to developing countries as donations or preferential credit, such as long-term loans at interest rates at least 25 per cent below the market value". But, the computation of interest rate and market rate results in profit for the donors. The net financial transfers from the Third World to the developed countries (1983–1995) totalled approximately $300 billion (World Bank, World Debt Tables).

Besides, ODA and other loan giving agencies like multilateral and bilateral aid givers (amount of loan given to the beneficiaries—$70 billion per year), 'take aid' scheme (amount of loan given in 1991 was $50 billion which increased to $159 billion in 1995) and NGOs (only 9% of the total loan given by all aid agencies for the global development). The Third World therefore still suffers from the disease of socio-economic and socio-political malnutrition. The prime reasons for such underdevelopment are excessive population increase, missing institutions, lack of capital formation, lack of entrepreneurship, debt burden, vicious circle of poverty, hunger and malnutrition and different endowment conditions (Siebert, 1999). Precisely, the context of underdevelopment focuses on (a) financial dependence, (b) overseas oriented economic system, (c) national economic dislocation, and (d) subordination of elite to foreign interests and influence of category classification (Gelinas, 1998). If we recall hymns from the Bhagavat Gita, i.e., love for the global kinsmen or *Sattvika* attitude i.e., "sincere desire having no demand of result or fruit", the disparity would be removed and globalization of humanity would dominate over such a globalization of non-altruism.

Rabindranath Tagore, the great poet and humanist social thinker said, "Thou powerful country! Don't lead us to the path of competition—lead ourselves to the arena of cooperation".

Altruism and Sociology of Humanity

India is the mother and seat of all true philosophy and metaphysics. Indian society would have been fractured and disintegrated had it not been the traditions of religion of humanity, the doctrine of *Atma* (self) and *Karma* (work is worship) the added positivistic features. The Indian social thinkers have analyzed these epistemological connotations. Sitting on a small rock of Kanyakumari at the southern part of India, Vivekananda, the great epistemologist, went into deep meditation not upon God but upon his nation. Engrossed in deep meditation he felt that India would rise only through a renewal and restoration of that highest spiritual consciousness and altruistic humanity. In spite of having development ulcer in its heart India is still alive in its religion and cultures. Vivekananda felt that India's only deficiency was poverty and it should have to learn from the world how to remove it. So, Vivekananda felt the necessity to learn western science and technology. Romain Rolland said that just as, at the call of Jesus, the dead Lazarus came to life, so also, at Vivekananda's call, a moribund India was infused with new life. So far as my view is concerned, the 1893 was the year of inception of the concept of globalization. On Monday, 11 September 1893, the Parliament of Religions as an adjunct of the World's Columbian Expositions, held in Chicago to celebrate the four hundredth anniversary of the discovery of America by Christopher Columbus with the mission to bring the countries of the world into a more friendly relationship. Vivekananda in 'Chicago Address' quoted a few lines from a hymn to "Sisters and

Brothers in America": "As the different streams having their sources in different places all mingle their water in the sea, so O Lord, the different paths which men take through different tendencies, various though they appear, crooked or straight, all lead to Thee." His 'calling' was the true calling of globalization in the spiritual and human sense: "Sectarianism, bigotry and its horrible descendant, fanaticism have long possessed this beautiful earth. They have filled the earth with violence, drenched it often and often with human blood, destroyed civilization and sent whole nations to despair. Had it not been for there horrible demons, human society would be far more advanced than it is now. But their time is come; and I fervently hope that the bell that tolled this morning in honour of this convention may be the death-knell of all fanaticism, of all persecutions with the sword or with the pen and of all uncharitable feelings ..." (Vivekananda, Chicago Address, 11 September, 1893). Doesn't this message symbolize the true form of altruism and essence of sociology of humanity? but, the reality depicts a very sordid picture now. The Third World has always assigned a marginal place in the international economic order and the prescriptions for advancement were either half-hearted or completely misguided. Although advances have been made for some, the pressing issues of global inequalities and poverty remain. The implementation of actually existing development has involved environmental destruction, exploitation, state oppression and impoverishment (Kiely, 1998). The philosophy of Indian society taught that a man ought to live in this world "like a lotus leaf, which grows in water but is never moistened by water; so a man ought to live in the world"—his heart to fellow men and hands to work. This philosophy of altruism best suits in ideal type globalization process where trade in love is a sin.

And, the trade in love makes such an inequality syndrome in our global society where coexistence does not transmit to synthesis. Here lies the philosophical crisis of globalization process. What is theory? What is especially social or sociological theory? It is merely the abstraction—the expression of thinking of one's self—expression of transcendental condition. When it blends with reality, the issue of applied theory comes into fore. And all the theories in sociology mostly stem from the humane attributes. It takes different shapes, forms and approaches only because of one's perception and sense of vision. So theory is just a travelling of one's mind, vision and angular axis, a coming up of different thoughts through various conditions and circumstances to the same goal, i.e., to crate a better human world. "It is the same light coming through glasses of different colours and there little variations are necessary for adaptations" (Vivekananda, Chicago Address, 1893). So, the positivistic approach, structural-functional approach, conflict approach, Interactionist approach, phenomenological school, structuration theory, modernization school and school of postmodernism came into being. The deductions or inferences of most of the schools (may be pragmatic, empirical, abstract, or applied) are humanistic and act as the effective force in the liberalization of the human spirit. But, the debate between realism and idealism continues. The exponents of the philosophy of science have renounced a tenet called metaphysics with which the Indian philosophers are mostly concerned. Herbert Feigl (1967) defends the scientific status of such metaphysical problems as the relationship between consciousness and the brain. Some believe it as the construction of scientific ontology. The rapid development of experimental science in the 18th and early 19th centuries was paused with the empirical methods of research. In 1830s positivism came out with a demand to oust idealistic philosophers from science and subjected idealism and religion to sharp criticism regarding them both a product of the mythological stage in the development of human spirit (Naletov, 1984). Comte considered it immaterial whether these personified abstractions were later turned into souls or fluids and thus Comte rejected metaphysics as it goes outside the limits of science. So he discarded metaphysics as an expression of mysticism, idealism or dialectics. But reality says that philosophy is always identical with metaphysics but accepted altruism as beyond the melting pot. The Vienna Circle launched struggle against metaphysics and they (Schlick, 1925; Wittgenstein, 1949) demanded verification of the metaphysical proof. But Carnap (1971) viewed that universal laws appear to be senseless from the philosophy of verification principle. His inductive logic (other name is 'logical empiricism') led him "beyond its limits right into the arms of metaphysics" (Naletov, 1984). Carnap (1971) regards metaphysics not as knowledge but rather as poetry with illusion of knowledge. But logical empiricism sometimes confines our thinking into the cage of narrow methodology to study man and society. Man is always a vain, fickle, unique and marvellous. A theory of science could not search for any general injunctions. Man can only be studied in terms of spiritual and practical activity. Here metaphysics blends with idealism and consider everything to be a function of reason and regard being in terms of man's mindset. Thus man's mental images produce man's practical activity. This might be called epistemological realism (Roger, 1980). Sociology of humanity emerged from such an epistemological realism or solipsism. Still a bipolar approach is in operation to study man in society: (a) scientific, and (b) anti-scientific. But, the author's view is that the scientific method of studying man in the era of globalization fails to achieve its humane target. The anti-scientific approach, which the author calls philosophic (real base of scientism!), could develop a view of studying man as the representative of the global human race. The practitioners of such a philosophy are the humanists, whereas a section of the sociologists views the doctrine of humanism as pseudo-study of man's real life or calls it the study of eternal and timeless values or a set of wishes or normative demands of the individual. But, the doctrine of globalization, which creates global malady now, demands humanistic assessment because scientism of globalization fails to achieve the need and demand of man's real life. Here scientism blends with aid trading. Therefore, how to guarantee protection of man's personal dignity, how to protect human rights, how to develop man's potentialities and capacities and how to make life without destructive wars, hunger, famine, poverty and disease—all demand altruistic and humane theory. Peter L. Berger (1963) states, "... there is a peculiar human value in the sociologist's responsibility for evaluating his findings, as far as he is psychologically able, without regard to his own prejudices, likes or dislikes, hopes or fears ... but it is especially different to exercise in a discipline that touches so clearly on the human passions". Under the pressure of scientific realism sociology's data are cut so from the "living marrow of human life" (Berger, 1963) that the basic and inherent sensitivity of humanism has lost its significance. Understanding of the humanistic place of sociology, as Berger (1963) views, implies an openness of mind and a catholicity of vision. The emergence of Renaissance was the beginning of such a humanistic philosophy in sociology. It is the theory, which tells about freedom. Edward Shils thought of man as a being with cognitive, aesthetic and moral capacities. Man is not a machine. He is soft and tender. He has sense of reasoning emotion, moral choice, aesthetic orientation, and creativity and sublime soul. The time backs again to write chapters or to build theory on the humanistic perspective because late modernism demands the analysis of self-interpretation of man. Shils (1961) quotes, "Sociology is humanistic because it attempts to understand whatever man does, in categories that acknowledge his humanity; his need for cognitive orientation; his capacity for rational judgement and action, for affectionate attachment, for aesthetic expression and response, for moral decision.... Sociology is a continuation and elaboration of the permanent and necessary effort of man to understand himself and his species". The humanistic sociological study now goes beyond the individual and is directing to the "trans-individual and trans-historical" network, the experimental sociology or scientism only attempt, to cast the result and procedure of this collective self-interpretation. Here lies the importance of applied sociological research. The bottom line of applied sociological research is not only to explore generalization in technical manipulation of data; it is like beyond a melting pot. Applied sociological research speaks of man's self-interpretation, assimilation and self-transmission and thus it helps the progress of humanity. But "every step forward faces a new danger. Every new virtue that renders if possible can all too readily become a vice that will undo it … love can turn to tyranny and then to hatred the sense of nationality can become a monstrous exclusiveness … Sociological analysis … is part of this movement. Without this movement, there would be no sociological analysis" (Shils, 1961).

In India, sociology of humanity emerged with the writings of the ancient sages, Vedantic philosophy, Brahmanical texts and social thinkers. They had attempted to study human being only in terms of love, interaction and goodness of human quality, which is always divine and transcendental. Sree Ramkrishna, a pious social thinker, said, "attainment of highest ideal of humanity is the attainment of divinity". Plato contended that cognition leads to love and love affects both morality and knowledge creativity. "Love does no wrong to God or man and suffers no wrong from God or man. For love does not suffer from violence, if it suffers, since violence does not touch love; and everyone becomes a poet when love touches him" (Plato's symposium). Plotinus (205–270 AD), the Neoplatonic philosopher has explained three types of love: (a) a God or divine love, (b) a demon, or human love, and (c) a passion or animal love. The divine-human-animal coexistence may create risky altruism but their synthesis may be a calling of postmodern Renaissance. The philosophical tradition in India posits the identity of man with the totality, i.e., entire cosmos. Thus universal love and compassion are based on metaphysics (it is difficult to denounce), which is the only basis of modern applied sociology. The oriental wisdom is defined not only by freedom from the egoism of the senses and comprehensiveness and sense of proportion of goals and values, but also by universal altruism and comparison (Mukerjee, 1960). The Bhagavata Gita, the sacred text of Hindus, written at the beginning of the millennium, develops a global religion of charity in terms of *sarva-avatara* (universal incarnation), *sarva bhute daya* (universal compassion) and *sarva mukti* (universal salvation). It is also evident from Indian philosophic texts that the charity, benevolence and compassion are the true identities of altruism and humanism, which are not only the expressions of metaphysics but lead to reality.

Bertrand Russell said, "I mean sympathy as an emotion, not as a theoretical principle". This altruistic metaphysics or metaphysical altruism changes its form and character from time to time and sociologists get maximum benefit from the changed version to build up new sociological theory. Comte's 'Positivism' is such a changed or metamorphosed version of metaphysics. Western philosophy mainly depends on Kantian theory of justice and equality. The post-Kantian thought introduced the notion of a tight cultural and economic determinism. The followers of this school of thought are Marx, Hegel and the like social philosophers. In India, the ethics founded on the pure metaphysics of the "indwelling of God in man fosters infinite charity and compassion for all sentient beings, and is egalitarian, buoyant and dynamic. In her non-theistic ethical systems it is introspection that establishes an inward continuity of self and the universe as a whole including more than man and generates reverence for man absolutely every common man" (Mukerjee, 1960).

With this view in soul, the Bhakti movement (egalitarian movement) gave the impetus of building theory of altruism in India. And, Comte's dictum of altruism has acted as fuel to light sociological theory of altruism in academic sphere in India. The kernel of Mahayana moral idealism is: "Can there be bliss when all that lives must suffer? Shalt thou be saved and hear the whole world cry"! A true world picture can be assessed in terms of scientific methodology or empirical verification, proof and principle. But it is more important to study the modern world picture in terms of humanity, love, interaction and moral values. The question of wisdom with the erasement of the boundaries of self is the true sense of altruism and humanism which global late modern society demands. The issue of universalism and impersonalism of wisdom and emotion is conducive to the promotion of the world community of today. Global cooperation rests far less on laws, conventions, treaties, institutions and aid-giver organizations, and far more on sympathies, habits and aspirations (Mukerjee, 1960). Indian sociologists recognize the philosophy of social sciences as the expressions of universal values, insight experiences and practices of man and moulds and shapes one community, one culture and one world. The Indian concept of *metaphysical triad*, i.e., man-self-transcendence-universe (Mukerjee, 1960) makes universal person and global community and builds sociology with the sociological triad like personality-transcendence-social universe. Cooley named it "growth of the larger mind". The 'triad' or the concept of the growth of the larger mind advocates the hidden philosophy of applied sociology. Because "man is not simply an organism bounded by an epidermis ... he is also an essence beyond the boundaries of skin and person" (Shils, 1961). Thus metaphysical thinking lies embedded in applied sociological research and denotes the true spirit of altruism and humanity. But Binoy Kumar Sarkar (1916), an Indian sociologist, was in favour of positivism. In Comte's judgement humanity has been marching towards a stage in which positive knowledge or scientific experience is dominant (Sarkar, 1916). In his essay, 'Asiatic Positivism' (1916) Sarkar states, "if the term (positivism) be applied to any inculcation of humanitarian principles or social duties and the like, every religion is surely positivistic and every human being is a positivist". In spite of such a bi-polar debate between metaphysics and positivism, Indian sociology tells the theory of humanism. To remove global malady, to use globalization for the better living and brighter tomorrow, the ability to understand and transmit 'species consciousness' (Weinstein, 2002) and wide-awake individual in utilizing world forces for a global village requires theoretical execution and humane mindset. Amartya Sen, in an interview (*Times of India*, 2 December 2001), expressed his discontent about the political situation in the world. He said, "The narrow categorization of civilization ... is a hazard to the human rights movement ... why are we boxing human beings on the basis of religion, gender and class?" Weinstein's (2002) version gives us a new dimension in this regard: "Learning about good neighbours as deviants may reveal much about the moral values and ethical boundaries of ordinary people. By insisting that we are all human beings, all part of one world, we may be able to be more effective actors." But, the Hindu-Muslim riots in 1947 or the cross-border terrorism in Kashmir do not depict such a bright picture of humanism. The rioters or the terrorists stop being workers or capitalists (Sen, 2001) and ultimately they are unable to set their home in order. "What do the religions of the world tell us? To love each other, to love everyone.... Religions authorities have regularly been a force for peace and tolerance, it is equally clear that they have regularly been a force for violence and intolerance. No doubt, God moves in mysterious ways, but we simple humans may feel impelled to try to make reuse of there days and, dare I suggest it, to draw conclusions from our faiths and our sciences than mere fatalism" (Wallerstein, 2000). Adopting global policy of benign altruism can only solve the problem of such religious dualism between peace and violence and between tolerance and aggressiveness. If sociological theories were used for such a social cause, the blend of theory with action would contribute to social progress in the world context.

The cooperation, transcendental interaction, coexistence and synthesis of aid and love can lead to a true globalization. Secondly, the policy makers, planners and initiators should have in mind not to trade aid and love. Thirdly, they start with what the people with Third World countries have, not with what they lack. There is a famous Chinese proverb, which strikes my mind again and again:

> "Give a man a fish and you feed him for a day,
> Teach a man to fish and you feed him for life".

Now, my question to the policy makers, aid givers and sociologists, what is the true sense of globalism? To give a man in the Third World a fish for a day or to teach him fishing for survival? The challenge of globalization is now facing such a strange interlude and the right answer will decide the future of globalization. After all, in this global age, only a truly global ethics can be of real value and the ethics with hunger, starvation and anxiety-ridden survival and economic uncertainty cannot be the discourse of humanity. The globalization with such global-local dichotomy and threat of exclusion is nothing but a deviant globalization.

9 Value Erosion and Defaced Humanity

A frog lived in a well. It was born there and brought up there. One day another frog that lived in the sea came and fell into the well. “Where are you from?” “I am from the sea.” “The sea! How big is that? Is it as big as my well?” and he took a leap from one side of the well to the other. “How do you compare the sea with your little well?” Then the frog of the well took another leap and asked, “Is your sea so big?” The frog of the sea said, “What nonsense you speak to compare the sea with your well?” “Well then,” the frog said, “nothing can be bigger than my well; there can be nothing bigger than this.” One may comfortably analyze the inner meaning of the story, as the debate on values. Someone claims that his values are great. Others say it devalued. It means what appears as moral and ethical values to someone may be devalued to other and vice-versa. Values are a powerful instrument to spur development. They are goals or standards that set the direction and mobilize the collective cultural energies of the society for great accomplishment. Over the last two centuries in countries around the world development has strengthened expansive values that encourage greater freedom, tolerance, individual initiative, self-confidence and self-respect, dynamism, risk-taking, efficiency, punctuality, organization, communication and cooperation, open-mindedness and respect for new ideas, innovation and creativity. At the same time, development has weakened values that support respect for tradition and hierarchy, seniority and authority, self-effacement and humility, patience and perseverance, generosity and self-sacrifice. The 19th century tolerated values based on the exploitation by people over people through slavery, colonialism and war, and the domination of nature by man. The guiding values for the coming century are freedom and respect for the individual, social equity, tolerance of human diversity and harmony with the environment.

Question of Values Uncertainty

I want to revisit to our customary root where there was love, passion, sympathy, devotion, clemency, lenience, honesty, loyalty to parents and other relatives, obedience and humane feelings. Here, there was no opportunity for technological despotism and value trafficking. One very crucial question comes into my mind: Does globalization disintegrate social solidarity and freedom of thinking and living? It has ingested our value-oriented interaction pattern and community living with our own local lifestyle pattern. For example, most of the people, who are chasing after globalization with the immense information technological components like cell phone and e-mail, and are subconsciously accepting global opportunities as the necessity of the era, have been disengaged from the local society. Once upon a time we were very much leaning with letter writing. It was an art in the arena of mental growth and creative mindset. But, immediately with the emergence of globalization process, we have been entered into the world of e-mail, SMS and Internet chatting. It invites a big problem in the passage of values. It not only begets the disease of language vertigo but it also squeezes our words from language, reduces our feelings and sentiments, narrows our freedom of expression and ultimately changes our value structure and value belongingness. Secondly, one may claim that changes are very natural in the era of globalization. The changes happened with the emergence of modernization and technological revolution. It is therefore the true story of space and time. The media has brought revolution in the arena of dress, fashion, style of living, custom, knowledge and culture. These are not the cases of value erosion. The local people have compelled to accept global phenomena either knowingly or unknowingly. It means globalization is interested in us. That is the story of success. But if a woman/mother rejects breast-feeding for keeping loveliness of her youth, it is value erosion. In our society the portraits and books of our great thinkers have been replaced by the portraits of Jennifer Lopez, Madonna, Maradona or the item boys and girls. Our kitchen has been a centre of fast food where there is no room for our traditional cooking artifacts. These are, as if, waiting for, to be placed in the archaeological museum. This is value erosion. In our traditional society there were folk plays, rituals and sacred ceremonies. These were the symbols of social togetherness and seats of the renewals of social and kinship bond and reunion. The question of social, ethical and moral values was associated with such traditional occasions. These have now been faded away. If it is being analyzed by the experts as the new form of globalization morality that we have to become accustomed with, I have nothing to say. Because sometimes it is said, "morality does not need codes or rules, reason or knowledge, argument or conviction.... Morality (in Levina's terms: being for the Other) has notoriously an awesome potential for love and hatred, for self-sacrifice and domination, care and cruelty"(cited in Bauman, 2001). It really signals value troubles.

The Tragic Metamorphosis of Values

A few days back it was reported in a newspaper in Kolkata that a pious Brahmin desired to sacrifice fruits and sweets as the offerings to a few Brahmin youth as the part of the death ritual of his father. The youths did not want to accept the offerings. They desired to have junk food like Pizza etc., with Pepsi. Finding no other alternative the pious man had to supply the junk food and soft drink to them as the offerings of the ritual.

When you will dissect and cross-dissect the rhetoric body of globalization, something occurs in your mind. Is it just a buzzword or real? If it is real, then, what are the realities? In the era of globalization some virtual images stand before us as the perils that deface the concept of humanity. And perhaps so an expected trauma is waiting for our doomsday when the clouds of uncertainty, economic insecurity and identity crisis will dominate over the sky of the world. Human species may be the replicants and will act like more human than human. The abstract identity of human existence will turn into simulacra-fashioned ecstasy. The impact of genetic engineering, a virtual innovation of postmodern science and technology, introduces such a simulacra, which has overcome the boundary of time, space and humanity. The dominance of information and communication technologies uproots the fetters of community feeling, family bondage and emotional interaction and community closeness. It seems to dominate over real-life individuals.

Bio-digital World

It is evident from the records that there are more than 3 million digital switches for every human being alive on the planet. There are nearly half a billion PCs over the world—one for every 13 human beings, if not more. The Internet and cell phone are spreading at high speed. In future these technologies will be more ultramodern. Is the hi-tech revolution virtual or real? Whatever it might be, it is certainly alarming for the comfortable growth of humanity, ethics and human values, which they possess and nurture, with the process of socialization and upbringing. Another important and alarming consequence of globalization is biological revolution—a product of interdisciplinary knowledge like chemistry, medicines, genetics, cloning, that are related to the 'bio-digital convergence'.

A True Story

A few days back an old rickshaw puller said, "Sir, have you seen sparrow or vulture very recently?" I was very careless of his saying and uttered in a very low and ignoring tone, "No". But something was happening in my mind and after a brief silence I asked, "You are right. The sparrows, vultures and a good number of traditional birds are not quite visible either in our courtyard or on the branches of trees or on the roof of our houses. But why?" The illiterate old rickshaw puller replied very excitedly, "I am an illiterate man. But I do feel it is mainly because of the overuse of cell phones, its magnetic dimension and towers of accesses". Yes, the traditional poor fellow was hundred per cent correct. The information technologies remove the spatial distance, links time over space and help a lot to spread the vision of global capitalism but side by side it has damaged not only the health and brains of the individuals but also invited a world of future without insects, birds and reptiles which always keep harmony with environmental equilibrium. This is perhaps the possibility of technological risk, which should remain outside the orbit of globalization, or it is itself the creation of globalization. This is the error of present-day globalization, which may give life to the volcano of globalization in future.

Language Game and Identity Crisis

Any one observing us from outer space might experience a feeling of disgust and pity at the same time, concluding that the human race on a global scale has fallen victim to social and cultural insanity and economic inequality. This is very much true when we explain postmodernism and globalization. For example, communication technology performs a vital role in storing knowledge. The students nowadays do not demand or require classroom lessons or extensive written study materials or books and journals. Learning is no longer be intertwined with the training minds with *Gurus*. Knowledge now can easily be borrowed and stored from the websites. One, who is economically weak, can have little knowledge from free versions like the abstract or the outline of the knowledge content. But he, who is economically capable, or has Internet access, can store the amount of knowledge he requires. He has to purchase it. Here two points are very important: knowledge selling and secondly, knowledge quantity. In future the storehouse of knowledge, I am afraid, will be computer with websites facility. A few days back I was in a doctor's chamber for medical check up. The nameplate showed a very interesting message: "My endeavour is to sign out pain and sign in happiness in your life." I thought that the nature of language now begins to suffer from globalization disease and consequently postmodern vertigo. The language of 'cure' and 'recovery', which should be the right word, has been deconstructed and gains technological code like sign out and sign in, which is unknown to the illiterate, the economically depressed and disadvantaged masses. This sort of technological-language vertigo in the Third World countries will create a dilemma between local and global language and knowledge nomenclature, which may create an off world to the local people. The concept of knowledge as the emancipation of soul or asylum of ideas and the taste of the last generation will be converted into knowledge commodity. Not only that for the transmission and storage of information will no longer depend on human beings but on computers. Information will be produced and sold. Nations and states will fight for information and it zip around the world at the speed of electricity, and people will try to steal it.

Different Names of Capitalism

Though postmodern society is based on the consumption of commodities—on buying and using things—this consumption can never make us happy". It was written in the Vedic scripture: Truth is one—but the sages call it by different names. Likewise, we can say that capitalism is one but people call it by different names: economic liberalization, reform and recovery, globalization, postmodernism neo-liberalization, fair globalization or civil society and good governance.

The ever-increasing economic gap between the West and the rest, global-local cultural conflict, upsurge of ethnic violence, vibrant intensity of cross-border terrorism, fundamentalism, religious bigotry and increase inequality within and between nations threaten the ethos and ethics of globalization process.

The crisis in the emerging markets has made it evident that globalization opportunities come with high risk. Hunger and poverty dominate over technology and communication.

Indian Philosophy of Humanity and Social Values

The philosophy of social science is facilitated by the triangular interaction or 'transaction' between man, communication and institution or between person, value and Culture (Mukerjee, 1960). Of the triad the crucial phase is values which, according to Mukerjee, are not only "motivations, underlying the behaviour of man in society, but also heuristic principles that explain both individual behaviour in relation to the physical and the social world as well as an objective social relationship, behaviour, institution and social system" (ibid.: 1). One should always analyze values dialectically, which brings truth not virtual image. All social interactions, behaviour and the values that "lie deep-seated in them embody polar principles and tendencies". Yet neither man nor society is conscious of the dialectical truth of all knowledge, values, human relations and social arrangements and institutions. Mukerjee observes that each system, each culture and each society keeps on stubbornly resisting its opponent and, in the midst of shattering new experiences and defeats, hopes for ultimate triumph though in the course of the struggle it goes through the new experience of accepting partially the opposite viewpoint and intention. In our society *I-think* and *I-transcend* concept excludes reality construction. Man is always divided in his mind, loyalties and ways of living. It is the reality that each society and culture maintains and bequeaths its myth regarding values, which have great emotional attractive power for social being (Mukerjee, 1960).

Values exist in an ascending series of planes, each higher plane being more powerful than the one before it. Physical values express in how carefully and reliably we handle material things. Vital values express in how pleasantly, harmoniously, generously we relate with other people. Mental values express in honesty, truthfulness, trustworthiness and idealism. Spiritual values express our faith, sincerity, patience, perseverance, goodwill and self-giving. Every act is a universe, which can express many values. The more it expresses, the greater its power and effectiveness. Milton Rokeal (1973: 5) writes, "A value is an enduring belief that a specific mode of conduct or existence is personally or socially preferable to an opposite or converse mode of conduct or end-state of existence". But no one can deny the relevance of social change and mode of development in the society. Some lament to say that our golden time has gone and we have stepped into an alien world. This is not highly logical. Values may only be devalued when one fails to comply with the modernization. Mind it, today always represents modernization with the values of that day but yesterday, to some people, may be signified as values with goodness and tomorrow will identify today as tradition. It means values are very much associated with the space and time. Globalization is not a new phenomenon that changes our culture and values. It has started with the emergence of colonialism. And since then our culture and values began to change. F. Fanon (1967) writes, "One of the gravest consequences of the colonialization of Africa, Asia and Latin America has been the systematic destruction of the cultures and historic value systems of each people.... Ferocious exploitation, misery, famine, discrimination, inferiority complexes and the loss of personality and self-respect are so many aspects of colonialism which induced a deep inhibition of cultures and knowledge".

What Sociologists Need to do for a Better Tomorrow and Ideal Humanism?

We say that academics and practitioners should combine their sociologies. In this global era such a patchwork is very necessary. Social scientists might well make special pleas for sociology as broad-ranging, daring, adapting and varying instruments for search, discovery, problem solving, model building and social struggle" (Lee, 1976: 934). Sociologists' calling is to make a better world. Yet most sociologists today are afraid to openly profess sociology. They disguise values and accept the premise that academic professionals should keep values out of their work. The whole culture is lost in this sea of relativism. But, as the early sociologists knew, value relativism disappears once we ground the enterprise with human needs as our referent. They saw progress and human betterment as the goals of social science. They continue, "Our values are the human agenda. The purpose of our knowledge is to promote human well-being. Lester Ward had pictured an applied national academy in Washington, D.C. to train lawmakers about how to create the good society. While the dire vision of conservatives maintains it is folly to hope for human betterment, Ward says the reason for lack of what he called *moral progress*."

The moral terrain of our society today should focus the widely held perception that the society is in moral decline. It looks at the question from a variety of angles, examining traditional, secular, religious, family and economic values, and others. Using unique data from the World Values Surveys, the largest systematic attempt has made to document attitudes, values and beliefs around the world, And, now it is the right time for the social scientists, particularly in the era of globalization, where postmodern values dominate over folk or traditional values, to evaluate the identity crisis of social and moral values. The gap between reality and perception does not represent mass ignorance of the facts or an overblown moral panic. Rather, the widespread perception of a crisis of values is a real and legitimate interpretation of life in a society that is in the middle of a fundamental transformation and that contains growing cultural contradictions. Instead of posing a problem, the author argues, this crisis rhetoric serves the valuable social function of reminding us of what it means to be American. As such, it preserves the ideological foundation of the nation.

Society has developed through three overlapping stages—physical, vital and mental. Over the course of tens of thousands of years humanity has evolved from a society mainly concerned with the *physical* realities, such as our survival, a life of fear and threat from without, and the need for complete deference to authority; to a stage in which our individual *vital* needs and wants, including our desire to expand and trade, come into their own; to the present emerging *mental* stage where peace, freedom, democracy, the fulfilment and empowerment of the individual, the emergence of fast, complex organizations, and the extraordinary power of thought to shape our world for endless progress emerges. Beyond that is the *spiritual* stage of social evolution, where mind is more fully developed to allow multi-sided awareness of truth.

The basic notion of applied sociology is the emancipation of humanity from value crisis, anxiety and dejection. Let us recall the note of Sorokin (1963: 3–11), which he quoted from Jesus' hymns: The Sermon on the Mount and Beatitude forecast happiness for those without wealth or comfort on earth: "Blessed are the poor, the sorrowful, the week, the hungry, the merciful, the faithful, the peacemaker, and the pure of heart, for they all shall be comforted and rewarded. Overcome anger, conquest, love your enemies, do not lie or Judge others" (pp. 3–11). Sorokin analyzes the social crisis and develops a blueprint for social construction. He perceives human pain and suffering and its relationship to social structure. Altruism, a sense of sociology of humanity, according to Sorokin, is an integral part and system of applied philosophy of sociology.

Sorokin's Harvard Research Centre in Creative Altruism is a product of professional concern. His studies show that sociologists and psychologists had ignored love and altruism. He criticizes the parochial view of most of the sociologists who are deeply concerned with narrow and specific social problems. He insists that interpretive inquiry be kept to a minimum. His paradigm of 'integral society' is the result of the searching of 'what' and 'why' through the connections of actions. By integral society, Sorokin means, a holistic approach to humanity, knowledge, values, and social organization (cited in Johnston, 1998).

The true altruism and social values mean, "do unto others what you would want others do unto you". The classical sociologists like Comte, Durkheim and Ozinga feel the need for altruism as a prerequisite for a better tomorrow. 'Doing good' is the inner motive of altruists. Sorokin's 'amitology' signifies "the applied science or art of developing friendship, mutual aid and love in individual and intergroup relations". His interpretation of altruistic love is unique. The 'good neighbours', he means, "a quest for sympathy, understanding, and inconsequent—the desire to find a co-sympathizer in either despair or loneliness—is just as strong in human beings as the need, for food or clothing". Jay Weinstein and Elvira del Pozo (2004: 119) in a recent study, observe, "altruism can mitigate if not solve many of the social problems encountered today, including such controversial issues as religious and ethnic intolerance welfare, aging, family crisis, health care, drug addiction, homelessness, and abortion".

Samuel P. Oliner (2007) deals with the relationship between altruism, empathy and forgiveness. Two hypotheses are relevant in this context. The respondents who score high on measures of altruism, spirituality/religiosity, empathy, social responsibility, moral identity and self-esteem are more likely to be forgiving and to help others and the respondents who score high on those same measures and who have been hurt or offended in some serious way will be more likely to forgive those who have harmed them. Respondents who receive high scores, and who have been hurt or offended, would be more altruistic and empathetic towards the harm-doers, was confirmed from his data. Although some studies show that 94 per cent of American people think that forgiveness is a very important part of healing in the community, only about 48 per cent have actually apologized and forgiven others. Oliner's study shows that 92 per cent of respondents have reported involvement in apology and forgiveness, stating that it helped restore good relationships with the harm-doer and also helped relieve their own pain and burden (cited in Dasgupta and Driskell, 2007).

William Kolb (1951: 268) rightly states, "The picture of modern society, which these men present, has tremendous relevance. Atomization, fragmentation, alienation, bureaucratization, terror, the loss of human choice—all are realities of our time... We must accept these predictions or show that sociology of possibility...". Similarly, Nelson Mandela (2003) states, "The world is undergoing a profound redefinition of values and modes of perception. The globalization of the world economy and the outstanding advances of communications technology have drawn all of us together into a smaller world. Those technical advances might, however, also have contributed to a growing confusion of values as people seek to find their localized places in that globalized world".

Globalization is not a new phenomenon. The seed of globalization sowed in 1893 with the happening of World's Columbian Exposition held in Chicago. It was aimed to present the truths and values of different religions of the world and to bring the nations of the earth into a more friendly interaction and unified values. Swami Vivekananda, the philosopher and the great monk in India, pointed out that the goal of human life is to become divine by manifesting the inmost divinity and moral and ethical values through every thought and action of ours. But sectarianism, bigotry, fanaticism and economic inequalization have possessed this beautiful earth. They have filled the earth with violence, drenched it with human blood, destroyed civilization and sent whole nations to despair. The speech of Swami Vivekananda is still alive to us. The ethics of globalization calls for individuals and communities that should care about the impact of one's actions on others—and the fairness of those impacts. It should unite peoples of common interests and values across nation-states. But, the mechanism of establishing the ethical interconnectedness that cares influence global actions to accord with its community and individual values, has not yet been explored. A few basic principles compose the foundation of human values upon which societies have been established. These are: the innate dignity of human life; respect and consideration for the 'other'; the interconnection between humankind and the environment and thus the need to care for and preserve the earth; the importance of integrity and service; an attitude of non-violence; the individual and collective quest for peace and happiness; and the movement to identify and promote the values shared by societies around the world is relatively new. It is only in recent years as globalization extended its reach to even remote corners of the earth that the need to refocus and build upon what we as a human society have in common, has become apparent.

Globalization has currently been seen to endanger cultural diversity and this would be a tragic loss for humankind. Increased contact between peoples and nations enhances awareness of our kinship and social bond and the shared code of ethics and conduct that underlies all civilization. It is these values that we must now promote to create a common vision and means for moving forward toward a more peaceful and sustainable world.

Amitai Etzioni (2004), in his outstanding work, *From Empire tc Community* speaks of 'good society'. The contemporary liberalists view that the formulation of 'good' should be left to each individual, and decisions as to what is right versus wrong should be left to the private realm. It means that the very notion of shared formulations of the good is at the heart of communitarian position, which, Etzioni argues, denies the difference between society and state. Etzioni, putting stress on communitarian conception of good society, mentions three basic features, viz., society that based on a crafted balance between autonomy and social order; re-examination of the balance and finally "the more the social order is based on moral; and informal social controls and the less on the state, and the more limited the scope of behaviors under the state's control, the closer the society is to a good one". I am very much convinced with Etzioni's (2004: 24) philosophical conviction that "the synthesis of autonomy with social order, a synthesis based largely on moral codes and normative controls, provides a better way". But who will take such a responsibility of making our society good? Is it civil society with good governance? But again I repeat how does it possible? How does a civil society control the moral and ethical consciousness of 'the rest'? In 1945, the founding of the United Nations gave the war-weary world a vision of what was possible in the arena of international cooperation and set a new standard by which to guide diverse peoples and nations towards a peaceful coexistence. Against the backdrop of the most calamitous war in human history, the creation of a world organization for the protection of the dignity, equal rights and security of all peoples and nations was an extraordinary feat of statecraft. Sixty years later, the questions that fuelled the San Francisco Conference assert themselves anew: Why have the current systems of governance failed to provide for the security, prosperity, and well-being of the world's people? What responsibilities do nations have towards their neighbours and their citizens? What fundamental values should guide relationships between and within nations to secure a peaceful future? What is more important is that the local values should be honoured and accepted by the global communities. A working balance between tradition and modernity should be included in the agenda of neo-globalization because both the value-orientation resides, in extreme opposite polls of time-space setting. Joseph Plummer (1989) compares traditional and new values. The pairs identified are: self-denial ethic/self-fulfilment ethic; higher standard of living/better quality of life; traditional sex roles/blurring of sex roles; accepted definition of success/individualized definition of success; traditional family life/alternative families; faith in industry, institutions/self-reliance; live to work/work to live; hero worship/love of ideas; expansionism/pluralism; patriotism/less nationalistic; unparalleled growth/growing sense of limits; industrial growth/information and service growth; and receptivity to technology/technology orientation.

Whether the issue is poverty, the proliferation of weapons, the role of women, AIDS, global trade, religion, environmental sustainability, the well-being of children, corruption, or the rights of minority populations—it is clear that none of the problems facing humanity can be adequately addressed in isolation from the other. Values and religious formulae have ceased to promote the welfare of mankind. The advancement of men and boys at the expense of women and girls has sorely limited the creative and material capacities of communities to develop and address their problems; the neglect of cultural and religious minorities has intensified ancient prejudices setting peoples and nations against one another; an unbridled nationalism has trampled the rights and opportunities of citizens in other nations; weak states have erupted in conflict, lawlessness and massive refugee flows; and narrow economic agendas exalting material prosperity have often suffocated the social and moral development required for the equitable and beneficent use of wealth. Such crises have laid bare the limits of traditional approaches to governance and put before the United Nations the inescapable question of values: which values are capable of guiding the nations and peoples of the world out of the chaos of competing interests and ideologies towards a world community capable of inculcating the principles of justice and equity at all levels of human society? The question of values and their inextricable link to systems of religion and belief has emerged on the world stage as a subject of consuming global importance, which the global initiators cannot afford to ignore. The emerging global order, and the processes of globalization that define it, must be founded on the principle of the oneness of humankind. The principle of the oneness of humankind does not seek to undermine national autonomy or suppress the cultural and intellectual diversity of the peoples and nations of the world. Rather, it seeks to broaden the basis of the existing foundations of society by calling for a wider loyalty, a greater aspiration than any that has animated the human race. Indeed, it provides the moral impetus needed to remould the institutions of governance in a manner consistent with the needs of an ever-changing world. Is there reason to worry about values as a result of the ongoing globalization? Thomas Friedman seems to think so. In his recent book, *The Lexus and the Olive Tree*, Friedman dramatizes the conflict of "the Lexus and the olive tree"—the tension between the globalization system and ancient forces of culture, geography, tradition and community.

Values and Postmodern Shock

Chaplin's film *Modern Times* is an ironical smile of the gift of modernization. The postmodern debate recently dominates over the intellectual arena. It mainly penetrates the cultural and aesthetic field and the focal theme of the debate is whether or not the tradition has closed its chapter. The postmodern specialty, rejecting the traditional social, cultural, moral and aesthetic versions, has now stepped into the world of new discourse and new rationality. In each and every era this process unfolds similarly. But analysis of postmodernism mostly pinpoints the surface rather than the depth of concerns. But it is the reality that people in any age always like the previous one and they always call the previous age golden. Likely, the people in the modern age following the instinctive paradigm of goodness of human quality favour traditional age and the postmodern men would like the previous one, i.e., modernity. Sociological theories therefore suffer from language vertigo. In society, polemics emerged over whether tradition in culture, economics and polity was dead or what sort of modernization was succeeding. In case of metamorphosis from modernism to postmodernism the same twist of rationality and communicative language happens. We are now on the crossroads of debate whether modernization has closed its chapter or emerged with new philosophy, new discourse and new rationality. Sociologists are mostly confused with the concept of such metamorphosis. First of all, we should know whether the metamorphosis happens only in the case of language, of thinking, or in the case of the reality of social living and moral values. Whether the realities of values are changing or should not be the prime concern of applied sociology. Practically, the time has come to examine the hidden nature of such value vertigo. If we back to our original roots, we could notice that sociology was very much concerned with the idea of progress, values, humanity, freedom and peace.

A fish cannot live without water. Likewise, a man cannot survive without his identity, social, moral and ethical values and tradition. T.S. Eliot quotes, "Tradition is not solely or even primarily the maintenance of certain dogmatic beliefs, these beliefs have come to take their living form in the course of the formation of tradition". Many people around the world fear that globalization brings the decay of social values. India is a multi-cultural, spiritually diverse country, now very much engaged in the global economy, culture and technology and a country where globalization is much more than a concept; it is the reality of our everyday lives. We are living in the era of profound social, economic and cultural change. Rapid changes are taking place not only in the institutional settings but also in the mental frame of human beings. Achievement, aspiration and motivation are shifting very promptly. Time has taken its place over space. It is running like *"Run Lola Run"*. Technology and knowledge dominate over humanity. All are suffering from a peculiar and unpredictable hyper real vertigo. The philosophers call it postmodern shock.

Starting by the end of the 1960s and rapidly accelerating into the 21st century, technological, economical, political and other forces have crafted a world in which this interdependence has reached an unprecedented level. In his 1999 Reith lectures, Anthony Giddens labelled this globalizing world a 'runaway world'. "We live," so he says, "in a world of transformations, affecting almost every aspect of what we do". It is my privilege to take note of a few cases in this runway world. When the values change with the emergence of a new society and new culture the value myth appears as a crisis. Globalization brings such a value crisis in our society. It not only violates the norms of culture tradition but also dislocates the old values from its orthodox orbit. For example, our family system has been changed radically; most of our families are becoming the cathedrals of consumerism; our interaction ties with our children has been turned into a new mode; the marriage system has been disintegrated and most of the young desire to lead a very restive life; our style of living has mostly become striving or vicarious; we are very much concerned with our heads not with our hearts; and our culture is becoming more and more malignant in terms of marginality arising from the postmodern vertigo. Below we can comfortably cite a few cases from our society, which represent how our traditional values are becoming devalued:

Case 1

By this time when I am writing this book a good number of married young in our country are compelling their old parents to take shelter in the old age homes. To have the opportunity of enjoying the taste of consumerism, runway world and technological gadgets, they are not ready to share those with their parents or other members of family. The rise of individualism and selfish attitude thus create value hazard. This is unthinkable for our predecessors and we people. Japan, a country with globalization boom, experiences such a value trauma. Recently, the elderly people in Japan are using Robots as their grandsons and granddaughters to get rid of the punishment of loneliness. This is really horrible than Jurassic Park or Blade Runner. Robots as grand kids are very much present to them in terms of virtual reality but in reality they are totally absent. Is this not value crisis in the era of globalization?

Case 2

The young of our society show a trend of ignoring their family of procreation. The parents are becoming the victims of poverty, loneliness and helplessness. Let me quote from Dante's "Inferno": "The motto on the gate of hell was: abandon all hopes, ye, who enter herein". Most of the parents across the world are likely subjected to such a paralysis of hopelessness and helplessness.

Case 3

Economy and love are the dual aspects of the same process. They are the kindred phenomenon. Let me narrate a story, which is not sociological but more than sociology: In a community there is a ritual. When someone dies, the neighbours supply grand food to the family members of the deceased for a few days. There was a family consisting of father, mother and two sons. The head of the family was a daily labourer. After his death there was nobody to look after the family. They were in great distress and were the victims of starvation. But they could not feel the future because of having meals from their neighbours. Only the expiry of the term of ritual they began to feel the pains of starvation and extreme poverty. One day the little boy asked his mother, "Can you say Mom when my brother will die?" This is not a story of either virtual reality or hyper reality. This is the actual value crisis that emerges from economic illness in the Third World countries.

The global dimension also influences communications and interactions on an individual and interpersonal level: (1) the one-sidedness (biased and limited) of economic globalization; (2) a generalized environmental crisis; (3) worldwide social and cultural disintegration; (4) the rise of racism and xenophobia; (5) the sclerosis of lifestyles and life forms; (6) the disruption of social protection; (7) the spreading of migration; (8) the violation of moral cohesion; (9) the erosion of the nation-state; (10) the growth of media dictated mass consumption; (11) a scientistic ideology; and (12) a strictly utilitarian obsessions of narrow material progress—all of them unaccompanied by a spiritual evolution and a moral development of mankind.

The social and political evolutions during this era of globalization, as has been said before, are giving rise to a moral disarray and cynicism, as can be heard in phrases and laments like 'the end of modernity', 'against ethics', 'the closing down of humanism', 'simulacra fashioned human existence', 'moral aestheticism and relativism', and so on.

Another factor fuelling this moral perplexity of our age is the radicalization of the tension between a much needed long-term vision for human aspirations on the one hand and the always threatening urgency and short-term applicability of policies, on the other. The moral perplexity of the era of globalization has rendered us, in the words of Jerome Bindé, a 'temporal myopia'.

Catastrophe Looming in the Third World

The dangers hanging over humanity are already clearly apparent in the dependent countries. Here, barbarism is already at work. Capitalism cannot be judged simply by looking at the living conditions of a small minority of the world's population—the middle classes and the highest paid workers in the richest countries—while closing one's eyes to the living conditions of the large majority of people in the capitalist countries.

Apart from a few exceptions, the semi-colonial and dependent countries have suffered a disastrous decline in living standards over the last ten years. A regularly employed wage worker often earns each year the equivalent of an average monthly or even weekly wage in the imperialist centres.

In the Third World countries, 15 million children die every year from hunger, malnutrition and the lack of health care and medicines.

Pollution is now being deliberately exported from the imperialist heartlands to Third World countries, which are becoming a cheap dustbin for dangerous, non-recyclable industrial waste. This means growing desertification, faster destruction of tropical rainforests and the transfer to these countries of industries that are particularly harmful to the environment, which rapidly creates even worse ecological disasters than those already affecting the richer countries. The population of South Asia (India, Pakistan and Bangladesh) has increased by 900 million since 1945, whereas Australia and Canada have still a combined population of less than 50 million.

While the Indian sub-continent of India, Pakistan and Bangladesh with 387.3 million hectares of land will see a population increase of 531 million between 1998 and 2025, the three quasi sub-continents of Australia, Canada, and Russia and Ukraine with 3,437.1 million hectares of land will experience a population decrease of 9.3 millions. The Indian sub continent is an area of great malnutrition, in which a good number of the 800 million undernourished people of the world live. The population of China increased from 927.8 million in 1975 to 1,255.7 million in 1998, and is estimated to be 1,417.7 million by 2015. This means an increase of 327.9 million in 23 years (UNDP Human Development Report, 2000; OUP, 2000). This has been at the human price of compelling this one-fifth of the human race not to have more than one child per family.

Due to population increases in the poorer countries, there is less land available for the agricultural production in spite of an increase in the total area under cultivation. Not only that some figures hide the hundreds of thousands of acres owned by

Western and Japanese multinational corporations in the poor countries.

Inequities in the relationship of population to land will worsen in the coming decades, because the populations of the affluent countries are not growing at all, or not so rapidly as in the countries of Asia, Africa and Latin America. Secondly, the 'more developed regions' have an ageing population. It is estimated that Europe will need an additional population intake of about 75 million in the coming 50 years in order to maintain its workforce and provide for the pensions and social securities for its elderly population. To meet this need European immigration policies encourage the immigration of skilled youthful human power from the southern countries. The USA, Canada and Australia follow similar immigration policies. This is a form of brain drain from the poor to the rich countries. What is the justice in this situation? It demands of human solidarity.

10 War Industry and Humanity

For over the hundreds of years great people like Jesus Christ, Mahatma Gandhi, Martin Luther King, Rabindra Nath Tagore, Nelson Mandela, Huzzarut Mohammad, Vivekananda, Dante, Goethe and others have been trying to say that, this planet does not belong to us and it is not our private property. Humanity belongs to the Universe. ... All things are connected like the blood that unites us all; like the rivers, forests, seas, waters of the Universe unite Planet Earth. Humanity did not weave the web of life, they are merely strands in it, and whatever they do to the web, they do to themselves.

In T1 and T2, the Terminator movies, showed an android that symbolized a whole world of computers and other robots that desired to annihilate or enchain humanity and remodel the planet to the machine's needs. And, interestingly this fiction comes into reality. Our world had witnessed two great Wars which invited modernity on the one hand and had damaged against human rights, on the other. Now, it may claim that modernization means a dehumanized enchanting world. Starting with the Jews to the hunting of Afghans and Iraqi people justifies that truth. The great bombing in Hiroshima and Nagasaki, the Japanese attack on Pearl Harbor, the Gulf war, the attack of Americans on Iraq and Afghanistan with bureaucratic and technologically enriched weapons and war machinery are the symbols of modernity. So it is undeniable that modernism began at the cost of human lives. During a single quarter century, for the first time in the world's history, imperialism unleashed two world wars. World War I claimed 20 million lives, more than all of the European wars for the three preceding centuries. During the 17th century 3.3 million persons, during the 18th century, 5.4 million persons and from 1901 to 1914, 5.7 million peoples died in wars on European territory (Dadayan, 1988).

During World War II, which was waged on the territory of forty countries, 55 million people were killed and 35 million were severely injured, of which 25 million remained physically handicapped for life. In the field of social science it may be argued that modernization has entered with a political power equation. Rise and fall of the superpowers, the trend of political domination and economic superiority are the prime but hidden causes and effects of modernization. So it can be assumed that political modernization with the help of technological innovations and diffusions shape and remake world economy. But what is the contribution of modernity to the human development? Is it a 'species-threatening' phenomenon? Is the other name for modernization *inequalization*? Dadayan (1988: 7) rightly states, "Viewed not from cosmic distances, but only on the ground, at the level they actually exist, socio-economic relations prove to be a web of striking and violent contradictions threatening to annual modern civilization altogether and tragicomic ones arousing an ironic smile like the films of the great Chaplin". The war industry appears as a demon in the era of globalization. It has already defaced humanity and closes the opportunity of opening up of dialogues with the global players. They have already placed globalization on trial. The global players' war against Afghanistan, Gaza or Iraq cannot be justified on the facts or the law. It is clearly illegal. It constitutes armed aggression. It is creating a humanitarian catastrophe for the people of those regions and creating dreadful regional wavering. "Lacking humility, will we ever apologize to the parents of those 5,00,000 children who starved as a result of our sanctions? Quite the contrary, we justify ourselves and claim that it was worth it: In addition, will we ever apologize for the birth defects accelerating cancers, or other toxic diseases caused by our depleted uranium weapons of mass inhumanity?" (Deanna Spingola, 2006, http://www.renewamerica.us/columns/spingola/060612)

It is irrefutable that one of the stimulating bonanzas of globalization is war. I call it globalization of war not humanity and the uncontrollable eruptions of overheated global war forebode tragedy for humanity. At present, we are suffering from food crisis and waiting for a doomsday. But we are two footstep advance regarding military expenses. We want war not food, we want to accumulate more and more money at the cost of human lives. By 1987–1996 the military expenditure in South Asian countries increased to 13 per cent and 90 per cent of this utilized in Pakistan and India. In case of Iraq, Iran, Israel, Jordon and other Middle East countries the military budget increased to nearly 11 per cent. In case of Thailand, Indonesia, Malaysia and Philippines it increased to 35 per cent of the total development budget. The following tables illustrate the global priority which shows the negative trend of development and it is implied from the priority list that global players want war, not humanity.

Table 1

Global Priority	*$US Billion*
Cosmetics in the United States	8
Ice cream in Europe	11
Perfumes in Europe and the United States	12
Pet foods in Europe and the United States	17
Business entertainment in Japan	35
Cigarettes in Europe	50
Alcoholic drinks in Europe	105
Narcotics drugs in the world	400
Military spending in the world	780

If we compare the priority from the human needs that we demand it shows that war is the opposite version of humanity which we now demand.

Table 2

Global Priority	*$US Billion*
Basic education for all	6
Water and sanitation for all	9
Reproductive health for all women	12
Basic health and nutrition	13

Source: The State of Human Development, United Nations Human Development Report 1998, Chapter 1, p. 37.

It would seem sarcastic that the world expends more on things to annihilate each other (military) and to destroy ourselves (drugs, alcohol and cigarettes) and some basic needs. James Madison (1795) states, "Of all the enemies to public liberty, war is, perhaps, the most to be dreaded because it comprises and develops the germ of every other. War is the parent of armies; from these proceed debts and taxes ... known instruments for bringing the many under the domination of the few.... No nation could preserve its freedom in the midst of continual warfare". Alarmed at the estimated $1 trillion in global military expenditures in 2004, Bangladesh's Foreign Secretary, in a 2005 debate of UN, said that "resources had been deployed to devise instruments of death, rather than for growth and prosperity, and there was no doubt about the direct relationship between disarmament and development. Most of those expenditures had been the result of an unfortunate arms race, which was negatively affecting the development agenda. The major military powers should curb military spending and devote part of the resources saved to the development of the developing countries".

If you assess inhumane and appalling impact of war, you cannot call globalization good; rather, it is a globalization error. If you could see the photographs of war, you will see that more than five crore of people are homeless and shelterless, and more than ten crore of people are the victims of extreme poverty. As we look at the Gaza killings with dismay, shocked at how the crisis is spiralling further out of control, one thing is clear—this hostility will only lead to further civilian anguish and a boom of the conflict.

It is evident from the call of Avaaz that after Gaza's bloodiest day in recent remembrance and eight or more years of ineffective US and global diplomacy, we need to ask world leaders to do more than just issuing statements if they are to ensure a lasting ceasefire. Through the international bodies, "the world can provide the help and pressure needed to stop the violence and change the situation on the ground in Gaza—preventing the rockets and incursions, re-opening crossing-points under international oversight so that instead of weapon-smuggling, the 1.5 million ordinary people of Gaza can get the fuel, food and medicines they so desperately need." It is the good task to work together to bring an end to this violence and establish global peace, which is the basis of humanity. It is the talk of the era that across the world, most people want stronger protections for the environment, greater respect for human rights, and intensive endeavours to wipe out poverty, illiteracy, violence, misgivings, corruption and war. Yet globalization faces a gigantic democratic dearth as international decisions are shaped by political elites and inexplicable corporations—not the visions and values of the global people.

The ethnic conflict of Rwanda between Hutu and Tutsi signalled a dark night of globalization. In this conflict only 8,000 Tutsis of the total 2,50,000 population remained left. The children were the most affected victims of war. It is reported from various sources that more than 20 lakh of children were killed in war; 1.10 crore became shelterless, 40 lakh became deformed and more than 1 crore are now mentally disbalanced. Is it humanity? A 16 years boy Susan wrote to the representative of UNICEF, "One boy tried to escape (from the rebels), but he was caught....His hands were tied, and then they made us, the other new captives, kill him with a stick. I knew this boy from before. We were from the same village. I refused to kill him and they told me they would shoot me. They pointed a gun at me, so I had to do it. The boy was asking me, "Why are you doing this'? I said I had no choice. After we killed him, they made us smear his blood on our arms.... They said we had to do this so we would not fear death and so we not try to escape... I still dream about the boy... I killed. I see him in my dreams, and he is talking to me and saying I killed him for nothing and I am crying. Is it humanity that we desire?" Kenneth Phifer declares, "Humanism teaches us that it is immoral to wait for God to act for us. We must act to stop the wars and the crimes and the brutality of this and future ages. We have powers of a remarkable kind. We have a high degree of freedom in choosing what we will do. Humanism tells us that whatever our philosophy of the universe may be, ultimately the responsibility for the kind of world in which we live rests with us".

In the era of globalization we are not only missing our humanity, we are also missing our humbleness, an accurate feeling of our affiliation to God and the other people who occupy an increasingly tainted earth. Albert Einstein says, "Since the advent of the Nuclear Age, everything has changed but the way people think, thus, we drift towards unparalleled catastrophe". Tolstoy speaks that war is an overwhelmingly wild human endeavour. Generals, journalists and politicians continue to assume it is a science, a matter of vectors and the measurement of force. The irrational must be made rational before men can feel themselves in control of events. Perhaps that is why war is so often portrayed as a game or sporting event, the battlefield as an extension of the playing fields of Eton. Tolstoy was right. War is irrational, and it is this aspect of the war that is so often lacking in the accounts written from and about the battlefields. "Viet Nam has been at blazing war for 27 years. There is hardly a person anywhere in Indochina who has not been touched directly, in one way or another, by the fighting. Mothers have lost sons and daughters. Sons have lost fathers and mothers. Farms, homes, towns, cities have been destroyed. The touches every young man between 18 and 35—except those who can bribe their way out. And the war, of course, touches everyone in subtle ways that erode the soul. Wives have lost husbands, brothers have lost brothers, and lovers have lost lovers. Yet it does not end, and does not even show signs of ending" (Stanley Cloud, 1972).

Source: (http://www.time.com/time/magazine/article/0,9171,877681,00.html)

Oscar Wilde states, "Most people are other people". This philosophy of human race creates the division of mindset and invites hostility and war. The division of we-people and other-people brings war catastrophe. From the inception of *Homo sapiens* we are cruel by nature. "There is a wolf in me". We have acquired both the traits of rationality as well as animality. Globalization process adds the fuel, and in the guise of creating humane communication and singleness, the global players stretch their hegemonic hands to dominate over the globe and they also begin snatching the natural resources from the Third World countries. The result is the war in Afghanistan, in Iraq. Now, the ruler rules not with virtue but with force. The Universal Declaration of Human Rights, in its first article, states that "all human beings are born free and equal in dignity and rights". But this contradicts with the wars in Afghanistan and Iraq. It is evident from a report (http://www.worldtribunal.org/main/) that "during the Gulf War in January 1991, the US Armed Forces dropped 320 tons of depleted uranium weapons on Iraq. Since after the war, there has been a high incidence of strange phenomenon not seen in Iraq before the war. There have been several incidences of such phenomenon as several members of one family developing cancer, or one patient having several types of cancer, etc., cancer that spreads fast, the outbreak of infectious diseases due to fast spreading cancer, leukemia, aplastic anemia, and malignant tumor, and immunodeficiency, massive herpes, and symptoms resembling AIDS, syndrome due to liver and kidney dysfunction, hereditary dysphasia (hereditary damage) due to gene defects. Children, especially infants, who cannot fight back and are blameless, have become the number one victims of this war. The southern city of Basra, which is near the battleground of the Gulf War, has been very seriously damaged, and according to a doctor at the Basra Educational Hospital, the number of people who have succumbed to cancer rose from 34 in 1988 prior to the Gulf War to the astonishing figure of 603 in 2001 that was 17 times larger". The humanitarian crisis in Iraq and Afghanistan is reaching shocking levels, says the International Committee of the Red Cross. The health care facilities and economic conditions are in a very grave condition. People suffer of food shortages and malnutrition. The conflict is inflicting immense suffering on the entire population. Iraq's death rate has risen sharply. A mounting figure of Iraqi population is being forced to depart their homes and most of the residents are now fatally at risk. According to UNHCR, there are 1.9 million internally displaced people in the country and 2 million refugees escaped to neighbouring countries, especially Syria and Jordan. Unemployment and poverty rose sharply, too. According to the United Nations Development Programme, one-third of the population now lives in poverty. Education has broken down. Further, Iraqis basic needs of drinking water, food, sanitation and electricity are not met. Hospitals lack basic medical supplies and are understaffed.

Source: (http://www.globalpolicy.org/security/issues/iraq/attack/crisisindex.htm)

It is evident from BBC News, November 8, 2007 that tens of thousands of people have died in Iraq since the US-led invasion of March 2003. But exactly how many Iraqi lives have been lost is a controversial issue. More than 4,000 coalition soldiers have died, but US forces do not keep complete records of civilians killed. Nor does the Iraqi government have a precise figure. Health ministry estimates in November 2006 ranged from 1,00,000 to 1,50,000 dead. This contrasts with a survey of Iraqi households in the Lancet, which suggested that by July 2006 about 6,55,000 Iraqi deaths were 'a consequence of the war'. Another survey published in September 2007 suggested that up to 1.2 million people might have died because of the conflict.

Source: (http://news.bbc.co.uk/2/hi/in_depth/629/629/7036068.stm).

The UNICEF report (2008) cites a tragic story of the crisis of humanity in Afghanistan. The report states, "Afghanistan has been in a state of complex emergency for over the past twenty years. The country's infrastructure and systems have been largely destroyed. An estimated 22 million Afghans, or 70 per cent of the population, live in poverty and substandard conditions. 40 per cent children less than three years old are underweight and 54 per cent of under five are stunted. Over 1,00,000 people—most of them children and women—remain displaced by conflict and drought. The security situation in the country is deteriorating; more areas have fallen into active military operation zones between the government/coalition forces and Anti-Government Elements (AGE), which hampers humanitarian operations and access to affected populations. In 2007, approximately 40–50 per cent of the districts in the country were not accessible to UN missions for extended periods due to insecurity and movement restrictions".

Source: (http://www.unicef.org/infobycountry/afghanistan_31224.html)

Violence in wars and ethnic conflicts have generated millions of refugees across the globe with unbelievable pictures of suffering and unnecessary death. Wars and civil conflicts are taking a massive toll on children. The numbers, though imprecise, are devastating: approximately 2 million children have been killed during the last decade, and between 4 million and 5 million disabled. Twelve million more have been uprooted from their homes, and countless others face the heightened risk of disease and malnutrition and of separation from their families (UNICEF, 1996).

War must be faced and checked, and such crimes against humanity must be brought to justice. How could this have been achieved without inflicting further violence and terror on more innocent civilians? Could global terrorism have been addressed more effectively by not calling it a new war, by not demanding that all other countries support the USA or be deemed "against the US?" Might the response of bombing Afghanistan prove less effective than many other diverse strategies? Why was the bombing combined with the now much-criticized dropping of surplus US packaged foods? And, as prominent Dutch business leader, Wouter van Dieren asks, "Would the 6,000 victims killed at the World Trade Center have wished that 5,00,000 innocent Afghan civilians should suffer so much vengeance in their name?" (Henderson, 2001)

Subcomandante Marcos (2001) states in a conference: "Who are they who dare to let their dreams meet with all the dreams of the world? What is happening in the mountains of the Mexican southeast that finds an echo and a mirror in the streets of Europe, the suburbs of Asia, the countryside of America, the townships of Africa, and the houses of Oceania? What is it that is happening with the peoples of these five continents who, so we are all told, only encounter each other to compete or make war? Wasn't this turn of the century synonymous with despair, bitterness, and cynicism? From where and how did all these dreams come to La Realidad?"

May Europe, Asia, Oceania, America and other countries across the globe speak and explain the causes of wars and motives of making the 'rest' the victims of inhuman war disaster. May humanity suspend for a moment its silence of shame and anguish! May humanity speak! May humanity listen! Why do each nation, each city, each village, each house and each person becomes a ground of conflict and violence? On the one side is neo-liberalism with all its repressive power and all its machinery of death; on the other side is the human being.

"In any place in the world, anytime, any man or woman rebels to the point of tearing off the clothes that resignation have woven for them and cynicism has dyed grey. Any man or woman, of whatever colour, in whatever tongue, speaks and says to himself, to herself: 'Enough is enough!'" (Marcos, 2001).

The anti-globalization movement is an effort to counter the perceived negative aspects of the actually existing process of globalization. Although adherents of the movement often work in concert, the movement itself is heterogeneous and includes diverse, sometimes opposing, understandings of this process, alternative visions, strategies and tactics. The neo-liberal capitalist administration has the wind in the sails with conquest of Afghanistan and Iraq. By globalization we mean a better tomorrow, not beating of swords or firing explosives into masses and ploughshares. By globalization we mean ethically and morally governance oriented industries, not expansion of military industries. Toffler (1993: 1) notes, "We appear to be plunging in a new dark age....... and wars multiplied by wars. How we deal with this threat of explosive violence will, to a considerable extent, determine how our children live or, perhaps, for that matter, die". Ideologies based on the extension of capitalism in the guise of perceiving diversity, space-time compression, free trade, altruistic aidocracy (aid industries!) humanism and singleness appear as a synonym of enmity and threat. The capitalist's regimentalism in recent Afghanistan and Iraq unmasked the anarchy of globalization. "Where innocents lost their lives because their only fault was to be different from their murderers, the large majority of humanity realized that no justification could be invented" (Picco, 2001: 35). The perpetrators of such attacks symbolize not the clash of civilizations but its end. Globalization has spawned multidimensional forms of uncertainty about ethnic identity, which create new kinds of ethnic and communal violence. In the large-scale ethnic wars of the 1980s and 1990s, cross-border movements of refugees, implosions of nationalist politics, fears of economic chaos and rumours of tyrannical autochtonies have produced large-scale ethnic violence involving extreme forms of bodily brutality. Widely dispersed terrorist networks now present one of the most serious challenges to the capitalists. Dauglas Kellner (2002) claims that the experience of September 11 points to the objective ambiguity of globalization, that positive and negative sides are interconnected, that the institutions of the open society unlock the possibilities of destruction and violence, as well as democracy, free trade, and cultural and social exchange. They attempt to use chemical, biological, radiological and nuclear weapons, which are the products of technological advance. The terrorist movements in the US, UK, Pakistan, Central Asia,

Southeast Asia, Africa, Gulf States. Afghanistan, Iraq, Libya, North Korea, Iran, China, Russia, and the potential regions for instability like Nigeria, Sudan, Brazil, Colombia, Costa Rica, Ecuador, Mexico, Nicaragua, Peru, and Venezuela, Columbia, Indonesia, Philippines where the risk of escalation, the sources think, is very high—all signify the expressions of deviant globalization where the rich can be more richer and the poor poorer. In a word the concept of 'war on terror' is just a buzzword to the depressed majorities and they are not thinking about the end of history or clash of civilization, rather they are afraid of economic and humane phobia. In the attack on the World Trade Center and in the continuing battering of the valleys, cities and caves of Afghanistan by the US-led alliance we see a state-led extension of these forms of vivisectionist violence which the capitalists or global initiators call 'diagnostic wars'. A diagnostic war is a war in which major acts of violence are intended to both discover and decimate the enemy. In the name of identifying masks they have done the brutal act of mass destruction. Is it for banishing terrorism, which is their creation, or to extend their touch of power to complete their unfinished project of globalization? The blueprint of American internationalism mainly focuses on the expansion of economic development which includes good governance, reduction of tariffs, removal of corruptions, proper utilization of capital and fair economic policies. The countries, which fail to achieve the policies, will be referred to as 'rogue state'. Is this the only reason to change regime in Afghanistan and Iraq? No, there was nothing to preach but only occupation with a view to material gains, i.e., oil. The Middle East is still viewed as the highest oil producing countries in the world (i.e., 66%).

The Bush Administration's war against Afghanistan, Iraq and others cannot be justified on the facts or the law. It is clearly illegal. It constitutes armed violence. It is creating a humanitarian upheaval for the people of Afghanistan. Boyle (2001) states, "It is creating dreadful regional instability. Right now we are having artillery barrages across the border between India and

Pakistan which have fought two wars before over Kashmir and yet today are nuclear armed. The longer this war goes on, the worse it is going to be not only for the millions of people in Afghanistan but also in the estimation of the 1.2 billion Muslims of the world and the 57 Muslim states in the world, none of whom believe the Bush administration's propaganda that this is not a war against Islam".

It can be assumed that the war on Afghanistan and Iraq is not just a war but a war for oil. Anti-globalization activists raised their heads against such a deadly war. The movement of anti-globalization across the world now transformed into an anti-war movement. The globalization on the one hand and war on the other are now the dual aspects of the same process of neo-capitalism and capitalistic expansion.

A friendly alliance is established between multinational corporations and global initiators, which is termed as 'crony capitalism'—a deadly friendship for the deprived majorities. Table 3 yields such a reality:

Table 3

Global Income of Some Multinational Corporations, 2001

($US billion)

MNCs	*Income*	*Capital*	*Wealth*
Wallmart	220	7	83
Exon Mobil	192	15	143
General Motors	178	0.6	323
British Petroleum	174	8	141
Ford Motors	162	– 5	277
Enron	139	NA	NA
Dailmer Critchler	137	– 0.6	185
Royal Dutch	135	11	112
General Elec	126	14	495
Toyota Motor	121	5	150
City Group	112	14	1,000
Mitsubishi	106	0.5	61

Cont'd...

Cont'd...

Mitsui	101	0.4	50
Shovran Texaco	100	3	76
Total fina Elf	94	7	79

Source: Fortune, July 22, 2002.

Nelson Mandela (January 31, 2003) writes, "All that [Bush] wants is Iraq oil". When the policies and ethics of neo-globalization are echoing the message of equality, new economic order, distributive social justice, and global anti-war sentiment, then, the third world is being driven 'into' a nearly dead end. This is perhaps for the first time the protestors are raising their voices: "human of this world, unite" against war. This episode might be the gift of globalization. Serious observers of the anti-globalization movement know that it is not just an anti-poverty crusade. It is not just about debt relief, fair trade, reducing the gap between rich and poor, or environmentally sustainable development, though all these are a part of it. It is about protecting and building democracy, community and identity.

Sharon Burrow, President of the Australian Council of Trade Unions, recently said at the World Economic Forum in Melbourne: "If companies continue to carve up the world and unchecked capital speculation makes the securities of communities increasingly volatile, then the tide of protest against globalization in its current form will grow". It is about changing a system that has been grossly unfair to the developing world, and has eroded individual and collective economic choices even in the industrialized world. The protest movement with the motive of viewing an alternative path of resisting capitalist implosion spread like fire in the global arena. The millions of protestors throughout the world gathered voicing anger and hatred against capitalist expansionism. In fact, so little protest that few people even remember. The present-day protest movement against war perhaps indicates either the positive sign of fair globalization or it is an expression of fear psychosis for uncertain and alien future. Of course, some activists in the movement are opposed to neo-liberalism, and international institutions that promote it, such as the World Bank, Organization for Economic Cooperation and Development (OECD) World Trade Organization (WTO), International Monetary Fund (IMF), and the North American Free Trade Agreement (NAFTA), Free Trade Area of the Americas (FTAA), the Multilateral Agreement on Investments (MAI) and the General Agreement on Trade in Services (GATS), the World Economic Forum (WEF), the Trans Atlantic Business Dialogue (TABD) and the Asia Pacific Economic Forum (APEC), as well as the governments which promote these agreements, institutions and policies. Still others argue that, if borders are opened to capital, they should be similarly opened to allow free and legal circulation and choice of residence for migrants and refugees. We stand at the threshold of an open door of global social order. The wave of globalization is rolling. The global initiators say, "The future is here". We have to settle how we will respond to such given movement? Will we struggle with the wave for an alternative? Or will we try to move ahead with the changing, always-moving-ahead world? Marshall McLuhan (1962) says, "When faced with a totally new situation, we tend always to attach ourselves to the objects, to the flavor of the most recent past. We look at the present through a rear-view mirror. We march backwards into the future". One futurologist argues that the future is permanently discontinuous from the past. It is no longer predictable. It is hardly forecastable. While we can't predict the future; it is the outcome of the present episodes, and actually existing orders. The late American President John F. Kennedy, himself a man of great vision, said, "Some men see things as they are and ask, 'Why?' Others see them as they could be and ask, 'Why not?' The vision of Kennedy was great and noble. But, such a rhetoric symphony is not acceptable to the deprived majorities who die in starvation and toil under broiling sun from morning till dusk for miserable rewards and always face a very slow and agonizing death. They always want to be one of the 'some' who see things as they are and ask 'why?' Why such a disparity? Wallerstein (2003) argues, "We move into the uncertain immediate future, and in moment of systemic anarchy such as the present, almost anything can happen". The tendencies, which Wallerstein foresees, are commitment of US government to a unilateral rather progressive foreign policy; European integration will proceed increasingly but with difficulty and there will be a distance between US and Europe; China, Korea and Japan will come more closer; nuclear proliferation in the South will continue and aggravate; and the Port of Alegre will be more militant and solid. He claims that the democracy will be in a state of uncertainty and the human society in the future will be more egalitarian.

The journey of humanity is the journey from darkness to light, from war to peace, from starvation to livelihood, from moral decay to moral cohesion, and from hatred to peace. Ness diazValentin (2006) notes:

> If humanity sees globalization as a method to help civilization become peaceful, honest, trustworthy individuals and really completely reorganize and reinvent what we know today as the economic system then globalization is the way to go. Civilization will learn to value humanity as well as the entire universe much more than a piece of paper (money), a rock (diamonds), metals (platinum, gold, cars), trees (houses, transportation)... Does humanity needs 10,000 different models of cars? Does humanity needs 19,000 models of computers? How much is too expensive? How much is too cheap? To me the word economy only means that we should economize (consume less) but to economize we need to consume not only less food but less electricity, less gasoline, less consumerism... Maybe, civilization as we know it today and had know it in the past, needs extinction like what happened with the dinosaurs so a more sophisticated, peaceful, honest civilization will emerge. Only 1 per cent of civilization is bad or how I refer to it they are making mistakes...the rest 99 per cent are good and teaching the 1 per cent how to correct the mistakes they are making.

The war of Afghanistan depicts a rather sordid picture of defaced globalization. Boyle (2001) states:

"Clearly, what is going on now in Afghanistan is not self-defense. Let's be honest. We all know it. At best, this is reprisal, retaliation, vengeance, catharsis—call it what you want. It is not self-defense. And retaliation is never self-defense. Indeed, that was the official position of the United States government. Even during the darkest days of the Vietnam War, when former Under Secretary of State Eugene V. Rosca tried to get the State Department to switch their position, they refused and continued to maintain, no, retaliation is not self-defense. And this is not self-defense what we are doing in Afghanistan." After the United States began its attacks against Iraq, FOX News actually reported the immediate comments of the Holy Father, made in an address at the Vatican to members of an Italian religious television channel, Telespace: "When war, as in these days in Iraq, threatens the fate of humanity, it is ever more urgent to proclaim, with a strong and decisive voice, that only peace is the road to follow to construct a more just and united society." John Paul said, "Violence and arms can never resolve the problems of man" (available at http://www.cjd.org/paper/jp2war.html). So, it is undeniable that "we are the juncture of the most serious crisis in modern history. The Bush Administration has embarked upon a military adventure which threatens the future of humanity."

The wars on Afghanistan and Iraq are part of a broader military agenda, which was launched at the end of the Cold War. The ongoing war agenda is a continuation of the 1991 Gulf War and the NATO-led wars on Yugoslavia (1991–2001). The post-Cold War period has also been marked by numerous US covert intelligence operations within the former Soviet Union, which were instrumental in triggering civil wars in several of the former republics, including Chechnya (within the Russian Federation), Georgia and Azerbaijan. In the latter, these covert operations were launched with a view to securing strategic control over oil and gas pipeline corridors. US military and intelligence operations in the post-Cold War era were led in close coordination with the 'free market reforms' imposed under IMF guidance in Eastern Europe, the former Soviet Union and the Balkans, which resulted in the destabilization of national economies and the impoverishment of millions of people" (Chossudovsky, 2003).

The global ethics, as conceived by the theoretical leaders, are longing and striving for peace, longing and striving for justice, longing and striving for partnership, longing and striving for truth. Human solidarity in the context of present-day globalization necessitates a radical transformation of the world order and relationships among peoples in the direction of sharing of resources and caring for all. In addition to changes at the national and regional levels, there has to be transformations at the world level too. It is in such a context that we can reflect on the personal and collective motivation that can foster the movements for transformation of the values of peoples and of the relationships and structures of the present capitalistic globalization. In this connection, we offer some thoughts on the lines of humanistic and spiritual reflection that can be an inspiration for a global solidarity of peoples to strive for the common good of humanity.

Spirituality is a human quest for self-realization of the noblest aspirations, for holiness and perfection in union with the Transcendent, the Divine, to the extent possible in our earthly existence. It engages a person and a community in the effort to overcome selfishness, to care for others, to share with others what each one has so that the human happiness and fulfilment of all may be increasingly realized. The world's religions and the best genuine humanistic thinking indicate that human happiness depends on the striving for love, sharing and understanding among persons and in society. As against glorified selfishness, the principle values of an alternative society should be the togetherness of all persons beyond divisions such as of gender, birth, income, wealth and status. There should be respect for all persons and a sharing of the earth's resources among all persons and communities. This can be summed up as 'human solidarity', the search for the realization of the values of love and sharing that are expounded by all the world religions and humanistic ideologies. I will quote a few lines from a hymn which Swami

Vivekananda cited in his Chicago Address: "As the different streams having their sources in different places all mingle their water in the sea, so, O Lord, the different paths which men take through different tendencies, various though they appear, crooked or straight, all lead to Thee." This, I mean echoes the ethical and altruistic version of globalization. This is the humane version of social cohesiveness and solidarity where the people in the world can mingle to be a whole or a universe.

The use of powerful technologies as weapons of destruction also discloses current asymmetries of power and emergent forms of terrorism and war, as the new millennium exploded into dangerous conflicts and interventions. As technologies of mass destruction become more available and dispersed, perilous instabilities have emerged that have elicited policing measures to stem the flow of movements of people and goods across borders and internally. It demands rethinking of the globalization discourse. Social scientists and altruists are divided over how globalization promotes homogeneity, integration and coexistence on the one hand and disparity, dejection, differences, dissonance and unevenness, on the other. It has become the focal point of attention in the social sciences since the late 1980s and has appeared as a paradigmatic concept in analyzing economic, social, political, environmental, ecological and cultural metamorphoses occurring in major parts of the modern world.

Until recently, the leading philosophical perspective on globalization emphasized crossing the economic and cultural divide. Ethically and morally, the purpose of globalization was to bring different races, cultures, ethnic groups and socio-economic classes into closer contact with each other. The rationale for the movement was altruistic: to replace hatred with love, violence with peace, destruction with construction, 'their' culture with 'our' culture, 'either' with 'or' frame of mind. The elements of this globalization model were the purging of antagonism, the construction of an ideal type civil society, the restructuring of a sick economy, and the integration of all cultures. Now, however, we fear the injuries that globalization can inflict in each and every facet of our economic, cultural, political and social lives. The concept demands revision, re-estimation, re-appraisal and re-projection. It demands reflections on diversity, an open vision of humanity and free discourse. It is a grim fact that many nations and peoples are now confronting reality with what appear to be two mutually contradictory faces: the global and the local. Along with the increasing pace of globalization in science, technology, economy, culture, education, the empowerment of women, and communication, local conflicts are also increasing at an unprecedented pace. This situation weakens the positive potentials of globalization that also affects traditional value system.

In terms of our temperament, institutional behaviour and self-identity we are neither global nor local. Globalization has thus created such an identity crisis, which is very dangerous for our mental and physical health. Man, overloaded with rapidly changing stimuli, starts reacting with his head, instead of his heart to protect himself against the sweeping currents that would uproot him. As a consequence, he reacts less to emotional response but respond more to the money economy and as a result money hollows out the core of individuality, devaluing the whole. The don't care attitude of children, commercial interaction among the family members, the rise of individualism, breaking down of family ties, domination of individual identity and spatial disequilibrium are coming into the fore. Either husband resides in India and wife in America or wife in India and husband in London. Culture of family and neo-culture that develops in fast food centres clash, the age-old people feels frustrated and alienated. They are now the victims of curse of loneliness. They feel economic and mental insecurity. On the other hand, they have become the potential burden to their sons who earn a little. Not only that the age-old boom will be a global burden very soon. All, these are the results and consequences of globalization and consumerism. The global people are running fast towards such a goal where tradition, sense of localism and community feeling have no room. The rat race of global civilization, the burden of money and hyper-real/mindset create mental disorder and emotional dislocation. It is the real crisis in the era of globalization and such a crisis may cause identity fragmentation in future if the runway world runs so faster.

In India, the breakdown of the joint family and the growth of consumerist culture, as the result of globalization, give rise to aspirations that often cannot be met, create mental strain and striving mental make up. Lacking the deep sense of belonging to a community, family or tradition, the individual will begin to seek meaning in various pseudo-solidarities.

The globalization bonanza that our family shares now are small family living with hyper electronic and modernized technological gadgets, frequent mobility from India to any other countries in the world having the facilities of tour package, vicarious and striving styles of living, adoption of alien culture, and don't care attitude of the kids. The qualities the families lack are identity crisis of family culture tradition, decomposition of family norms, respect to the elders, emotional mindset, and values and cultural identity. We are getting hyper medicines which we now call life-saving drugs at a very high price but getting Viagra at a very low price. We are taking borderless education but ignoring traditional ways of teaching and learning. We have become very restive, vicarious but alienated, rat racers but dejected. We have forgotten mostly to forgive, love and show kindness to others. All human traits have mostly become the things of the past and meaningless.

In the era of globalization the problems relating to social exclusion appear as a local and national barrier. The time has ripen to contextualize the issues of social exclusion, especially in Indian society associated with multiple group identities like caste, ethnicity, religion, gender and other forms of exclusion. Social exclusion has been defined as the process through which individuals or groups are wholly or partially excluded from full participation in the society within which they live. Two defining characteristics of exclusion are particularly emphasized: the societal relations (or institutions) that cause exclusion and its consequence of deprivation in several spheres through the denial of equal rights. In the era of globalization the re-making of policy regarding the uplift of the exclude or disadvantaged group has not yet been so advanced. The re-designing of policy is still in an imperfect and unequal stage. So, the exclude remain as yet 'the exclude'. They could not enter into the mainstream orbit of our society. Social exclusion is not coterminous only with poverty. It is very much associated with a broader view of deprivation and disadvantage in the matters of health, education, and access to human development, social, political and cultural arena. Social exclusion focuses attention on central aspects of deprivation, is equally relevant to analysis and policies, and directs us to the fact that deprivation is a multidimensional phenomenon. Such injustice and discrimination leads to deprivation and dejection.

Amartya Sen notes, "The exclusion lead to the impoverishment of human life through their casual consequences (such as the denial of social and economic opportunities that would be helpful for the persons involved)". He also differentiates between 'active' and 'passive' exclusion. For causal analysis and formulating policy responses, Sen argues that "it is important to distinguish between 'active exclusion'—fostering of exclusion through deliberate policy interventions by government or other agents (to exclude some people from some opportunity)—and 'passive exclusion', which works through the social process. There are no deliberate attempts to exclude but the process may result in exclusion from a set of circumstances." Social exclusion not only generates tension, violence and disruption but also perpetuates inequality, helplessness, identity crisis and deprivation in society.

When we are loud of saying 'global village' then side by side several types of exclusion such as exclusion from land and other natural resources, exclusion from agricultural livelihood, exclusion from formal and informal employment, exclusion from organization and representation, exclusion from social services and exclusion from physical infrastructure are also living with globalization process. The marginalized or disadvantaged communities, by virtue of having no access to education, politics, culture and economy, cannot enhance their skill, capabilities and efficiency and ultimately become the 'other-faces' of our society. And they cannot enter into the arena of socio-economic and cultural mainstream. Here, we can feel the lacunae of distributive social justice in the era of globalization. Dante, in his famous 'Inferno' writes, "The motto on the gate of Hell was: Abandon all hopes, ye, who enter herein". And, the exclude in the Third World countries are still likely to be subjected to the paralysis of hopelessness and helplessness.

This is really inhumane globalization where the lives, humanity and right to live are not included in their agenda. Today, pharmaceutical companies talk of capitalist corridors of power. The multinational corporations sell Viagra across the world mainly because of the serving the people who are very much addicted to sex pleasure. Are we getting back to the root of promiscuity? This poses a basic question to the values of our future society.

In this era of globalization some virtual images stand before us as the perils that deface our ideal value system and of humanity. And perhaps so an expected trauma is waiting for our doomsday when the clouds of uncertainty, economic insecurity and identity crisis will dominate over the sky of the world. Human species may be the replicants and will act like more human than human. The dominance of information and communication technologies uproots the fetters of community feeling, family bondage and emotional interaction and community closeness. It seems to dominate over real-life individuals. Even after thirty years Toffler's future prediction of society is more contextual. The Internet and cell phone are spreading at a high speed. In future these technologies will be more ultramodern. Is the hi-tech revolution virtual or real? Whatever it might be, it is certainly alarming for the comfortable growth of humanity, ethics and human values, which they possess and nurture, with the process of socialization and upbringing. All affects the traditional value system and in this context one cannot claim that we are sinking into the problems of de-values that are endangered. De-value is one of the value systems of present-day society. It is the saying of the people of yesterday. Today's people say it values. We can easily comment that the moral terrain of our global society today is in moral decline. It looks at the question from a variety of angles, examining traditional, secular, religious, family and, economic values, and others. Many of these matters are under fierce debate. They include pre-emptive war, women's rights, terrorism, civil liberties, homosexuality, abortion, death penalty, science and religion, environmental degradation, nuclear arsenals, America's global image, fundamentalism, and the melding of religion and politics.

What would be the future of ideal social and moral values? Will it be gray and the old values will emerge with a new taxonomy and a reversed but a parallel value structure of two contending value forces (traditional values and modern values) will be in conflict? Will the postmodern value enchantment gobble up our identity of humanity? Will it be human more than human? Will morality be a sin? I am afraid, we are going deep into such a new dark age of hate, mistrust, intolerance, violence, greed and lustre, family disaster, interaction-fragmentation, poverty and global-local disarray. Carol Brouillet notes, "The Earth is not dying; it is being killed, not by corporations or institutions, although they certainly play their roles, but by real people, with names, faces and addresses, (1) whose actions and decisions mean 'war', 'death', 'starvation', 'illness', 'deforestation', 'flooding', 'drought', 'the expansion of the Ozone Hole', 'climate change', 'violent storms', 'the end of the Cenozoic Era". (2) ... Fascism and the struggle against fascism shaped the twentieth century. Ostensibly, we have been told, "Democracy triumphed" (http://www.communitycurrency.org/deadly.html). Humanity has been experiencing complex global-scale problems, crises and threats in the 21st century. This includes global violence, fundamentalism, religious bigotry, value erosion, rat racing for career, a kind of imperialist attitude of the global players, crisis of confidence, ethnic and religious intolerance, hunger, poverty, illiteracy, environmental pollution, excessive price of life-saving drugs, sexual sin, breaking down of joint family tie, emotional uncertainty, lack of human passion and kindness, technological and digital mend set, desperate consumerism, quick change of family values, divided self, lack of love, affection, neighbourhood feelings, charity, empathy, compassion, mercy, altruism, forgiveness, kindness, appreciation, sincerity, friendship, helpfulness, humbleness, nurturing, humility, modesty, affection corruption, sexual abuse, violation of human rights, global and local disparity, injustice, nuclear threat, war in Iraq and Afghanistan and so on.

The health hazards and technological risks may anytime swallow the dejected majorities; the age-old people may be completely frustrated due to the social, economic and moral sound of silence, alienation, deadly loneliness and insecurity. The women may be the symbol of sex commodities and virtual images. The epidemics may anytime engulf any country of the Third World. The unobtrusive and deadening poverty and hunger always warn them. The enchanting style of imaginary living is being always threatened by technological risks and hazards. The losers are always working hard for the winners under broiling sun from morning till dusk for miserable rewards and premature death even not knowing the reasons why. They are really at the crossroads of puzzle. All these are the result of globalization fear. Are we then waiting for a doomsday? Beck (1992: 19) argues that we are living on the "volcano of civilization, the contours of the risk society". And in the context of modernity and globalization he notes, "In advanced modernity the social production of wealth is systematically accompanied by the social production of risk". Setting aside the romantic and rhetoric discourse, can we manage the problems?

We are afraid that the liberal intellectuals and academics are taking over the anti-globalization movement as rhetoric discourse. But, the reality tells that the ultimate fate of such a struggle may be a discourse of confrontation between hegemony of the global initiators and hegemony of the anti-globalizers. W. Bello in a 'Report on Alternatives to Corporate Globalization', notes that two contradictory and opposite blueprints were opened to the post-cold War visionaries, i.e. "centralized socialism and corporate capitalism". But, the emerging process of de-globalization with the notions of remaking of local economies towards domestic markets, reorientation of income and land distribution, policies de-emphasizing growth and maximizing equity and remaking of a policy that subordinates markets to social justice are getting new entries in the arena of alternative globalization. When anti-globalizers are protesting against corporate capitalism replacing its neo-liberal principles and call for an alternative architecture, the global initiators are speaking about 'fair globalization' with the mission of 'good governance'. And, the wave of such a discourse continues.

"The sustainability challenge for the new millennium is whether global economic man can move out of the world-view based on fear and scarcity, monocultures and monopolies, appropriation and dispossession and shift to a view based on abundance and sharing, diversity and decentralization, and respect and dignity for all beings" (Shiva, 2002). The people of the Third World feel to be de-trapped from the economic globalization, because the ethics of globalization are undermining the ethics of justice and sustainability, of compassion, love, altruism and sharing. The alternative way, some suggest, is moving from market totalitarianism to an earth democracy. Gandhiji states, "The Earth has enough for everyone's needs, but not for some people's greed".

It is undeniable that people are the starter and end product of any movement. And, the end product of such a conflict may be either total global dominance of capitalism and abolishment of socialism or degeneration of capitalism and rebirth of neo-socialism. But as yet the future is unpredictable. What is the future of globalization then? What are the alternatives? Will it be only a few words like cooperation and diversity, democratic and ecologically sustainable economic relationship, neo-transnational good governance and civil society, democratization of local economic relationship, local governance and globalization from below (Wiseman, 2000)? What would be the future of neo-globalization? Will it be faded away and the old capitalism will appear with a new nomenclature and a reversed but a parallel globalization for the deprived majorities will appear and two contending forces will be in conflict? I am afraid, we are going deep into an era, where there will be only wars and anti-wars, globalization and anti-globalization. Are we going to be plunging into such a new dark age of hate, intolerance, violence, poverty and global-local disorder? Will the postmodern simulacra engulf our identity of humanity? Will it be human more than human? I don't know. We can only say we are in transition and the nightmare of alien future frightens us.

At the Global Compact Leaders Summit on 24th of June, 2004, United Nations Secretary-General Kofi Annan said: "Let us be true global citizens. Let us not rest until we have truly succeeded in bringing positive change into the lives of people, and laid the foundations for peaceful, well-functioning, sustainable societies throughout the world... Rarely has there been a moment in recent history when it has been so critical for all of us to protect our common space, building on what unites us. Again, I ask, if not us, then who?..."

Even amidst worry over the possibility of war, the heart of the global players should quest for economic development, moral solidarity and traditional-emotional identity and social justice, so that each and every human being can live in dignity, peace and security. Rabindra Nath Tagore feels, "Love gives beauty to everything it touches. Not greed and utility; they produce offices, but not dwelling houses. To be able to love material things, to clothe them with tender grace, and yet not be attached to them, this is a great service. Providence expects that we should make this world our own, and not live in it as though it were a rented tenement. We can only make it our own through some service, and that service is to lend it love and beauty from our soul. Your own experience shows you the difference between the beautiful, the tender, the hospitable, and the mechanically neat and monotonously useful. Love is an endless mystery, for it has nothing else to explain it. Love is not a mere impulse; it must contain truth, which is law. Love is the only reality and it is not a mere sentiment. It is the ultimate truth that lies at the heart of

conflicts or are there alternatives to the endless repetition of such catastrophes?" Karakas' paradigm of global humanity symbolizes a rosy dawn of optimistic humane globalization. He developed nine path paradigm of values and humanity: (1) path of truth (objectivity, truthfulness, ethics, order, quality, perfection, truth, conscience, self-discipline, idealism, judgment, consistency, efficiency, discipline); (2) path of compassion (love, affection, service, charity, empathy, gentleness, compassion, mercy, altruism, forgiveness, kindness, appreciation, sincerity, friendship, helpfulness, humbleness, nurturing, humility, modesty, affection); (3) path of devotion (conscientiousness, striving, persistence, perseverance, ambition, development, ethical success, effort, work, achievement, diligence); (4) path of inspiration (self-awareness, creativity, inspiration, sensitivity, emotional honesty, aesthetics, depth, authenticity, equanimity, beauty, self-expression, reflection); (5) path of wisdom (science, comprehension, insight, knowledge, understanding, intellectual mastery, enlightenment, learning, foresight, curiosity); (6) path of trust (loyalty, trust, commitment, faithfulness, reliability, obedience, dedication, caution, responsibility, dependability, trustworthiness, honesty, integrity); (7) path of hope (exploration, openness, thanksgiving, hope, enthusiasm, gratefulness, positive thinking, resilience, innovativeness, novelty, flexibility); (8) path of will (magnanimity, courage, decisiveness, initiative, action, determination, justice, freedom, equity, willpower, assertiveness, confidence, zeal); (9) and path of harmony (patience, acceptance, dialogue, receptivity, tolerance, courtesy, peace, balance, moderation, harmony, naturalness, wholeness, tranquillity, interdependence, interconnectedness).

The Holy Pope Benedict XVI in his message (January 2008) says that it is essential to 'sense' that the earth is 'our common home' and, in our stewardship and service to all, to choose the path of dialogue rather than the path of unilateral decisions. Further, international agencies may need to be established in order to confront together the stewardship of this 'home' of ours; more important, however, is the need for ever greater conviction about the need for responsible cooperation. The problems looming on the horizon are complex and time is short. In order to face this situation effectively, there is a need to act in harmony. One area where there is a particular need to intensify dialogue between nations is that of the stewardship of the earth's energy resources. The technologically advanced countries are facing two pressing needs in this regard: on the one hand, to reassess the high levels of consumption due to the present model of development, and on the other hand, to invest sufficient resources in the search for alternative sources of energy and for greater energy efficiency. The emerging countries are hungry for energy, but at times this hunger is met in a way harmful to poor countries which, due to their insufficient infrastructures, including their technological infrastructures, are forced to undersell the energy resources they do possess. At times, their very political freedom is compromised by forms of protectorate or, in any case, by forms of conditioning which appear clearly humiliating. R.R. Diwakar (2007) argues that one world and world peace are practically synonymous. Neither of them can exist without the other. The strong desire and the frequent attempts for both are rooted in the hunger of the human heart for peace and happiness. How heartening it is to imagine that when there is one world, all the natural and human resources, all the sciences and technology, which are today being marshalled and arrayed for destructive purposes, will be used for the elimination of poverty, ill-health and ignorance. They shall be used for promoting goodwill and for creating better conditions of life for the whole of humanity. Though this rosy picture is today the privilege only of the poets and the dream of idealists, there is no doubt that this is the cherished hope of everyone who strives for peace. It has been the living faith of persons like Gandhi. He once wrote: "Not to believe in the possibility of permanent peace is to disbelieve in the godliness of human nature."

Source: (http://www.tamilnation.org/oneworld/diwakar.htm)

Gandhi's comment is noteworthy in the era of defaced globalization: "You must not lose faith in humanity. Humanity is an ocean; if a few drops of the ocean are dirty, the ocean does not become dirty." This is the right time for us to call for humanity, love, forgiveness peace and solidarity. It is the time to feel for the have nots, destitute and starved. It is not the time of "I entreat you not to be turned by the call of vulgar strength, of stupendous size, by the spirit of storage, by the multiplication of millions, without meaning and without end. Cherish the ideal of perfection, and to that, relate all your work and all your movements. Though you love the material things of earth, they will not hurt you and you will bring heaven to earth and soul into things". The global players, Remember! "We come nearest to the great when we are great in humility".

Our great poet Rabindranath Tagore accepts love as the true spirit of humanity: "Life is perpetually creative because it contains in itself that surplus which ever overflows the boundaries of the immediate time and space, restlessly pursuing its adventure of expression in the varied forms of self-realization".

Life, like a child, laughs and shakes its rattle of death as it runs. Life's errors cry for the merciful beauty that can modulate their isolation into a harmony with the whole. Love adorns itself; it seeks to prove inward joy by outward beauty. Love does not claim possession, but gives freedom.

Love gives beauty to everything it touches. Not greed and utility; they produce offices, but not dwelling houses. To be able to love material things, to clothe them with tender grace, and yet not be attached to them, this is a great service. Providence expects that we should make this world our own, and not live in it as though it were a rented tenement. We can only make it our own through some service, and that service is to lend it love and beauty from our soul. Your own experience shows you the difference between the beautiful, the tender, the hospitable, and the mechanically neat and monotonously useful. Love is an endless mystery, for it has nothing else to explain it. Love is not a mere impulse, it must contain truth, which is law.

Love is the only reality and it is not a mere sentiment. It is the ultimate truth that lies at the heart of creation. Love is the only reality and it is not a mere sentiment. It is the ultimate truth that lies at the heart of creation… . Your mission is proving that a love for the earth, and for the things of the earth, is possible without materialism, a love without greed… In love all the contradictions of existence merge themselves and are lost. Only in love are unity and duality not at variance.

Prometheus was punished by the Gods because he was worshipped by primeval Greeks who challenged Zeus. He stole the fire from the chariot of Goddess Phoebus Apollo and brought it down to earth. For this reason only Prometheus was punished. It was the verdict of the Goddess that an Eagle would devoir the Titan's liver. And yet he carried on his rebelliousness amid his sufferings. This is the source of the humanist challenge to authority. Echoing Gandhiji's great proclamation I may enunciate that if someone chop off someone's nose that will not kill him; if someone pluck out someone's eyes that will not kill him but if the global players kill belief in humanity then the common people will be die.

If we follow this paradigm, the globalization of poverty will turned into the globalization of love and globalization of humanity not globalization of disparity and terrorism. It would not be then an enchanting discourse rather it would be the reality talk of the 21st century.

Bibliography

Abramov, L.S. 1975. "Natural Disaster", in L.S. Abramov (ed.), *Man, Society and the Environment*. Moscow: Progress Publisher.

Afshar, Haleh and Stephenie Barrientos. 1999. "Introduction: Women, Globalization and Fragmentation", in Haleh Afshar and Stephanie Barrientos (eds.), *Women, Globalization and Fragmentation in the Developing World*. London: Macmillan.

Albrow, Martin. 1990. "Introduction", in Martin Albrow and Elizabeth King (eds.), *Globalisation, Knowledge and Society: Readings from International Sociology*. London: Sage.

Albrow, Martin. 2001. "Globalization after Modernization: A New Paradigm for Development Studies", in Frans J. Schuurman (ed.), *Globalization and Development Studies*. New Delhi: Vistaar Publications.

Amin, Samir. 1997. *Capitalism in the Age of Globalization*. London: Zed Books.

Annon, Kofi A. 2001. "Foreword", in Giandomenico Picco (ed.), *Crossing the Divide*. New Jersey: School of Diplomacy and International Relations, Seton Hall University.

Appadurai, Arjun. 1990. "Disjuncture and Difference in the Global Cultural Economy", in Mike Featherstone (ed.), *Global Culture: Nationalism, Globalization and Modernity*. London: Sage.

Appadurai, Arjun. 1996. *Modernity at Large*. Minneapolis: University of Minnesota Press.

Archer, Margaret S. 1991. "Seeking for One World: Unity and Diversity", in *International Sociology*. Vol. 2.

Avino, Elvira del Pozo. 2006. "Social Movements in a Globalized World", in Samir Dasgupta and Ray Kiely (eds.), *Globalization and After*. New Delhi: Sage. Available at http://www.lean.net.au/thoughts/1127057684_32682.html

Barry, Kathleen. 1995. *The Prostitution of Sexuality*. New York: New York University Press.

Baudrillard, Jean. 1970. *La Societe de consommation*. Paris: Gallimard (English citation in Powel, Jim. *Postmodernism for Beginners*. India: Orient Longman).

Baudrillard, Jean. 1980. *De la seduction*. Paris: Galilee (English citation in Powel, Jim). *Postmodernism for Beginners*. India: Orient Longman).

Bauman, Zygmunt. 1998. *Globalization: The Human Consequences*. Cambridge, Polity Press.

Bauman, Zygmunt. 2001. *The Individualized Society*. Cambridge: Polity Press.

Beck, Ulrich. 1992. *Risk Society: Towards a New Modernity*. London: Sage.

Berger, Peter L. 1963. *Invitation to Sociology: A Humanistic Perspective*. Harmondsworth: Penguin Books.

Bharucha, Rustom. 1999. "Politics of Culturalisms in an Age of Globalisation", *Economic and Political Weekly*. Feb. 20.

Bishop, Ryan and Lillian S. Robinson. 1998. *Night Market*. New York: Routledge.

Boss, Shira. 2007. "Women want Wives", in *Times of India*. Kolkata.

Bradshaw, Y.W., J.F. Healey and Rebecca Smith (eds). 2009. *Sociology for the New-Century*. California: Pine Forge Press.

Brouillet, Carol 2008. Available at http://wgns.net/ICR/Library/PolSocAction/PDF/UnansweredQuestions911.pdf

Bruce, Steve. 1999. *Sociology: A Very Short Introduction*. Oxford: Oxford University Press.

Bruno, Amoreso. 1998. *On Globalization: Capitalism in the 21st Century*. London: Macmillan.

Carnap, Rudolf. 1971. "A Basic System of Inductive Logic", in R. Carnap and R. Jeffrey (eds.), *Studies in Inductive Logic and Probability*. Berkeley: University of California Press.

Castells, M. 1996. *The Risk of the Network Society*. Oxford: Blackwell.

Chew, Sing C., 2004. "Globalization and Ecological Crisis", in Samir Dasgupta (ed.), *The Changing Face of Globalization*. New Delhi: Sage.

Chossudovsky, Michel. 2001. *The Globalisation of Poverty*. Goa: Other India Press.

Cloud, Stanley. 1972. "The Futility...: the Unspeakable Inhumanity", in *Time CNN*. May 1.

Cogswell, David. 1996. *Chomsky: For Beginners*. Hyderabad: Orient Longman Limited.

Comte, Auguste. 1855. *The Positive Philosophy of Auguste Comte* (H. Martineau translation). New York: Blanchard.

Cornell, D. 1991. *Beyond Accommodation*. New York: Routledge.

Corsaro, W. 1997. *The Sociology of Childhood*. Thousand Oaks, CA: Pine Forge Press.

Dadayan, Vladislav. 1988. *The Orbits of the Global Economy*. Moscow: Progress Publishers.

Dasgupta, Priyanka. 2006. "Woman of Substance", in *Times of India*. Kolkata.

Dasgupta, Samir. 2006. "Globalization and its Future Shock", in Samir Dasgupta and Ray Kiely (eds.), *Globalization and After*. New Delhi: Sage.

Dasgupta, Samir. 2008. "Globalization and Environmental Menace", in Samir Dasgupta (ed.), *Understanding the Global Environment*. New Delhi: Pearson Longman.

Dasgupta, Samir. 2008. "Introduction", in Samir Dasgupta (ed.), *Understanding the Global Environment*. New Delhi: Pearson Longman.

Dasgupta, Samir (ed.), 2004. *The Changing Face of Globalization*. New Delhi: Sage.

Dasgupta, Samir and Ray Kiely (eds.), 2006. *Globalization and After*. New Delhi: Sage.

Dasgupta, Samir and Ray Kiely. 2006. "Introduction", in Samir Dasgupta and Kiely Ray (eds.), *Globalization and After*. New Delhi: Sage.

Dasgupta, Samir and Robyn Driskell. 2007. "Introduction", in Samir Dasgupta and Robyn Driskell (eds.), *Discourse on Applied Sociology: Theoretical Perspectives*. London: Anthem Press.

Diwakar, R.R. 2007. "One World and Mahatma Gandhi", at www.musicforworldpeace.com/node/29

Dreze, Jean and Amartya Sen. 1995. *India: Economic Development and Social Opportunity*. New Delhi: Oxford University Press.

Driskell, Robyn. 2004. "Empowerment versus Development: The Effects of Women's Empowerment and Economic Development on Children's Nutritional Well-Being", in Samir Dasgupta (ed.), *The Changing Face of Globalization*. New Delhi: Sage.

Dube, S.C. 1990. *Indian Society*. New Delhi: National Book Trust.

Edwards, M. and Hulme, D. (eds). 1995. *Non-Governmental Organization: Performance and Accountability Beyond the Magic Bullet*. London/West Hartford: Earthscan/Kunarian.

Edwards, Frederick. 1989. *What is Humanism?*

Ellwood, Wayne. 2001. *The No-Nonsense Guide to Globalization*. Oxford, England: New Internationalist.

Enright, Robert. 1998. *The Enright Forgiveness Inventory User Manual*. Madison, WI: The International Forgiveness Institute.

Enright, Robert D. and Joanna North (eds.), 1998. *Exploring Forgiveness*. Madison, WS: University of Wisconsin Press.

Eriksen, T.H. 1995. *Small Places, Large Issues: An Introduction to Social and Cultural Anthropology*. London: Pluto Press.

Escobar, A. 1995. *Encountering Development*. Princeton: Princeton University Press, p. 3.

Etzioni, Amitai. 2004. *From Empire to Community*. New York: Palgrave Macmillan.

Fanon, Frantz. 1967. *A Dying Colonialism* (Trans. by H. Chevalier). New York: Grove.

Fedosov, E. 1980. *Man and Nature*. Moscow: Progress Publishers.

Feigl, Herbert. 1967. *The "Mental" and the "Physical"*. Minneapolis: University of Minnesota Press.

Fitzsimons, Patrick. 2002. "Globalization: The Politics of Corruption in the 21st Century". Available at http://globalzation.icaap.org/content/v2.1/07_fitzsimons.html

Foster, J.V.B. 1999. *The Vulnerable Planet: A Short Economic History of the Environment*. London: Carnes Stone Books.

Foucault, Michel. 1982. *The History of Sexuality*. Harmondsworth: Penguin.

Gelinas, Jacques B. 1998. *Freedom from Debt*. Dhaka, Bangladesh: The University Press Limited.

Gerasimor, I.P. et al. (eds.), 1975. *Man, Society and the Environment*. Moscow: Progress Publishers.

Giddens, Anthony. 1989. *Sociology*. London: Polity Press.

Giddens, Anthony. 1990. *The Consequences of Modernity*. Cambridge: Polity.

Giddens, Anthony. 1991. *A Contemporary Critique of Historical Materialism*. London: Macmillan.

Gilman, Charlotte Perkins. 1966. *Women and Economics*. New York: Harper and Row.

Grapard, Ulla. 2001. "The Trouble with Women and Economics", in Stephen Cullenberg, Jack Amariglio and David F. Ruccio (eds.), *Postmodernism, Economics and Knowledge*. London/New York: Routledge.

Gray, J. 1997. *Endgames: Question in Late Modern Political Thought*. Cambridge, U.K.: Polity Press.

Greenspan, Alan. 1947. Globalization and Finance, available at www.cato.org/speeches.

Hagood, Caroline. 2007. Documentary "Thinking XXX" takes an Unconventional Look at the Porn Industry. http://www.campusprogress.org/filmtv/2041/not-your-fathers-porn-flick

Hassan, Ihab. 1982. *The Dismemberment of Orphans: Toward a Postmodern Literature*. New York: Oxford University Press.

Heidegger, M. 1971. *The Thing. In Poetry, Language, Thought*. New York: Harper & Row.

Heinrich Heine's citation quoted from Samir Dasgupta and Ray Kiely (eds.), *Globalization and After*. New Delhi: Sage.

Henderson, Hazel. 2001. "Preventing War and Global Recession: Change Globalization to a Win-Win Game". Available at http://www.hazelhenderson.com/editorials/preventingWar10-02.html

Hewitson, Gillyan. 2001. "The Disavowal of the Sexed Body in New-classical Economics" in Stephen Cullenberg et al. (eds.) *Postmodern Economics and Knowledge*, London: Routledge.

Hirst, P. and G. Thompson. 1995. "Globalization and the Future of the Nation-State", in *Economy and Society*. 24 (3): 408–42.

http/resurgence.gn.apc.org/issues/contents/202.html

http/www.jubilee 2000 uk.org/debt.html

http/www.labormet.org.uk/so/current.html

http://global_india1.tripod.com/negative.htm

http://jwsr.ucr.edu/

http://news.bbc.co.uk/2/hi/in_depth/629/629/7036068.stm

http://www.cjd.org/paper/jp2war.html

http://www.communitycurrency.org/deadly.html (01.02.08)

http://www.globalissues.org/article/75/world-military-spending

http://www.globalization101.org/issue/woman/

http://www.globalresearch.ca/articles/BOY111C.html

http://www.gseis.ucla.edu/faculty/kellner/kellner.html

http://www.infidels.org/library/modern/fred_edwords/humanism.html

http://www.nacoonline.org/Quick_Links/Women/

http://www.rcgg.ufrgs.br/gp002bas.htm (01.11.08)

http://www.religion-online.org/showarticle.asp?title=1108

http://www.springerlink.com/content/dbvytcxgae6l2mrg/

http://www.tamilnation.org/oneworld/diwakar.htm)

http://www.un.org/News/Press/docs/2005/gadis3298.doc.htm

http://www.uri.edu/artsci/wms/hughes/siii.htm)

http://www.vatican.va/holy_father/benedict_xvi/messages/peace/documents/hf_ben-xvi_mes_20071208_xli-world-day-peace_en.html

http://www.voteswagon.com

http://www.worldtribunal.org/main/

Hughes, Donna M. 2000. "The Internet and Sex Industries: Partners in Global Sexual Exploitation", in *Technology and Society Magazine*. Spring.

Huizer, Gerrit. 2003. *Globalization from Above and from Below: A Dialectical Process*. Inhoud.

Hunter J.D. and Yates J. 2002. "In the Vanguard Globalization: The World of American Globalizers", in Peter L. Berger and Samuel P. Huntinghton (eds) *Many Globalizations: Cultural Diversity in the Contemporary World*. New York: Oxford University Press.

Jeffreys, Sheila. 1999. "Globalizing Sexual Exploitation: Sex Tourism and the Traffic in Women", *Leisure Studies*. 18 (3), July: 179–186.

Johnston, Berry. V. (ed). 1998. *Pitirin Sorokin: On the Practice of Sociology*. Chicago: University of Chicago Press.

Kellner, Douglas. 1995. *Media Culture*. London: Routledge.

Kellner, Douglas. 1998. "Globalization and the Postmodern Turn". Available at www.gseis.ucla.edu

Kellner, Douglas, "Theorizing Globalization", Available at http://www.gseid.ucla.edu.

Khatami, Mohammad. 1998. "Education and the Dialogue among the Civilizations". Discussion organized by United Nations University, Japan. Available at http://www.unu.edu/globseminar/2001/shimane/rector.pdf

Kidney, Sean. 2005. "Amazing Climate Change Facts".

Kiely, Ray. 1998. *Globalization and the Third World*. London: Routledge.

Kiely, Ray. 2005. *Empire in the Age of Globalisation: U.S. Hegemony and Neo-Liberal Disorder*. Michigan, USA: The University of Michigan Press.

Kiely, Ray. 2006. "Business As Usual or Radical Shift" in Samir Dasgupta and Ray Kiely (eds). *Globalization and After*. New Delhi: Sage Publications.

Kolb, William. 1951. "Review of Social Philosophies of an Age of Crisis", in *American Sociological Review*. No. 16: 267–268.

Korten, D. 1990. *Getting to the Twenty-First Century: Voluntary Action and the Global Agenda*. West Hartford, CT: Kumarian Press.

Krishnakumar, Asha. 2003. "Importing Danger", in *India's National Magazine*. Issue 25, December.

Laffey, Mark A. and Jutta Weldes. 2005. "Anti-globalization Protests and the Future of Democracy". Available at http://upress.kent.edu/Nieman/Antiglobalization.htm

Lee, Alfred McLung. 1976. "Sociology for Whom?" in *American Sociological Review*. Vol. 41, No. 6.

Luther King, Martin (Jr). Citation available at http://www.metanexus.net/Magazine/tabid/68/id/8271/Default.aspx

Lyon, David. 2002. *Postmodernity*. New Delhi: Viva Books Pvt. Ltd.

Madison, James. 1795. "The Most Dreaded Enemy of Liberty", in *Freedom Daily*. Available at http://www.fff.org/freedom/0893e.asp

Mandela, Nelson. 2003. "All Bush wants is Iraqi oil" in *Independent*. (www.news.independent.co.uk.)

Marchand, Marianne H. and Anne Sisson Runyan. 2001. "Feminist Sightings of Global Restructuring: Conceptualizations and Reconceptualizations", in Frans J. Schuurman (ed.), *Globalization and Development Studies: Challenges for the 21st Century*. London: Sage.

Marcos, Subcomandante. 2001. "Tomorrow Begins Today", in *New Internalist*. Available at http://www.articlearchives.com/environment-natural-resources/ecology-environmental/813735-1.html

Martinez, O. 1997. Speech delivered at International Meeting of Workers Against Neoliberalism and Globalization. Havana Convention, Cuba, August 6. Available at www.labor.org

McLuhan, Marshall. 1962. *The Gutenberg Galaxy: The Making of Typographic Man*. Toronto, Canada: University of Toronto Press.

McMichael, Philip. 1994. *Development and Social Change: A Global Perspective*. Thousand Oaks, CA: Sage/Pine Forge Press.

Mirkinson, J. 1994. Red Light, Green Light: The Global Trafficking of Women. Available at www.armory.com.

Moore, DG Mike. 2000 WTO NEWS: "Trade, Poverty and the Human Face of Globalization", London, June 16, Reuters/Carnegie Public Policy Series, London School of Economics. Available at http://www.wto.org/english/news_e/spmm_e/spmm32_e.htm

Mukerjee, Madhusree. 1995. in *Scientific American*. June and July.

Mukerjee, Radhakamal. 1960. *The Philosophy of Social Sciences*. London: Macmillan & Co. Ltd.

Naletov, Igor. 1984. *Alternatives to Positivism*. Moscow: Progress Publishers.

Offe, Claus. 1985. "New Social Movements: Challenging the Boundaries of Institutional Politics", in *Social Research*. Vol. 52, No. 4.

Ohmae, K. 1991. *The Borderless World*. London: Fontana.

Ogburn, W.F. 1964. *On Culture and Social Change*. Chicago: Chicago University Press.

Oliner, Samuel P. 2007. "Unlimited Love, Compassion and Forgiveness: Acts of Moral Exemplars", in Samir Dasgupta and Robyn Driskell (eds.), *Discourse on Applied Sociology: Theoretical Perspective*. London: Anthem Press.

Ozinga, James R. 1999. *Altruism*. Westport, Conn.: Praeger, p. 64.

Patnaik, P. 1995. *Whatever Happened to Imperialism and other Essays*. New Delhi: Tulika.

Petras, James. 1999. "Globalization: A Socialist Perspective", in *Economic and Political Weekly*. February 20.

Petras, James. 1999. *America Latina: De La Globalizacion a La Revolucion*. Rosario: Homo Sapiens Ediciones.

Petras, James and Veltheyer. 2007. *Globalization Unmarked*. Delhi: Madhyam Books.

Picco, Giandomenico (ed.), 2001. *Crossing the Divide*. New Jersey: School of Diplomacy and International Relations.

Pieterse, J. 2001. *Development Theory*. New Delhi: Vistaar Publication.

Pieterse, J.N. 2006. "Oriental Globalization: Past and Present" in Gerald Delanty (ed). *Europe and Asia Beyond East and West: Towards a New Cosmopolitanism*. London: Routledge.

Plummer, Joseph. 1989. "Changing Values", in *The Futurist*. January–February, pp. 8–13.

Powel, James. 1998. *Postmodernism*. India: Viva Publications.

Purkayastha, Bandan and Jayme Schwartzman. 2008. "Mother-Work and the Work of Mothers: Contemporary Globalization and the Labour of Poor Women", in Samir Dasgupta et al. (eds.), *Gender and Power in Global Context*. (Forthcoming).

Raghavan, Chakravarthi's speech in accepting the 1997 G77/UNDP Award for TCDC/ECDC, January 12, 1998.

Ritzer, George. 1996 (Fourth edition). *Modern Sociological Theory*. McGraw Hill: McGraw Hill Publishing Co.

Ritzer, George. 2002. *The Mcdonaldization of Society*. New York: Pine Forge Press.

Robertson, Ronald. 1992. *Globalization: Social Theory and Global Culture*. London: Sage.

Roger, Trigg. 1980. *Reality at Risk: A Defence of Realism in Philosophy and the Sciences*. New Jersey: Barnes & Noble Books.

Rose, F. 1997. "Sex Sells—Today's Sex Industry, Tomorrow's Mainstream" in wired 5, December 12. available at www.wired.com/wired/archive/5–12

Rostow, W.W. 1960. *The Stages of Economic Growth: A Non-Communist Manifesto*. Cambridge: Cambridge University Press.

Sahtouris, Elisabet. 1998. "The Biology of Globalization", adapted from first publication in *Perspectives in Business and Social Change*. September.

Salih, M.A. Mohamed. 2001. "Globalization, Sustainable Development and Environment: A Balancing Act", in Frans J. Schuurman (ed.), *Globalization and Development Studies*. New Delhi: Vistaar Publications.

Sandler, Todd. 1997. *Global Challenges*. Cambridge: Cambridge University Press.

Sarkar, Binoy Kumar. 1985. *A Positive Background of Hindu Sociology*, Book 1. New Delhi: Motilal Banarsidass (First Print, 1937).

Schlick, Moritz. 1925. *Allgemeine Erkenntnislehre*. Berlin: Springer.

Sefidvash, Farhang. "The Concept of Globalization", Federal University of Rio Grande do Sul, Porto Alegre, Brazil.

Sen, Amartya. 2002. "How to Judge Globalization", in *The American Prospect* Online, http://www.prospect.org/print/V13/1/sen-a.html

Sen, Amartya. 2002. "On Environment", in *Environment: Dimensions and Change*. Kolkata: Visions Publications.

Sen, Amartya. 1981. *Poverty and Famines*. New Delhi: Oxford University Press.

Sen, S. 2004. "The Fantasy of Fair Globalization" in *Peoples' Democracy*. July 15.

Shils, E. 1961. "The Calling of Sociology", in Talcott Parsons et al. (eds.), *Theories of Society*. New York: The Free Press of Glencoe.

Shiva, Vandana. 2002. "Economic Globalization has become a War against Nature and Poor", in *Resurgence Issue*.

Shmelyov, N.P. 1970. *Problem of Economic Growth in the Developing Countries*. Moscow: Progress Publishers, p. 22.

Siebert, Horst. 1999. *The World Economy*. London and New York: Routledge.

Silverste, Ken. 1999. "Millions for Viagra, Pennies for the Diseases of the Poor", in *The Nation*, July 19.

Singh, Yogendra. 1973. *Modernization of Indian Tradition*. Delhi: Thompson Press (India) Ltd.

Smith, Dorothy. 1978. "A Peculiar Eclipsing: Women's Exclusion from Men's Culture", in *Women's Studies International Quarterly*, Vol. 1, No. 4.

Spingola, Deanna. 2006,thttp://www.renewamerica.us/columns/spingola/060612

Sorokin, Pitirim. 1954. *The Ways and Power of Love: Types, Factors and Techniques of Moral Transformation*. Boston, Mass.: Beacon Press.

Sorokin, Pitirim. 1950. *Altruistic Love: A Study of American "Good Neighbors" and Christian Saints*. Boston: Beacon Press.

Sorokin, Pitirim and Barry V. Johnston. 1963. *On the Practice of Sociology*. Chicago: University of Chicago Press.

Stanton, Elizabeth Cady, Susan B. Anthony and Matilda Joslyn Gage (eds.), 1881. *History of Woman Suffrage*. Vol. 1, New York: Fowler and Wells.

Stephen Post's. 2003. Available at http://www.unlimitedloveinstitute.org/publicaions/pdf/UL_What_and_Why.pdf

Stiglitz, Joseph. 2004. "Consensus is Emerging on the Destructive Effects of Globalization", in *Guardian*.

Stiglitz, Joseph. 2002. *Globalization and Its Discontents*. Great Britain: The Penguin Press.

Sule, Surekha. 2007. "Neutralising Industrial Waste with Worms", in *India Together*. February.

Swaminathan, M.S. 2000. "World Trade: Employment and Poverty-1", in *The Hindu*. p. 12.

Tagore, Rabindranath. "History of India", in *Viswa Bharati*.

Tagore, Rabindranath. 2003 (Third edition). *Gitanjali*. Delhi: Sahni Publications.

Tanuro, Daniel. 2008. "Humanity, Society and Ecology: Global Warming and the Ecosocialist Alternative". Available at http://climateandcapitalism.com/?p=567

Tempest, Metthew. 2003. "Noam Chomsky on the Anti-War Movement", in *Their War Our Will*. Kolkata: Foset.

The Bhagavad Gita (The Sacred Text).

Tickel, Adam and Peek, Jamie. 2003. 'Making Global Rules: Globalization on Neoliberalization', in Jamie Peek and Henry Young (eds) *Remaking in Global Economy: Economical, Geographical Perspectives*. London: Sage.

Tinbergen, Jan. 1976. *Reshaping the International Order* (A Report to the Club of Rome). New York: E.P. Dutton & Co., Inc.

Todaro, M. 1977. *Economic Development*. Harlow: Longman.

Toffler, Alvin. 1970. *Future Shock*. New York: Random House.

Toffler, Alvin. 1993. *War and Antiwar*. London: Warner Books.

Tolba, M.K. and O.A. El-Kholy. 1992. *The World Environment 1972–1992: Two Decades for Challenge*. London: Chapman and Hall.

Tomlinson, John. 1999. *Globalization and Culture*. Cambridge, U.K.: Polity Press.

Tuna and Tong, 1995 cited in Y.W. Bradshaw et al. (eds.), *Sociology for the New Century*. California: Pine Forge Press.

United Nations Human Development Report. 1998. Chapter 1, p. 37.

Vivekananda, Swami. 2001. *Chicago Address (1893)*. Kolkata: Advita Ashrama Publications Department, 29th Impression.

Walia, Nona and Amartya Sen. 2001. "A Nobel Cause", in *Times of India*. December 2.

Wallerstein, Immanuel. 2003. "Entering Global Anarchy", in *New Left Review*. No. 22, August.

Wallerstein, Immanuel. 2000. "Cultures in Conflict?" Y.K. Rao Distinguished Chair Lecture, Hongkong, September 20.

Wallerstein, Immanuel. 1974. *The Modern World System*. New York: Academic Press.

Ward, Ms. Olivia. 2006. "Globalization and Disparities in Global Wealth", in *Toronto Star Issue*. December. Available at www.thestar.com

Waters, Malcom. 1995. *Globalization*. London: Routledge.

Weinstein, Jay. 2002. "The Place of Theory in Applied Sociology: A Reflection", in *Theory and Science*. U.S.A.

Weinstein, Jay and Elvira del Pozo, Avino. 2004. "Altruism and the Prospects for a Common Humanity", in Samir Dasgupta (ed). *The Changing Face of Globalization*. New Delhi: Sage.

Wiseman J. 2000. "Alternatives to Oppressive Globalization", in S. McBride and J. Wiseman (eds) *Globalization and Its Discontents*. London: Macmillan Press Ltd.

Wittgenstein, Ludwig. 1949. *Tractatus Logico Philosophicus*. London: Routledge and Kegan Paul.

Yale Global Forum. 2006. Advantage of Globalization by NDVC (Ness diazValentin). Posts: 1/From: USA/Registered: April.

Yan, Yunxiang. 2002. "Managed Globalization: State Power and Cultural Transition in China", in Peter L. Berger and Samuel P. Huntington (eds.), *Many Globalizations: Cultural Diversity in the Contemporary World*. New York: Oxford University Press.

Yearley, Steven. 1996. *Sociology, Environmentalism, Globalization*. London: Sage.

Zizek, Slavoj. 1997. "Multiculturalism or The Cultural Logic of Multinational Capitalism", in *New Left Review*. 225, September/October.

Index